The Woke Mind-Set: A Historical Psychoanalysis.

by

Steffen Skovmand

Contents

Prologue: 4

Part I: The Origin and History of Woke 9

Chapter 1: The Woke Philosophers. 9
Part I: The Origin and History of Woke 21

Chapter 2: The Three Stages of Woke 21

Stage I: the 60s. 22
Stage II-The 1970s and '80s. .... Error! Bookmark not defined.
Stage III-2008-today: Woke´s long march through the institutions. .... Error! Bookmark not defined.
Part I: Summary. .... Error! Bookmark not defined.

Part II: Transforming the Consciousness of Society .... Error! Bookmark not defined.

Chapter 1: From Individualism to Identity Politics. .... Error! Bookmark not defined.

Part II:Transforming the Consciousness of Society .... Error! Bookmark not defined.

Chapter 2: Transgenderism: Gender as Social Construct on Steroids. .... Error! Bookmark not defined.

Part II: Transforming the Consciousness of Society: 71
Chapter 3: Race as a Social Construct. 71

Part II: Transforming the Consciousness of Society 89

Chapter 4: Feminism: The Identity Politics of Moral Superiority. 89

Summary: Part II: 106
Part III: Woke´s Long March Through the Institutions 107

Chapter 1: Woke´s One World Internationalism: the EU. 107
Part III: Woke´s Long March Through the Institutions 116

Chapter 2: The European Union and the Soviet Union: Woke´s March from Idealism to Authoritarianism 116

Part III: Woke´s Long March Through the Institutions 122

Chapter 3:   Woke´s One World Internationalism: the UN and Open Borders 122

Part III: Woke´s Long March Through the Institutions 138

Chapter 4: Woke´s One World Internationalism: the UN and Climate Change Panic ... 138

Part III:Summary 167

Part IV: From Free Speech to Hate Speech-How Woke Crushes Dissent 167

Part V:Epilogue. 184

Prologue:

The philosophy of Woke so far has not been taken seriously as an organized attempt at explaining the world. Right-of-center political movements, like that of Florida Governor, Ron De Santis, denounce it as a temporal, short-lived bout of social lunacy and left-of center believers while spouting Woke narratives of gender identity, transgenderism and anti-racism hesitate to openly recognize its Marxist roots in Central European schools of philosophy which reject traditional Judeo-Christian Enlightenment orthodoxy in favor of outright secularism and atheism.

This book sets out to right that wrong by arguing that Woke is not just a passing fad but a genuine political and moral philosophy that already has had and if fully implemented will have even bigger real world consequences.

Clearly, Woke is offering a moral and political belief-set that millions of ordinary people can agree upon and believe in today.

The unprovoked and brutal attack by Hamas, Gaza´s democratically elected government, on October 7,2023, on unarmed civilians, women and children in Israel led to huge demonstrations all over the West, from Boston to Brussels in support of …..Hamas.

Why?

It is an important part of the book´s argument that people supporting progressive woke policies and millions of their fellow travelers do not decide *spontaneously* what to believe in morally, politically, and ideologically. A mass political movement requires that much cultural groundwork be done over the course of many years. And this is where intellectuals do their work. A culture´s intellectuals develop and articulate a culture´s ideals, its goals, its aspirations…It is intellectuals who write the opinion pieces in the mass newspapers, who are the professors at the universities, the universities where teachers and preachers are trained, where politicians and lawyers and scientists and physicians get their education.

It should have come as no surprise, therefore, that college campuses one of the most consistently pro-Woke demographics all over the West erupted in sometimes violent demonstrations against Jews, But it did.

Equally, it should have come as no surprise that Hamas received massive mainstream political support from hundreds of thousands of ordinary citizens. But it did.

This book sets out to explain why.

Woke has voted Woke leaders like Angela Merkel in Germany, Emanuel Macron in France, Justin Trudeau in Canada, and Barack Obama in the U.S. into power again and again because voters believe in Woke ideas.

It is an astounding fact, f.ex.,that more than 80 million people voted for Joe Biden in 2020, the biggest number ever in American history and more than 10 million more than woke President Barack Obama´s record of 69.5 million. Donald Trump received a little more than 74 million, the second largest vote for a president ever even as he argued that he would have won if it had not been for Democrat- organized fraud.

This is highly unlikely.

Biden was certainly considerably less charismatic than Obama and virtually conducted no campaign at all during the Covid-19 pandemic but sent out messages from his basement. But these messages and daily briefings made it very clear that he would govern on a typical and woke Democratic platform of doing away with fossil energy, increasing international cooperation after the Trump years, reforming the electoral college and the Supreme Court and last but not least give more power to the Government to redistribute wealth from the rich to the poor.

That the elections were free but not fair, has been suggested by subsequent events and research such as Mollie Hemmingway's book Rigged [1], showing that the media connived to keep damaging material to Joe Biden about his son Hunter Biden from the public, that Democratic state administrations sometimes unconstitutionally passed legislation doing away with stringent controls on mail-in voting and voter-harvesting, and a that a concerted effort to get out the (Democratic) vote by Democratic philanthropists such as Facebook´s Mark Zuckerberg sometimes bypassing official election laws took place.

Similarly, by the Durham Report [2] which concluded that the FBI in its anti-Trump zeal rushed to investigate a collusion with Russia in the 2016 presidential election that had no basis in factual evidence but was a plant by the Democratic party and its leader Hillary Clinton.

That may all be true. But is unlikely to have changed the end result substantially. Millions of woke voters may be ultimately proved by history to be wrong, but so are millions of anti-woke ones: but they are unlikely to have been deluded.

That ideas matter was borne out by the fact that Joe Biden, despite his personal popularity being in the tank and after 2 years of woke policies going far beyond his more centrist election promises, at the midterm-elections in the U.S. in November 2022 managed to reverse the trend of the ruling party almost always losing these elections by *increasing* his majority in the Senate and only barely losing the House.

And that Macron was recently reelected to a second term, despite massive working class protests, the mishandling of the Covid 19 crisis and deep popular unpopularity and that Merkel became the longest serving Chancellor of Germany, ever.

Ideas matter and this book argues that Woke as a set of coherent ideas and as an ideology, has been extremely successful, all be it as we shall see later, by stealth.

Therefore, whether we like it or not, Woke, as a philosophy and a political program is with us to stay.

Which makes the story of how and why that came to happen even more pressing.

The book traces Woke´s philosophical roots back to Nietzsche and a later fusion in the early and middle parts of the 20th century of 3 neo-Marxist schools of thought: the Frankfurt School of Critical Theory, Existentialism and French Postmodernism.

---

[1] Mollie Hemingway, Rigged, How the Media, Big Tech, and the Democrats Seized Our Elections (2021 Regnery Publishing)

[2] The Durham Report on the Russian Collusion Investigation published by Special Counsel John Durham in May, 2023.

Nietzsche and all three schools of philosophy were grounded in a critique of Enlightenment philosophy´s ideal of rationality, scientific discourse, and individualism and as such were antithetical to traditional Anglo-Saxon philosophy which until the youth rebellion of 1960s constituted the predominant philosophical strain in the West.

Classic Marxism is first and foremost an economic analysis of capitalism. It failed because its main economic predictions including that of endless class struggle, stagnant real wages and increasing inequality would lead to the overthrow of capitalism, did not fare well in the real world.

Classic Marxism still has its proponents who preach the same message of the rottenness of the capitalist system and its inequalities such as Bernie Sanders and Liz Warren in the U.S and economists like Thomas Piketty in France, but by and large traditional Marxism has lost its intellectual credibility among Western elites.[3]

While classic Marxism today is on life-support, its successor movement, Woke, has retained a crucial component, namely the concept of pitting various sections of society against each other in a ruthless struggle for power.

Except class warfare now has been replaced by a relentless and irreconcilable confrontation between *oppressed and oppressor*, with white men being the oppressors and just about everyone else, including women, belonging to the oppressed.

Woke has become the favorite philosophy of former Marxists and Socialists, the Left and progressives in general.

Why?[4]

Because, faced with the obvious failures of Marxism and Socialism in places as different as the Soviet Union, Mao´s China, and Cambodia in the 20th century, and today´s Cuba and Venezuela, it had to change its line of attack on capitalism and democracy. It went from one of exploitation of the working class (which obviously was doing rather well in the West compared with other parts of the world) and the coming victory of the proletariat (which not even the Marxist terrorist movements of the 1960s and ´70s, like the infamous German Baader-Meinhof Group, had managed to bring about) to one of relativism and subjectivism.

Put simply, because *facts* and *reality* told the Woke that capitalism and democracy and its belief in the common sense of the common man had created hitherto unknown wealth and health for everybody, Woke, had to change its line of attack. And it did, so by reverting to philosophies like those of the Frankfurt School of Critical Theory and Postmodernism, that had hitherto been limited to college campuses and philosophical specialist schools, philosophies which in effect argued that the reality and the facts of progress that everyone claimed to see were not *real*.

Woke ideology decided so to speak to challenge the very concept of reality and fact. Its denial of biology and human nature in favor of a social-constructionist interpretation of political problems, as well as its rejection of individualism for a collectivist perspective that sees human beings as intrinsically shaped by the gender/race/group/class, they were born into, was Marxism redux.

---

[3] For a devastating critique of Classic Marxism see <u>Anti-Piketty,Capiral for the 21sr Century</u>, edited by Jean- Phillipe Delsol et.al.
[4] Hick,Explaining Postmodernism,p.47.

This book traces this transition over 3 stages from *protest to power*, a journey from the youthful exuberance of telling truth to power and opposing any social, political, moral and cultural constraints, to Woke itself coming into power in most Western nations at the beginning of the 21st century.

Stage I: the 60s, the stage of idealism, sexual liberation, and protest.

Stage II: On the one hand this stage describes Woke´s revolutionary attempt to violently overthrow the Western capitalist system in favor of Marxism in the 1970s and 80s.On the other, Woke going *underground* into introspection, self-realization drugs, and political apathy.

Stage III: The post-cold- war period from 1991 until today, where the end of the Cold War and manifest failure of Marxism led proponents of woke ideology to a change of tactics and a gradualist approach to taking over the institutions of the West.

The book demonstrates how Woke succeeded in taking power, namely by infiltrating the main *cultural* institutions of the West, such as anti-racism, identity politics, feminism and transgenderism; but also by hijacking of international *institutions* such as the UN and the EU to further Woke´s political One World Order as exemplified by its open borders, globalization, and climate change policies.

Finally, the book examines Woke´s reaction to criticisms of the obvious shortcomings of its system and its narratives, a reaction that most charitably can be described as a deliberate and ham-fisted attempt at crushing *any* dissent; and Woke´s subsequent descent into intolerance, arrogance, and authoritarianism vis-à-vis those who insist on claiming the right to the same freedoms, including free speech, which Woke once demanded, fought for and obtained.

A note on the methodology of the book.

Historical psychoanalysis is a tool used by philosophers, sociologists, historians, economists and yes, psychologists.

It is the theory underlying Erich Fromm´s, Escape From Freedom(1941)a Neo-Freudian psychologist´s attempt to explain why people sometimes turn to authoritarianism like Hitler and Nazism, because, in his view, they cannot handle the responsibility and challenges of freedom; it is the tool used by the sociologist Robert Putnam in his book Bowling Alone(2000) in which he argues that civic life is collapsing - that Americans aren't joining, as they once did, the groups and clubs that promote trust and cooperation, a development which in turn undermines democracy; and it's the tool used by Canadian psychologist, Jordan B.Peterson in 12 Rules For Life: An Antidote to Chaos(2018) , which among other things debunks the theory of the glass ceiling which is alleged to hold women back, by referring to the historical fact that women in Scandinavian countries in spite of government-paid daycare and no social or educational barriers in a state funded University system, still shy away from STEM(science, technology, engineering and mathematics) jobs because they, in his opinion based on his own clinical psychoanalytic experience, have other priorities: children and family.

It is tool based on the Swiss psychologist, Carl Jung's, theory of *the collective unconscious*. He believed that human beings are connected to each other and their ancestors through a shared set of experiences. And that humans use this collective consciousness to give meaning to the world. And lose it at their mental peril.

Finally, it is a premise of the book that culture is downstream from politics: culture impacts politics, not the other way around.

American and European culture though not synonymous are seen as interdependent. When a young Black man, Michael Brown was shot by a white police officer in Ferguson, Missouri, in 2014, European demonstrators carried signs around saying "Hands Up, Don't Shoot" allegedly Brown´s last words.

It turned out to be a hoax, but the demonstrators didn´t care: culturally Woke has captured the West on both sides of the Atlantic, and though America may be ahead of the game, Europe was quick to get its own sub-chapters of #MeToo and Black Lives Matters and arguably is successfully exporting its Woke green environmentalism, like Extinction Rebellion and Stop the Oil, and its violent Antifa movements, the other way across the pond..

Part I: The Origin and History of Woke

Chapter 1: The Woke Philosophers.

xxxxxxxxxxxxxxxxxxxxxx

God is dead.

Friedrich Nietzsche, German philosopher (1844-1900)

xxxxxxxxxxxxxxxxxxxx

Life has no meaning a priori, It is up to you to give it a meaning, and value is nothing but the meaning that you choose.

Jean Paul Sartre, Existentialist philosopher

xxxxxxxxxxxxxxx

"The psychoanalytic liberation of memory explodes the rationality of the repressed individual. As cognition gives way to re-cognition, the forbidden images and impulses of childhood begin to tell the truth that reason denies."

Herbert Marcuse, Frankfurt School of Critical Theory

xxxxxxxxxxxx

"It is meaningless to speak in the name of-or against-Reason, Truth or Knowledge" [because] "reason is the ultimate language of madness",

Michel Foucault, Postmodernist philosopher.

xxxxxxx

"Reason and power are one and the same",

Jean-Francois Lyotard, Postmodernist philosopher.

xxxxxxx

Postmodernism "seeks not to find the foundation and the conditions of truth but to exercise power for the purpose of social change", and its task is to help students "spot, confront, and work against the political horrors of one´s time".

Frank Lentricchia, Postmodernist philosopher.

Xxxxxxxxx

Who Guards the Guards?"

Juvenal, Roman poet in Satires, 2nd century.

xxxxxxxx

"Politics is *downstream* from culture. In other words, popular culture drives politics, not the other way around"

Jerome Hudson, 50 Things They Don´t Want You to Know.

xxxxxxx

" You never let a serious crisis go to waste. And what I mean by that it's an opportunity to do things you think you could not do before."

Rahm Emmanuel, Chief of Staff of Presidents, Barack Obama.

xxxxxxx

" We need to create fear"

Albert Gore, former US vice-president when asked how to teach people the seriousness of climate change.

From Hans Rosling, Factfulness.

xxxxxxx

God is dead.

Philosophically, Woke started with the German philosopher, Friedrich Nietzsche in the 19th century. [5]

"God is dead is his famous dictum" by which he meant mankind is like the orphaned child who no longer has a father to rely on. How do we face that challenge?

Nietzsche´s answer is that it depends on who we want to be, masters or slaves. To Nietzsche all organic nature is divided into two broad species. herd animals and those that are loners, those that are prey and those that are predators.

The divide is between the strong and the weak.

Those that follow their own path and rebel against social pressure, conformity and yes, religion, and those that believe in conformity and stick together for a sense of security just like herd animals.

---

[5] The underlying premise of Woke as an attack on Enlightenment philosophy and a "philosophy of hate" is inspired by a book by two Danish philosophers, The Bourgeois Order-On the Attack On Everyday Man(Den Borgerlige Orden-Om Angrebet På Det Almindelige Menneske),Eksistensen,2023.

Historically, Judaism and Christianity survived the enslavement of the Egyptians and the Romans by obeying their masters, by suppressing their natural impulses and internalizing a humble, patient obedient self. By turning the other cheek.

God is dead, Nietzsche, says because the morality of Christianity is the morality of the sheep and of the weak.

God is dead so *we* must become gods and create our own values. But only a few are able to embrace the responsibility. Such individuals will raise mankind out of religious and social bondage. They are the Ubermensch, the Overman.

Relativism or anti-rationalism.

A second important part of Nietzschean philosophy was a lack of belief in reason, with Nietzsche describing higher reason as a "state of relations between different passions and desires".

Here is an excerpt from Nietzsche's journals (1886-1887) :

"We believe in reason: this, however, is the philosophy of gray concepts. Language depends on the most naive prejudices. Now we read disharmonies and problems into things because we think only in the form of language - and thus believe in the "eternal truth" of "reason".

"Rational thought is interpretation according to a scheme that we cannot throw off."

Needless to say, this nihilist philosophy sat uneasily with the budding democratic movements in Central Europe at his time, not to say the classic human rights Enlightenment Philosophy of Francis Bacon, John Locke, Edmund Burke and Adam Smith predominant in the Anglo-Saxon world of England and the U.S.

In fact, it represented a fully-fledged counter argument to traditional Enlightenment philosophers.

As such it remains an integral part of Woke philosophy with its sometimes only skin-deep commitment to popular democracy and its disdain for "the masses", the populists and the "deplorables"

The authentic human being.

If all objective and rational values as Nietzsche says are dead and we must create our own values, we must know who we are; and to know who we are we must be authentic.

To the Frankfurt School of Critical Theory, this was the supreme philosophical question whose answer has become one of the main pillars of Woke. How do we live authentic lives?

Its main philosopher, Martin Heidegger, continues Nietzsche's attack on rationality believing reason to be a superficial phenomenon and that words and concepts were obstacles to our coming to know reality. Only by being ourselves and not following rational external influences and stimuli can we live authentic lives.

However, the main influence on Woke, *the* philosopher of the Woodstock generation, was Herbert Marcuse, a neo-Marxist member of the Frankfurt School of Critical Theory.

Church, Family and Capitalism: the evil trifecta.

In *Eros and Civilization* (1955) Marcuse argues that strict morality is designed to repress sexual instincts.

What is commonly understood as "morality", he says, echoing Nietzsche, is actually just a complex shame system designed to make people repressed so that they are more dependable workers. Including religion that shames sexually liberal behavior.

An erotic life is an enjoyable, fulfilling life. By rejecting the moralism and social pressure against sex, and by adopting a more optimistic view of sexuality, Marcuse argues that people could find fulfillment in the way nature intended.

Marcuse in One Dimensional Man(1964)strongly criticizes consumerism and modern "industrial society", which he claims is a form of social control. He argues that while the system we live in may claim to be democratic, it is actually totalitarian. Modern industrial societies have furthermore created an "affluent society", which in increasing comfort have disguised the exploitative nature of the system, and have therefore strengthened means of domination and control. Modern "affluent society" therefore limits opportunities for political revolution against capitalism.

In modern consumer societies, Marcuse argues, a small number of individuals are empowered to dictate our perceptions of freedom by providing us with opportunities to buy our happiness. In this state of "unfreedom", consumers act irrationally by working more than they are required to in order to fulfill actual basic needs, by ignoring the psychologically destructive effects of consumerism, by ignoring the waste and environmental damage it causes, and by searching for social connection to other people through material items.

The individual, Marcuse says, in the process loses his humanity and becomes a tool in the industrial machine and a cog in the consumer machine. Additionally, *advertising* sustains consumerism…..telling the masses that happiness can be bought is an idea that is psychologically damaging to their identity, their authenticity.

Revolution is Marcuse's´ answer, rebellion against the Church, against Family and against Capitalism which suppresses our sexuality, our natural instincts, our desire to do what we want.

 One-Dimensional Man and *Eros and Civilzation* from the perspective of the origins of Woke are some one of the most important templates from which to carry out its deconstruction.

Existentialism.

Nietzsche knew that in a world rid of God and of moral idols, man is now alone and without a master. No one has been less inclined than Nietzsche to believe that such freedom would be easy. In fact, he himself admitted suffering from its most painful by-product:*anguish.*

Existentialism and its main proponent, Jean Paul Sartre,is *the* philosophical movement which articulated this anguish. Sartre´s main work, Nausea (1938)is a direct reference to Nietzsche and his description of the nauseousness of being. Its main character, Antoine Roquentin, is tired of life and in an existential crisis. Everything seems meaningless, pointless, and false and translates into a physical feeling of nausea. Where is his authentic self?

Together with Albert Camus,whose main protagonist in The Stranger(1942) is also an ordinary man who does not care about anything, remains indifferent to his mother´s death, treats women diabolically, and ends up killing an Arab for apparently no reason at all, Existentialism exercised an enormous influence on contemporary thought after the horrors of the Second World War.

Existentialism´s influence on Woke is hard to understand today where it has vanished almost totally from the curricula of universities` psychology faculties, but Sartre and cohorts popularized Nietzsche and Heidegger more than anyone else because they turned a philosophical discourse into a successful literary and cultural movement.

Existentialism´s influence on Woke is seen most keenly today in that staple of Woke philosophy: feminism.

Sartre´s life-long partner (among many others in a life of debauchery), Simone de Beauvoir´s, main contribution to Existentialism was The Second Sex(1949) a fierce attack on the bourgeoisie and patriarchy. The overwhelmingly dominant premise of the book is that the world is dominated by men. Women are the second gender because they are formed by men. Or as she says: One is not borne a woman but becomes one.

It is part of the story of Woke, that as a true existentialist. Simone de Beauvoir lived her own truth. Like Sartre she had many lovers both men and women and like Sartre she had a predilection for young ones.

As a teacher at a lycée in Paris she seduced a young student, Bianca Lamblin and persuaded her to enter into a menage á trois with Sartre.

The parents of one of her students, Natalie Sorokin, filed charges against her for having seduced their daughter, a minor at the time, and she lost her teacher´s license for life.

Perhaps not coincidentally, she campaigned-unsuccessfully- together with Sartre and a postmodernist philosopher, Jaques Derrida,whom we shall meet below, for abolishing the statutory age limit for sex between adults and minors in 1977.

It is a sign of how Woke´s template of oppressor (white men) vs. oppressed (women and everybody else) has taken over our cultural institutions that though their campaign to lower the age of statutory rape went nowhere, Sartre and de Beauvoir in their day were feted as literary and philosophical icons.

Whereas today the high-society couple of Ghislaine Maxwell and rich financier, Jeffrey Epstein, for whom Maxwell, like de Beauvoir for Sartre, groomed underage girls throughout the first two decades of the 21st century, both ended in jail, the latter eventually taking his own life.

Postmodernism.

Woke´s philosophical end stage is Postmodernism: The fusion of Nietzsche´s nihilism, Heidegger's attack on reason, Marcuse's´ Neo-Marxist criticism of capitalism, and Existentialism.

One of its foremost critics has called it "the first ruthlessly consistent statement of the consequences of rejecting realism"[6]:

Postmodernism is as the name indicates a philosophical movement *following* Modernism. Modernism is the world view of the Enlightenment-period of the 18th century, based on reason, objectivity, individualism, and truth, ideas which saw mankind liberate itself from the shackles of political oppression by the elite, the political classes of the day, and escape from the tyranny of religious irrationality and superstition.

---

[6] Stephen C.R.Hicks,Explaining Postmodernism,p.81,Connor Court Publishing,2019.

Woke is best seen as a Counter-Enlightenment movement. And its main point of attack was its attack on reason.

Why?

Because reason is at the core of the Enlightenment project which saw the West bypass all other nations in liberal democracy, capitalism and wealth, science, and medicine.

Reason, the Enlightenment philosophers like Francis Bacon and John Locke argued, is a faculty of the individual which makes individualism as opposed to collectivism a key theme of our ethics. Individualism applied to politics yields liberal democracy, individual freedom against government encroachment and decentralized power to individuals.

Individualism applied to economics yields free markets and capitalism, the outstanding example of that being the Industrial Revolution. Reason applied to science yields engineering and technology. And science applied to human beings yields medicine.

But Postmodernism rejects the entire Enlightenment project as shown by the quotes above.[7]

The most prominent Postmodernists are three French philosophers, Michel Foucault, Jacques Derrida and Jean-Francois Lyotard and an American one, Richard Rorty. Whenever you see or hear anyone quoting or referring to these guys drop everything you have got and run for the hills.

What do you do with a philosophical world view, the pre-dominant one of the Woke world, that *admits* it does *not* seek the truth and is actively political at the same time in its insistence on working "against the political horrors of one's time"? You can ask, of course, "what political horrors" and "compared to what" but you cannot trust their answers because the Postmodernists themselves admit they do not believe in truth or facts and that their words are "rhetoric" to "exercise power for the purpose of social change".

Their philosophical and political world view has been debated and debunked by eminent thinkers like the linguist Noam A. Chomsky, who finds them incomprehensible over the cultural critic, Camille Paglia, who considers Postmodernist professors "frauds and poseurs"[8], by the journalist Douglas Murray in his recent book <u>The War on the West</u> with the significant subtitle, <u>How to Prevail in the Age of Unreason</u>, to my own favorite, Stephen R. C. Hicks, professor of philosophy.

But despite taking a vicious beating it is still around. In fact, some would argue that the riots and mass demonstrations in the summer of 2020 organized by Black Lives Matter which garnered huge popular support all over the West and whose leadership is constituted of self-declared Postmodernist neo-Marxists, is an indication that it is stronger than ever and ready to take over political power.

The Corona-crisis has shown that Postmodernism is the prevailing ideology of our elites at the present time mainly in the West. Andrew Breitbart, the late editor-in-chief of Breitbart News, along with Jerome Hudson, always said:" Politics is downstream from culture", meaning culture drives politics, not the other way around. I agree. Postmodernism is the culture of our elites, and it drives the absurdities of the Woke world.

---

[7] The content of the summary of what Enlightenment stands for in the preceding 4 paragraphs above is from Hicks, <u>Explaining Postmodernism</u>, pp.7-13.
[88] Jordan B. Peterson, <u>12 Rules of Life</u>, p. 310

Don't let a serious crisis go to waste, Obama's right hand man said. What crisis? The financial crisis of 2008 and the Corona-crisis of 2020.That was the crisis of capitalism that Postmodernists had been waiting and hoping for. That's the years when Postmodernism started its move from being an intellectual fad at the university faculties of art and humanities to being mainstream. The Postmodernists didn't let a good crisis go to waste and their success in bringing issues which hitherto had been considered marginal into the mainstream like gender identity, transsexuals, same-sex marriage, gay marriage, climate change and open borders was stunning and swift.

Just a few examples: President Obama, one of the most left-wing presidents in US history, when taking power in 2008 considered marriage a union between a man and a woman. He approved of *civil* unions between same-sex couples but not marriage. 7 years later while he was still President , the Supreme Court made same-sex marriage legal citing changes in popular perceptions and attitudes.

The emergence of Bernie Sanders, an avowed Socialist and until the 2016 US presidential elections an obscure member of the US Senate and not even a member of the Democratic Party, as one of the front-runners of the Democratic Party's presidential candidates for the 2020 US presidential elections is yet another example of Postmodernism going mainstream.

Climate change had been a concern for earnest tree-huggers before 2008, but not the focus on global *warming*. In fact, the climate crowd in the 1970s warned the world about the climate getting *colder*.

But the Postmodernists saw an opening between the anxieties brought on by the financial crisis and the climate change debate and used it as a vehicle for their attempt to attack the capitalist order. And succeeded brilliantly. Teen-ager Greta Thunberg chastising the world's leaders at the United Nations' general Assembly in the fall of 2019 for not doing their job on climate change and ruining the life for her generation being the high-water mark.

In the process, the Postmodernists took Vice-president Gore's somewhat Machiavellian instructions of creating fear to heart. Indeed, the hallmark of Postmodernism is fear morphing into mass hysteria.

The *purpose* of this mass hysteria is to make us afraid, so alarmed, so desperate so panicked that we will accept anything…. everything, to radically change, re-order, re-arrange the world we live in. As the quotes above demonstrate, this mass hysteria does not come about by accident; on the contrary, it is carefully manufactured by Woke which uses the panic, *our* panic, to further their own political and personal careers and…fortunes.

Marxism and Communism viewed everything through the prism of money and class. After the Gulags and the fall of Communism not even the Communists themselves could stand up for Communism, but the fact remains that the philosophical fathers of Woke all considered themselves Marxists. Same brand, new label. The only change is that Postmodernism, instead of viewing everything through the concept of money and class changed its form but not its substance to view everything, and I mean everything, through the prism of *power*.

As Jordan B. Peterson says of the change from Marxism to Postmodernism: "Society was no longer oppression of the poor by the rich. It was oppression of everyone by the powerful".[9] To give an example: the French Postmodernist, Derrida claims that this oppression is built right into everything, even including the language: there is a linguistic group called "women" only because

---

[9] Jordan B. Peterson,12 Rules For Life-An Antidote To Chaos, Allen Lane 2018, p.310.

another hierarchical group called "men", the supposedly more powerful group, gain by excluding women from power. Science exists only to benefit scientists, etc. etc.

You would have thought that after the man-made disasters of collectivist Utopian thinking in Mao´s China, Pol Pot´s Cambodia and Soviet Russia, these Utopians would have learned their lesson. No such luck: What we´re up against is *another* Utopian experiment. Only this time, the new Utopia, which literally in Greek means "the place that isn´t there", is called internationalism, globalism, anti-nationalism, anti-racism, collectivism, open-borders, goodbye to biological determination of our gender to be replaced by a variety of gender identities where you get to make your own pick of which among at least 56 genders you "identify as", etc., etc.

Postmodernists, to justify the need for a new Utopia, have to present a *distorted* picture of the world.

In a democratic presidential candidates' debate in February,2020, Bernie Sanders said: "people ... after 45 years of work are not making a nickel more than they did 45 years ago."

Now that is a statement that is falsifiable and has been falsified time and time again. Yet, Sanders keeps lying about it.

What is the truth?

For those who were not alive then, David Harsanyi, senior editor at The Federalist says, the 1970s were largely a crime-ridden decade of stagnant economics, city bankruptcies, crushing energy prices, sky-high interest rates, institutional rot, garbage and retirement-destroying inflation.

And a big part of the post-'70s economic boom we're still experiencing today -- the one that certain progressive and some statist right-wingers like to disparage -- was propelled by policies that freed most people in the West from overbearing technocratic oversight, intrusive regulations and stifling taxes that undermined growth.

The alleged "wage stagnation" to which Sanders and others are constantly referring is a myth. For one thing, "wage stagnation" fails to consider the health care benefits, pensions, vacations, family leave and other perks now embedded in job packages -- somewhere around 30% of an employee's overall benefits. Once those benefits are added, most people probably have seen about a 45% wage increase since 1964.

In the past 50 years, spending on food and clothing as a share of family income has fallen from 42% to 17%.

The year Sanders graduated from college, less than 6% of his fellow Americans -- most of them wealthy, very few of them minorities or women -- were enrolled in higher education. In 1975, only around 11% were enrolled in college. According to the Federal Reserve study, Millennials are the most educated generation, with 65% of them possessing at least an associate degree.

In 1970, around 14,000 workers were killed on the job in the United States. That is somewhere around 10,000 more deaths yearly than the number of those who perished in the entire Iraq War. Although the workforce had more than doubled since then, the number of occupational deaths in the United States has dropped to around 5,100.

There's a decent chance that Sanders' heart attack would have killed a 78-year-old man in 1975. If not, it would have required dangerous surgery. Despite a small dip recently, life expectancy has skyrocketed in the West over the past 45 years -- adding more than six years since 1975. The cancer casualty rate has fallen more than 27% in the past 25 years. We've been able to mitigate the damage of so many diseases and ailments over the past 45 years -- allowing millions to lead longer, more active and less painful lives -- that it would take a book to lay out the miraculous number of advances properly.

We are, in short, by nearly every quantifiable measure, collectively better off today than ever before. Including Sanders himself because as Harsanyi says: "It's not in every country that a professional revolutionary like him can afford to buy a dacha on Lake Champlain."[10]

Women are prime ministers, CEOs, and heads of mass media-corporations all over the West. Ask the question, *compared to what*, and the obvious answer is that women in the West were the first to get the vote and gain equality under the law and career opportunities that most women in the world are still without.

But what do you do when you are of the Postmodernist persuasion and have been indoctrinated to think that women and blacks by definition are oppressed? You make it up. What do you do when the world you want to revolutionize and turn into a Socialist paradise, like Sanders, already is the closest thing to it? You lie.

If economic and social progress is manifestly everywhere, provable, and factual, there's only one way out for the Postmodernists: lie about it.

Language, as Chomsky says, is not infinitely malleable and we are in a situation where the "double-speak" that George Orwell warned about in his book, <u>1984</u>, has become reality. "Doublespeak is defined as lie by the writer <u>Edward S. Herman</u> in his book *Beyond Hypocrisy*:

"What is really important in the world of doublespeak is the ability to lie, whether knowingly or unconsciously, and to get away with it; and the ability to use *lies* and choose and shape facts selectively, blocking out those that don't fit an agenda or program".

Indeed. And that's the kind of "agenda or program" this book is all about. It's called Woke.

When Woke calls language, it doesn't agree with "violence", the answer to this is of course that although it is true that speech propagates through air and impinges on our ears which are physical organs and when Woke claims that therefore there are only differences of *degree* between someone hitting me with a baseball bat and someone calling me an idiot, there is another major difference: control. I don't have any control over someone wanting to attack me with a baseball bat, but I *can* choose to ignore someone calling me something which in my own opinion I am not.[11] Woke mixes the two vocabularies, the physical and the linguistic into one, to advance its real agenda: getting rid of free speech for those who disagree with them. It's a power play.

If we ignore Orwell's warning and do twist language to our purposes, there's a psychological price to pay: delusion. Woke not only takes away our freedom to express our thought without censorship, it drives us crazy because it distorts reality, the textbook definition of mental disorder.

---

[10] David Harsanyi, Bernie's Wrong: We Are Better Off Today Than We Were 45 Years Ago, Real Clear Politics, Feb.21,2020
[11] Hicks, Explaining Postmodernism, p. 242

If "white privilege" studies are not racism but a way to *combat* racism we have come full Orwellian circle, " Black is indeed the new white" and if you can´t see it, you are not just blind but…a racist.

By demonizing words like "nigger" we don´t make racism go away.

Just like we don´t eradicate racism by removing statues of Robert E. Lee, general of the Confederacy´s Army. We distort reality and the history of our own nature.

It isn´t that Postmodernism doesn´t have a point in warning against the dangers of just blithely accepting the way we use language. "Nigger" is and was historically a way of expressing racism and disrespect for people of color.

It is that Postmodernism´s real target never was racism but changing society according to their ideological beliefs by replacing our language by a new language which is totalitarian and whose purpose is to take away our freedom of *thought*. It is a politically based linguistic exorcism that wants us to believe that by cutting away the devils and demons that make humans do evil deeds we can create the illusion that deep down we are better than that. And somebody else made us do it.

Only we aren´t and nobody else did.

We must face our own human nature and sometimes dark history realistically.

Denying human nature and its history will not help us live happier lives.

The truth, on the other hand, linguistically, scientifically, psychologically and socially *will* set us free and keep us sane.

How do you spot a Postmodernist? Do they wear French berets and speak English like the actors in Allo, Allo, an English sitcom about a French café owner during German occupation?

 They might, but it is not foolproof. A more useful tool is language. If someone's speech is full of them vs. us, wrong side of history, oppressor vs. oppressed, villains and victims, there is good chance you´ve got yourself a Postmodernist. Secondly, all Postmodernists believe in not just equality of opportunity and equality before the law, but equality of *outcome*. They call it equity.

Western society's doctrine of equality of opportunity is based on the biological fact that talent is widely distributed. Some people, not groups of people but individuals, are much better at doing a given task than others, and it is in society's interest to allow such differences in talent to be played out.

Not so, say the Postmodernists. The difference in outcome between social groups, men and women, blacks and whites, that , they postulate, can only be explained by systemic discriminations. What Black Lives Matters, in the face of all evidence, call *systemic* racism.

It is no coincidence that President Joe Biden's first act on his first day in office was to sign an Executive Order instructing all federal agencies to promote equity.

And that's a totally different ball of wax. Why? Because if taken seriously it leads to totally different policy solutions, namely massive state interventions in all areas of life.

Take jobs, f.ex. The work categories, in the U.S. that favor men the most are vehicle technicians, mechanics, and electricians, (above 99%).

What Biden is doing may sound innocuous but it isn´t. The Federal government is a huge employer of private companies and Postmodernists, like Biden, are effectively compelling companies to hire more women .But since not enough female electricians are around, Biden would be "forced " to make drastic changes to post-secondary education, possibly involving strict quotas, justified by ,as Jordan B. Peterson, author of 12 Rules of Life, says, "the obvious "fact" that the reason this pipeline problem exists is the absolutely pervasive sexism that characterizes all the programs that train such workers(and the catastrophic and prejudicial failure of the educational system that is thereby implied".

Furthermore, policies of eradicating differences in outcome have already been tried. And failed. In the U.S through more than 50 years of years of positive discrimination in favor of African Americans and against whites with the Orwellian name of affirmative action. And elsewhere such as in my country, Denmark, and the rest of Scandinavia.

As Jordan B. Peterson says, "Countries that have pushed the laudable doctrines of equality of opportunity most assiduously (that would be the Scandinavian states) have the lowest level rates of STEM enrolment among females in the world, as it turns out that freed females, given free choice, do not often voluntarily become engineers and mathematicians and physicists".[12]

The fact is that Utopian experiments, from the Soviet Union to Mao´s China, from Lenin´s Communist revolution in 1917 to the dictatorship of Victor Chavez and his successors in Venezuela have all ended in failure.

The Woke will wave this argument away with the claim that real socialism has never been *really* tried. And that Venezuelans have a better health-care system and less inequality than the US, so never mind the lack of freedom of speech and its political prisoners.

But it is a lie. Venezuela´s health-care system lacks basic medicines and medical technologies that even a non-insured US citizen enjoys on a trip to the emergency room; and while it is true that inequality ratings are lower in Venezuela it is only because *everybody* is dirt poor.

And it´s a lie because democratic Socialism really has been tried and failed in countries from Israel, over China to India. All three countries started the first part of their nationhood in the 1940s as decidedly socialist. Just think Mao´s Great Leap Forward, Kibbutzim in Israel and Nehru´s 5-year plans.

Today, all three countries have escaped the grinding poverty of their early years by adopting capitalist models of production. And for those who still aren´t convinced, socialism is still being *really* tried in unfree places like North Korea and Vietnam. And it is *still* not doing well. Only the very naïve, or willfully blinded ideologues and Postmodernists, can ignore the bloody history of socialism and its destruction of democracy and the deaths of millions of individuals in each and all of the countries in which it has been implemented; people who tempted fate by allowing their hearts to rule their heads.

Having established where Woke came from philosophically, we must now tell the story of the *people* who made Woke´s transition from the halls of Academe to everyday life possible.

---

[12] All quotes from Jordan B. Peterson, When the left goes too far-the dangerous doctrine of equity, They don´t care that there are well-documented reasons for unequal outcomes in occupational choice and pay in addition to whatever role genuine prejudice plays, National Post, May 10,2019

Part I: The Origin and History of Woke

Chapter 2: The Three Stages of Woke

This book is about the world my parents' generation, the woke generation, left me: the men and women who promised freedom, sexually, socially, culturally, and politically but who when they came to power delivered angst, hypocrisy, polarization, and panic.[13]

It is about deconstructing their concept of themselves, their narratives.

In modern psychology, narrative has a special meaning. It's not a spin or an angle or a lens through which to interpret the politics of the world nor is it your autobiography.

It is who you are.

This book sets out to deconstruct Woke's road from protest to power in the West and explain how the movement's original idealism and enthusiasm ossified into authoritarianism and elitist arrogance.

Woke's favorite analytical tool is deconstruction. It has deconstructed the Founding Fathers of America as being slaveowners (which they were) and racists(which they weren't) leading to the now ubiquitous charges of white privilege and systemic racism; it has deconstructed Hitler and Mussolini as right wing (which they were not, Hitler being the founder of the NSDAP, as the Nazi-party was officially called and which stands for National *Socialist* German *Workers'* Party and was a believer in eugenics, a racial "health "theory, which was the brain-child of the Left, and Mussolini being a member of the *Socialist* Party in Italy before founding the Fascist Party)and fanatical rabble-rousing populists,(which they were); which has led to the now stock accusations by the Left against conservative politicians like Trump or other members of the GOP in the U.S. or Victor Orban in Hungary of being "fascists" or "nazis" or comparing them with Hitler.

But Woke has been strangely hesitant to deconstruct its *own* narrative. This book will do the work for them.

Woke won't like it but only by deconstructing woke ideology's narratives of identity politics, internationalism, radical environmentalism, and a new McCarthyism will we be able to understand and change today's culture and its politics.

Let's start at the beginning.

---

[13] This sentence paraphrases the subtitle of Boomers, a book by Helen Andrews: Boomers-the Men and Women Who Promise Freedom and Delivered Disaster, Sentinel,2021.

Culturally, proponents of Woke are the founders and unrepentant apostles of one of the greatest countercultural movements in history: the 60s.

The first thing that strikes me when deconstructing the woke narrative is that even after *becoming* the system, the Woke, the Civil Rights icons still around like Jesse Jackson or even former Democratic Presidents like Barack Obama and Bill Clinton, confusingly, still act and talk as if they are *fighting* the system.

Obviously, both cannot simultaneously be true, and the conclusion this book arrives at is that Woke, its set of political values, and thus those of our day and age, was the result of much more complex philosophical and historical developments than it will have us believe.

Developments, which are far less flattering to its own self-serving narrative, and which essentially played out not just in the 1960s but in three stages lasting until today:

Stage I: the 60s.

---

xxxxxxxxxxxxxxxxxxxxxxxxxxxxxxxxxxxxx

"We were young, we were reckless, arrogant, silly, headstrong-and we were right".[14]

Abbie Hoffman, student leader and activist, in 1989.

xxxxxxxxxxxxxxxxxxxxxxxxxxxxxxxxxxxxxx

"The sixties produced an anarchic mind-set that is great for imagining a world not yet in existence."

Walter Isaacson in his book, Steve Jobs: The Exclusive Biography.

Xxxxxxxxxxxxxxxxxxxxxxxxxxxxxxxxxxxxxx

"We ended a war, toppled two presidents and desegregated the South".

Tom Hayden, Freedom Rider and civil rights activist.[15]

Xxxxxxxxxxxxxxxxxxxxxxxxxxxxxxx

"Hey,hey,ho,ho. Western Civ has got to go."

---

[14] Boomers, p. 195
[15] Idem.

Civil Rights icon, Jesse Jackson, and around 500 protesters on January 15,1987, protesting Stanford University's introductory humanities program known as "Western Culture." For its lack of "diversity."

Xxxxxxxxxxxxxxxxxxxxxxxxxxxxxxx

"Don´t trust anybody over 30".

<u>Jack Weinberg, Student activist during the free speech movement at Berkely</u>.

Xxxxxxxxxxxxxxxxxxxxxxxxxxxxxxxxx

In the US The 60s are the Woodstock generation. Flower Power Generation, The Hippies.

In France the 60s are named after the series of students' revolts and strikes in France in May 1968: les soixante-huitards.

But the best word to describe it is in Danish: Ungdomsoprøret: the Youth rebellion.

For that is what it was.

The 60s were above all an adolescent rebellion. Woke rebelled against authorities whether in the shape of parents, church, family, teachers, anybody in authority laying down rules.

It was pubescent, irrational and .at least initially, almost wholly driven by biology. The politics of it came later, such as the anti-war movement driven by the war in Vietnam, the Anti-Nuclear Movement in Europe, Women´s Lib etc.

All youth throughout history has rebelled against their parents.

What is historically exceptional about the 60s' cohort of youths was its sheer numbers and in consequence its voting power as the post-World War II generation came of voting age in the 1960s.Combined with the emergence of new technologies, starting with TV and after that computers and I-phones which made the woke generation a highly sought after class of consumers.

All of this translated into power "far beyond the normal generational allotment" as one prominent Millennial critic of the Boomers, Helen Andrew, has expressed it.

"Since they came of age" she says, they have been America´s largest voting bloc, the largest advertising demography, the most important readers, drivers, diners, concertgoers. They were dominant in their youth when elders flattered their idealism and advertisers chased their dollars, and they clung tenaciously to their dominance for the next half century".[16]

It was a time when the most energetic and ideological leaders of the West made a bid to reform and change their world in a more humane and just way, rallying around various" loosely linked moral crusades " [17]such as the civil rights movement, the anti-nuclear energy movement, women´s lib and last but not least a sexual revolution "untethered to tradition and prudery", all

---

[16] Boomers, p.1 &2.
[17] Christopher Caldwell, The Age of Entitlement, Simon, and Schuster,2020.

revolutionary changes that taken together constituted the "most dramatic sundering of Western civilization sine the Protestant Revolution".[18]

Let's deconstruct the most sacrosanct element of the woke narrative: the Civil Rights Act of 1964.

Politically, the Civil Rights Act of 1964 is the top prize in the woke trophy cabinet is. But if our woke parents "solved" racism in America and civil rights activists are still dining out on their 1960s heroics, why have race riots become increasingly frequent since then, indeed, why did the biggest race riots in U.S. history, the George Floyd riots, take place all over America including its biggest Southern cities not too long ago in the summer of 2020?

Firstly, more Republicans voted for the Civil Rights Act than Democrats. There is an explanation for that namely that Southern Democrats were in political power and had been since the Civil War all over the South and they weren't about giving it up without a fight.

But it does paint a more complex picture than the one our progressive parents want us to believe, namely that of the civil rights as a battle between good and evil, progressivism v. conservatism, Democrats v. Republicans.

Secondly, the Civil Rights acts have proved an unmitigated disaster that continues to split America down the middle.

Why?

Because the Civil Rights Act of 1964 and its successors not only banned discrimination on the *basis of color* in public places from voting booths to hotels and restaurants and swimming pools but empowered the federal government to reform and abolish institutions that stood in the way of racial equality. It expanded the power of the Civil Rights Commission enormously, by subjecting to bureaucratic scrutiny any company or institution that received government money; it laid out hiring practices for all companies with more than 15 employees, created a new agency the Equal Employment Opportunity Commission with the power to file lawsuits, conduct investigation and order redress and in the process emboldened and incentivized bureaucrats, lawyers, intellectuals and last but not least political agitators like the Woke cohort to become the foot soldiers of civil rights enforcement.

But worst of all, Section 706(g) of the Civil Rights Act introduced the concept of positive discrimination, its somewhat Orwellian name is "affirmative action", which allowed the government to compel the hiring of black people, if a company had engaged in "unlawful practices" which not only flew in the face of constitutionally mandated equality before the law but opened almost all American businesses to lawsuits for discrimination.

Not unsurprisingly ,the scope of the Civil Rights Act of 1964 was quick expanded to include not just the discrimination on the basis of color but also the discrimination on the basis of sex, effectively moving the goalposts from civil rights to human rights, meaning that employers accused of sexism in hiring practices of women could expect the full force of the expansive new powers of the federal government to come down on them; and from then Woke expanded its scope to include people with disabilities and recently, transgender people.

---

[18] Boomers, p.2.

So now, Woke was assimilating society's. white men's, treatment of women, handicapped and transgender people as on a par with slave owners´ institutionalized plantation- based slavery during a historically limited period of time and in specific geographic region of the U.S.

The Civil Rights Act in fact became a template, not just to do away with one heinous exception in American culture, the racism of the South, but one that broke with every political tradition of equality before the law in America and became The New Constitution. [19]

Somehow, I don´t think that discriminating against white Americans in favor of black Americans through affirmative action is what Woke´s Freedom Riders, originally 7 black and 6 young white men who set out to enforce two Supreme Court rulings, which declared that segregated bathrooms, waiting rooms and lunch counters were unconstitutional, and that it was unconstitutional to implement and enforce segregation on interstate buses and trains, had in mind.

But that is what Woke created and what we are stuck with.

The same development happened in Europe with the adoption in 1950 of The European Convention on Human Rights (ECHR) which protects the human rights of people in countries that belong to the Council of Europe.

The idea for the creation of the ECHR was proposed in the early 1940s while the Second World War was still raging across Europe. It was developed to ensure that governments would never again be allowed to dehumanize and abuse people's rights with impunity, and to help fulfil the promise of 'never again'.

Woke´s implicit premise was that existing *institutional* guarantees to protect human rights on a *national* level were insufficient just as traditional *constitutional* guarantees in the U.S. had proved ineffective in enforcing the human rights of black Americans in one part of country.

But just as with the Civil Rights Act, the woke cure proved worse than the disease.

Civil rights activist and their NGOs used their lobbying power to bring cases to the court implementing the ECHR, the European Court on Human Rights, and in the end captured the court completely by having their own activists appointed judges, sometimes adjudicating cases that they themselves had brought before the court.

Today, the Court´s reputation lies in tatters and countries all over Europe are routinely ignoring its decisions with impunity.

Politically, the founding document of Stage I is the Port Huron statement, written by the President of the most influential student group of the 60s, Students for a Democratic Society, SDS, Tom Hayden, at a SDS conference of students in 1962. The Port Huron Statement is significant because by criticizing America's faith in technology, affluence, and above all mindless consumerism and materialism, the statement provided a foundation for the counterculture of the 1960s and beyond."[20]

---

[19]This argument paraphrases Civil Rights Act subchapter, p.9, in The Age of Entitlement by Christopher Caldwell, Simon and Schuster,2020.
[20] David Krugler, Students for a Democratic Society, The Port Huron Statement (New York: The Student Department of the League for Industrial Democracy, 1964).

Philosophically, the philosopher most frequently associated with this first stage of Woke's narrative, the 60s, its guru so to speak, was Herbert Marcuse, the neo-Marxist member of the Frankfurt School of Critical Theory discussed above whose philosophical message of throwing off the shackles of capitalism, materialism and consumerism and throwing off your clothes in the process proved an irresistible drug for the Woke.

Culturally, Stage I is the Hippie stage of radical individualism, frank hedonism and sexual excesses; it is the one we all know, and it constitutes the initial phase of the rebellion. And the initial phase of the initial phase, was, quite possibly, one of the schmalziest ever.

It is the flower-power stage and the lyrics of the Scott McKenzie song 1967from say it all:

"If you are going to San Francisco
Be sure to wear some flowers in your hair
If you are going to San Francisco
You are gonna meet some gentle people there

For those who come to San Francisco
Summertime will be a love-in there
In the streets of San Francisco
Gentle people with flowers in their hair.

All across the nation such a strange vibration
People in motion
There is a whole generation with a new explanation
People in motion people in motion.

For those who come to San Francisco
Be sure to wear some flowers in your hair."
If you come to San Francisco
Summertime will be a love-in there.

If you come to San Francisco
Summertime will be a love-in there.

"Gentle people with flowers in their hair" were staging a "love-in "there in San Francisco, and those people were "a whole generation with a new *explanation*". That explanation was love and that love conquers all and The Beatles, in agreement, were singing "All you Need is Love".

There was messianic quasi-religious tone to it all, perhaps best illustrated by one of the seminal books of the `50s and ´60, and a forerunner to the Woke, The Catcher In the Rye, whose main protagonist finds growing up very hard to do, struggles with school, sex and love and ends up telling us what his real ambitions are from a mental health sanatorium in L.A.:

> "I'm standing on the edge of some crazy cliff. What I have to do, I have to catch everybody if they start to go over the cliff—I mean if they're running and they don't look where they're going I have to come out from somewhere and catch them.
>
> That's all I'd do all day. I'd just be the catcher in the rye and all."

The flower part of stage I quickly came to an end and running headfirst into reality, turned to revolt on a personal scale against parents, consumerism and societal conventions.

No work of art encapsulates this stage of Woke's revolt better than the 1967 movie, <u>The Graduate</u>. And no movie has been more mislabeled than this film, which has respectively been said to be about "A disillusioned college graduate[who] finds himself torn between his older lover and her daughter" or an "American romantic comedy-drama film".

Let's deconstruct what message Woke was sending us through this movie.

The film is based on a book by Charles Webb and is partly autobiographical-Mrs. Robinson for example is based on a real-life neighbor, Jane Ericsen. Webb, accepted no financial benefits or royalties, distanced himself from the movie adaptation's huge success, throughout his life championed an anti-materialist philosophy and ended up living in poverty.

The key to the film is its soundtrack, mainly the Simon and Garfunkel song, "The Sound of Silence".

Hello darkness, my old friend
I've come to talk with you again
Because a vision softly creeping
Left its seeds while I was sleeping
And the vision that was planted in my brain
Still remains
Within the sound of silence.

In restless dreams, I walked alone
Narrow streets of cobblestone
'Neath the halo of a street lamp
I turned my collar to the cold and damp
When my eyes were stabbed by the flash of a neon light
That split the night
And touched the sound of silence

And in the naked light, I saw
Ten thousand people, maybe more
People talking without speaking
People hearing without listening
People writing songs that voices never shared
And no one dared
Disturb the sound of silence

"Fools" said I, "You do not know
Silence like a cancer grows
Hear my words that I might teach you
Take my arms that I might reach you"
But my words, like silent raindrops fell
And echoed in the wells of silence

And the people bowed and prayed
To the neon god they made
And the sign flashed out its warning
In the words that it was forming
Then the sign said, "The words on the prophets are written on the subway walls
In tenement halls"
And whispered in the sound of silence.

The sound of silence is what Buddhists call a koan. Zen Buddhist masters use these paradoxes to force their pupils to abandon reason in favor of sudden enlightenment. As such it invites irrationalism or distrust of reason as the way forward towards spiritual health. In this, as discussed earlier, the Graduate is truly Woke.

The Graduate, therefore, is only superficially, a romantic comedy- drama film or about the transition from childhood to adulthood, but rather, once deconstructed, it constitutes Woke's representation of what in its opinion was and still is wrong with Western Society.

When one of his fathers' business friends says to Benjamin, the Graduate,"I just have one word for you: Plastics! , it may be a well-meant piece of a career-advice, but what it really constitutes is a comment on a society that just like plastic- a material that can be shaped into anything you want-has no intrinsic moral values other that money-which is not a moral value. When Simon and Garfunkle satirize "the people [who]bowed and prayed to the neon god they made" they are criticizing capitalism and consumerism for being non-human, artificial and phoney, at odds with who we really are as human beings. After all, neon is as artificial a light-source as plastic is artificial material.

When at the beginning Benjamin is standing at the bottom of the pool in a diver's outfit and helmet, the symbolism is clear: there is nothing of value to search for in Western society just as little as in the bottom of a sterile swimming pool.

The Graduate, thus deconstructed, is a search for spirituality, a search which becomes a dead-end when it is just about sex, transactional like a business relationship of quid pro quo as in Ben's loveless affair with Mrs. Robinson; and symbolically ends with the love-struck rejecting society- and traditional Christian values-by barring *their* parents inside a church-while running away to another and better world.

Stage I is the stage which its leaders like Abbie Hoffmann consider the real and only 60s.But what they are hiding from us is that there were two more stages to Woke's narrative:

Stage II-The 1970s and ´80s.

I think we are constantly faced with the same decision. The decision to be blindly obedient to authority versus the decision to try and change things by fighting the powers that be is always, throughout history, the only decision.

-Abbie Hoffman, student leader and activist.

xxxxxxxxxxxxxxxxxxxxxxxxxxxxxx

"Protest is when I say I don't like this. Resistance is when I put an end to what I don't like. Protest is when I say I refuse to go along with this anymore. Resistance is when I make sure everybody else stops going along too."
Ulrike Meinhof Founder of the Red Army Fraction or Baader-Meinhof Group.

Xxxxxxxxxxxxxxxxxxxxxxxxxxxxxxxxxxxxxxx

"Dr. King's policy was that nonviolence would achieve the gains for black people in the United States. His major assumption was that if you are nonviolent, if you suffer, your opponent will see your suffering and will be moved to change his heart. That's very good. He only made one fallacious assumption: In order for nonviolence to work, your opponent must have a conscience. The United States has none."

Stokeley Carmichael, Black Power Leader

"Wir sagen natürlich, die Bullen sind Schweine. Wir sagen, der Typ in Uniform ist ein Schwein, kein Mensch. Und so haben wir uns mit ihnen auseinanderzusetzen. Das heißt, wir haben nicht mit ihm zu reden, und es ist falsch, überhaupt mit diesen Leuten zu reden. Und natürlich kann geschossen werden."

(We say, of course the cops are pigs. We say, the guy in uniform is a pig, not a person. And that is the way we have to deal with them. That means we don´t have to talk to him, it is wrong even to talk to these people. And of course, we can shoot) (my translation)

Ulrike Meinhof
xxxxxxxxxxxxxxxxxxxxxxxxxxxxxxxx

By the 1970s Woke turned both radical and inward.

The SDS, the epicenter of the 1st stage of Woke, logically, quickly became the focal point in the Hippie movement's transition from non-violent democratic methods to open revolutionary revolt. Thus, Weatherman, or the Weather Underground Organization, co-founded by Barack Obama's friend and colleague, Bill Ayers, was a faction of the SDS and "the first and by far the largest group of people to launch a nationwide campaign of underground violence on American soil."[21]

As an SDSer named Dotson Rader put it:

"The meaninglessness of non-violent,"democratic" methods was becoming clear to us in the spring of 1967.The Civil Rights Movement was dead. Pacifism was dead. Some Leftists, the Trotskyites, Maoists, radical socialists…some of the radicals in SDS, Stokeley Carmichael, Rap Brown, Tom Hayden-knew it early. But it took the rest of us awhile to give up the sweet life of the democratic Left for revolt."[22]

In Denmark a similar development took place starting with a musical festival in 1970 in Thy,a remote part of Western Denmark, which turned into a 74 day love-in experiment that ended brutally when radical Marxist elements in the camp took over and initiated the occupation of a near-by church,Hjardemål Kirke, which forced the police into a violent stand-off and the subsequent closing of the camp.

In Germany, a similar transition took place led by Wilfred Willi Rudolf "Rudi" Dutschke, a German sociologist and political activist who, until severely injured by an assassin in 1968, was a leading charismatic figure within the Socialist Students Union in West Germany, and that country's broader "extra-parliamentary opposition."

Philosophically, as discussed above, the philosopher most frequently associated with this first stage of the Woke narrative, the 60s, its guru so to speak, was Herbert Marcuse, a neo-Marxist member of the Frankfurt School of Critical Theory which in turn was the main philosophical inspiration for the French neo-Marxist Postmodernists which laid the philosophical foundations for Woke.

An unlikely hero, the bespectacled German philosopher believed and persuaded his followers that, unlike traditional philosophy until then which had largely stayed away from politics, his brand of philosophy, the Frankfurt School of Critical Theory, saw itself in direct conflict with capitalism and posited that consequently it was the duty of the proletariat, including the

---

[21] Bryan Burrough's <u>Days of Rage-America's Radical Underground, the FBI, and the Forgotten Age of Revolutionary Violence,</u> Penguin Books,2015, p.55.

[22] Quoted in Bryan Burrough's <u>Days of Rage-America's Radical Underground, the FBI, and the Forgotten Age of Revolutionary Violence,</u> Penguin Books,2015, pp.59-60.

dispossessed and students, to overthrow the existing capitalist system and its institutions like the Family and the Church which were all suppressing people's natural instincts s and desires.[23]

These were the days of radical revolutionary Marxist terrorism when bombing by domestic, often student-based, terrorist groups were daily occurrences in the West. The days of the Symbionese Liberation Army, the Weathermen and the Black Liberation Army in the U.S.as described in Bryan Burrough's Days of Rage-America's Radical Underground, the FBI, and the Forgotten Age of Revolutionary Violence [24]; and of the Red Brigades of Italy ,the Red Army Fraction or Baader-Meinhof Group in Germany, or of the Basque separationist movement, ETA, in Spain, the most murderous terrorist movement of them all which killed mor than 800 people during its reign; all neo-Marxist movements(there is a reason they called themselves red!) with deep roots in the counter-culture of the 60s as shown by recent academic research.[25]

Why did Woke turn to terrorism in the 1970s and `80s?

There are 5 main reasons[26]:

-*Epistemologically*, the prevailing academic and intellectual climate was either anti-reason, ineffectual in defending reason, or saw reason as irrelevant to practical matters. Nietzsche and Heidegger spoke the new language of thought. Reason is out, the intellectuals were teaching, and what matters above all is will, authentic passion and non-rational commitment.

Practically, after a century of waiting for the revolution, impatience had peaked, especially among the younger generation who wanted decisive action *now*.

Morally, there was the extreme disappointment of the failure of the classic socialist ideal, the fact that Marxism had failed to materialize. There was widespread rage at the betrayal of the utopian dream in the Soviet Union.

Psychologically, in addition to this disappointment, there was the supreme insult of seeing the hated enemy, capitalism, flourishing.

Politically, there was the justification of violence in the theories of the Frankfurt School, as applied by Marcuse. The revolutionary knows that the masses are oppressed but held captive by the veil of capitalist false consciousness. So, he knows with Nietzschean certainty that it will take individuals with special insights and special courage to break down the capitalist system.

The 1970s,it is easily forgotten, saw a concerted attack on *democracy*, including the murders of Prime Ministers in Italy(Aldo Moro killed by the Red Brigade) and Spain (Carrero Blanco killed by ETA)and leading members of government(Detlef Rohwedder, Head of Treuhand, an organization charged with integrating East German businesses into West Germany after

---

[23] Explaining Postmodernism by Stephen C. Hicks, p.154, Connor Court Publishing 2019.
[24] Bryan Burrough's Days of Rage-America's Radical Underground, the FBI, and the Forgotten Age of Revolutionary Violence, Penguin Books,2015.
[25] , Die Rote-Armee-Fraktion: Irrweg in die Gewalt "(The RAF-Lost Road to Violence),PhD-thesis by : Anna-Katharina Zahrl,Vienna,2012.
The Red Brigades-The Story of Italian Terrorism, by Robert C. Meade Jr.,Palgrave Macmillan,1990.
El Desafio: ETA (ETA: The Challenge) an Amazon Prime Video Documentary laying bare its Marxist roots.
[26] Paraphrasing Hicks,in Explaining Postmodernism,The Rise and fall of Left Terrorism,p.166-168

Germany´s Unification in 1989) and industry (industrialist HannsMartin Schleuer,Head of the German Employers 'Federation and banker, Alfred Herrhausen, Head of Deutsche Bank)killed by RAF in an attempt to install a new Marxist system in the West. Woke failed, but only just, and not for want of trying.

The poster child in the U.S. of this transition from flower-power to gun-power is Patricia Hearst, the rich heiress of the powerful Hearst-family who went underground in the 1970s only to emerge on a blurred CCTV picture robbing a bank as an armed member of the Symbionese Liberation Army.

Bob Dylan anticipated the angry violence of the 1970s in his <u>Subterranean Homesick Blues</u> the first track of his LP, <u>Bringing It all Back Home</u>(1965),for these were the days when Woke literally went underground, subterranean, to continue its protests with violence and bombs, and what Johnny is doing in the basement is mixing up the medicine, the bombs, to be used against the soulless society, dysfunctional, police state("the man in a trench coat, badge out", "watch the plainclothes ")Woke imagined were all around it: Look out, kid, Don't matter what you did, Walk on tip toes, Don't tie no bows, Better stay away from those, That carry ´round a fire hose, Keep a clean nose, Watch the plainclothes, You don't need a weather man,To know which way the wind blows.

> Johnny's in the basement
> Mixing up the medicine
> I'm on the pavement
> Thinking about the government
> The man in a trench coat
> Badge out, laid off
> Says he's got a bad cough
> Wants to get it paid off
>
> Look out, kid
> It's somethin' you did
> God knows when
> But you're doin' it again
> You better duck down the alley way
> Lookin' for a new friend
> A man in a coon-skin cap
> In a pig pen
> Wants eleven dollar bills
> You only got ten.
>
> Maggie comes fleet foot
> Face full of black soot
> Talkin' that the heat put
> Plants in the bed but
> The phone's tapped anyway
> Maggie says that many say
> They must bust in early May
> Orders from the DA

Look out, kid
Don't matter what you did
Walk on your tip toes
Don't tie no bows
Better stay away from those
That carry around a fire hose
Keep a clean nose
Watch the plainclothes
You don't need a weather man
To know which way the wind blows.

Ah, get sick, get well
Hang around an ink well
Ring bell, hard to tell
If anything is gonna sell
Try hard, get barred
Get back, write Braille
Get jailed, jump bail
Join the army, if you fail

Look out kid
You're gonna get hit
By losers, cheaters
Six-time users
Hanging 'round the theaters
Girl by the whirlpool is
Lookin' for a new fool
Don't follow leaders
Watch the parkin' meters.

Ah, get born, keep warm
Short pants, romance, learn to dance
Get dressed, get blessed
Try to be a success
Please her, please him, buy gifts
Don't steal, don't lift
Twenty years of schoolin'
And they put you on the day shift

Look out kid
They keep it all hid
Better jump down a manhole
Light yourself a candle
Don't wear sandals
Try to avoid the scandals
Don't wanna be a bum
You better chew gum

> The pump don't work
> 'Cause the vandals took the handle.

In Europe there are many examples of how the summer of love of 1968 turned sour, the best description being the 2-Volume Danish history of this mythical countercultural revolution called <u>The Hippies</u>.[27]

The iconic image remaining in most people's memory is that of a Marxist radical student leader, pushing the Dean of the University of Copenhagen which the students forcibly occupied for months, Mogens Fog, aside with very little resistance. Fog in fact declared himself in agreement with the students and thus legitimized their actions while hiding the fact that he sympathized with the Danish Communist Party, whose interests he served even after leaving the party, and whose members, of course, welcomed any chance to challenge the capitalist system.

On the other hand, this was the time when those believers in Woke who could neither abide the underground terrorism nor the existing materialistic, consumerist society around them, which they thought had lost its way, turned into self-imposed internal exile.

Often with help of drugs.

Early conservative social criticism has focused on the hedonistic getting-high aspects of drug taking.

But psychologically Woke's explanation and justification for drugs was spiritual: self-actualization, a truly Woke psychological concept, as discussed in the preceding chapter, namely that our senses do not adequately tell our mind the real story about the world.

Woke was told that it needed to expand its mind, and drugs were just one of many ways, including Yoga, meditation, mantras and Zen Buddhism. A University of Minnesota professor called Robert Pirsig wrote a book about a long motorcycle journey with his son along the backroads of America called <u>Zen and the Art of Motorcycle Maintenance</u> and for a while starting with Timothy Leary being ejected from Harvard for his demonstration of the "benefits" of LSD, drugs were the spiritual solution with which Woke tried to turn away from the sameness of suburbia, the wasteland of Western consumerism and seek new identities in internal exile.

Culturally the high point of this self-imposed internal exile was the Coen Brothers' cult movie movie, <u>The Big Lebowski</u>.from 1998.

Let's deconstruct this cult classic and see what it really says about Woke's narrative about itself.

Firstly, the main character, the Dude, literally personifies the internal exile from society that is so characteristic of Woke's transition into the 1970s, in that in most of his scenes he is either wearing pajamas or clothes that look like ones.

Another thing this part of the Woke did not take seriously was school.

When talking to Brandt, the Big Lebowsli's secretary, the Dude, when asked whether he went to college, answers:

---

[27] Mads Øvig, Hippie 1, 3 År og 74 Dage Der Forandrede Danmark (3 Years and 74 Days That Changed Denmark), and Hippie 2-Den Sidste Sommer (The Last Sommer (published by Gyldendal in 2011 and 2012 respectively.

> " Yeah, I did, but I spent most of my time occupying various administration buildings, smoking a lot of thai stick, breaking into the OTC and bowling. Tell the truth, Brandt, I don´t remember most of it."

Many critics have wanted to identify the genre of the movie and struggled; and the reason for that is simple: there isn´t one.

Ethan Coen the co-director-writer together with Nathan of the movie, wrote his senior thesis of philosophy on Ludwig Wittgenstein, an Austrian philosopher who was deeply influenced by the same anti-Enlightenment philosophical movements that shaped Nietzsche, Critical Theory and Postmodernism discussed earlier.

His theories of the meaning of language run through the movie like a red thread, And to cut it short: he didn´t think much of it. In fact, he thought of language as a game that can be played according to certain rules but says very little about the actual world.

And I think that's the point of *The Big Lebowski* as well: at its heart it is existentialist; it is about the meaninglessness of life.

Funny and charming, its meaningless banter caught the tenor of Woke´s retreat from taking life seriously.

Almost every character in the movie engages in some form of empty rhetoric including Maude, who bandies words "vagina" and "Johnson" around for no other purpose than to see if they make the Dude uncomfortable. (Which they don´t). And over and over scenes end when the Dude's conversation with another character slips into just moving words around detached from any meaning, at which point the Dude loses interest and just walks away.

Walter, the Vietnam veteran, is the epitome of language and communication as game-playing. And the Dude´ subsequent frustration

When Walther and the Dude discuss what to do about the two thugs, one of whom is Chinese, peeing on the Dude´s carpet mistakenly thinking he is the Big Lebowski not the small one and the Dude says:

> "The Chinaman, I can´t just go out and give him a bill, Walter, what the fuck are you talking about" "I'm talking about drawing a line in the sand, Dude" after which Walter, ever the arbiter of language says: "Also, Dude, Chinaman is not the preferred nomenclature, Asian-American ‚please".

Whenever confronted with a problem, he starts moving words around emptily and meaninglessly, and that is meant to solve it. "I got this. They're amateurs, dude." "Not to worry. These men are nihilists, Donnie." "They kidnapped that woman. That woman – that *slut* – kidnapped herself!"

Furthermore, in *The Big Lebowski,* the meaninglessness of language is illustrated by the fact that a number of phrases occur throughout the movie, but spoken by different characters: "this aggression will not stand, man", (President Bush, the Dude);"where´s the fucking money, Dude"..

The German nihilists, of course, are ridiculed by Walter and the Coen Brothers and caricatured as just ideological mercenaries, although philosophically Nietzschean nihilism is probably as close a description of the consequences of Wittgenstein´(and Ethan Coen´s) philosophy as anything: "Say what you want about the tenets of national socialism, dude. At least it's an ethos", says Walter,in another word game play.

Significantly, the one who really makes Walter blow his cool, is Larry Sellers, the kid who just stares at him blankly refusing to engage in any language games whatsoever. This is what finally sends Walter over the edge and makes him start smashing the sports car with the golf club.

Furthermore, Wittgenstein was not an outlier among postmodernist philosophers, as illustrated by a debate he had with philosopher Karl Popper at Cambridge about whether there are philosophical problems at all. Wittgenstein thought that all difficult philosophical problems were at their core language puzzles, and Popper thought they actually did represent meaningful issues in the world. Wittgenstein got so mad at one point that he picked up a poker from the fireplace and started waving it around.

Golf club? Fire poker? Walther exemplifies Wittgenstein´ s language games which is the lens through which the Coen Brother and Woke saw and see life.And to the Dude and to Woke, life, truth, meaning and love, is just a word game.[28]

Or as Bob Dylan would say: Love is Just a 4-Letter Word.

---

[28] Eddie Brawley,'The Big Lebowski', Wittgenstein, and the Garbage Pile That Is Online Discourse, Vulture, SEPT. 16, 2015,

Stage III-2008-today: Woke´s long march through the institutions.

"_Socialism_ is precisely the religion that must overwhelm Christianity. ... In the new order, Socialism will triumph by first capturing the culture via infiltration of schools, universities, churches, and the media by _transforming the consciousness of society_."(my underline)

 Antonio Gramsci, neo-Marxist Italian political philosopher

     Xxxxxxxxxxxxxxxxxxxxxxxxxxxx

The Revolution won't happen with guns, rather it will happen incrementally, year by year, generation by generation. We will gradually infiltrate their educational institutions and their political offices, transforming them slowly into Marxist entities as we move towards universal egalitarianism.

 Max Horkheimer, Prominent Philosopher of the Frankfurt School of Critical Theory

     xxxxxxxxxxxxxxxxxxxxxxxxxxxxxxx

"You go into these small towns in Pennsylvania and, like a lot of small towns in the Midwest, the jobs have been gone now for 25 years and nothing's replaced them. And they fell through the Clinton administration, and the Bush administration, and each successive administration has said that somehow these communities are gonna regenerate and they have not. And it's not surprising then they get bitter, they cling to guns or religion or antipathy toward people who aren't like them or anti-immigrant sentiment or anti-trade sentiment as a way to explain their frustrations."

 Barack Obama,U.S.President 2008-16, at a fundraiser in 2008.

     Xxxxxxxxxxxxxxxxxxxxxxxxxxxxxxxxx

"You know, to just be grossly generalistic, you could put half of Trump's supporters into what I call the basket of deplorables. Right?" The racist, sexist, homophobic, xenophobic, Islamaphobic—you name it. And unfortunately, there are people like that. And he has lifted them up".

 Hillary Clinton,Presidential Candidate at a private fundraiser in New York.2008.

     xxxxxxxxxxxxxxxxxxxxxxxxxxxxxxxxxxxxx

"The world is made up of people with either killer instincts or without killer instincts, and the people that seem to emerge are competitive and driven with a certain instinct to win".

 Donald Trump,U.S. President 2016-2020,in **Trump:An American Dream(Netflix)**

xxxxxxxxxxxxxxxxxxxxxxxxxxxxxxxxxxxxx

"Transforming the consciousness of society", as Gramsci calls it, in the above quote is the key to analyzing Woke's transition from outsider to insider, from rebels to Establishment, from students to teachers, from nobodies to the elite.

Stage III sees a change of tactics from the open attempts at overthrowing the political system of the West by terrorism and revolutionary actions to *gradualism*. In short, when Woke's rebellion failed in openly and politically taking over the democratic institutions of the West in the 1970s, it changed its *tactics* but not its *goal* of transforming capitalist democracies into socialist nirvanas.

For Woke could not come out in the open and admit that it had learned its lesson, namely that popular support for its narrative dwindled once the true revolutionary and violent nature of its anti-establishment protests became clear. It knew it couldn't' come clean about the real purpose of its politics: system change.

So Woke did it *gradually*. By infiltrating the West's Post WWII *cultural* institutions like the gender-identity movement including the transsexual and gay-rights movements, the feminist movement and the Civil Rights Movements and its *political* institutions of climate change (IPCC-International Panel for Climate Change), internationalism and open borders: the UN and the EU.

In the process, it subverted the Post WWII's system of individualism, of Enlightenment rationalism, of liberal democracy, of objectivity and science, into a Neo-Marxist collectivist struggle between oppressed and oppressors, between white privilege and oppressed people with historically justified grievances, between bigoted populists and principled democrats and between narrow minded-nationalists and open borders.

The story begins in 1928, when Mussolini's regime sentenced a young Antonio Gramsci, then the leader of the Communist Party in Italy, to 20 years in prison, hoping to "stop his mind from ever working again," in the prosecutor's own words. Imprisonment instead afforded him a quiet retreat to refashion Marxism for the future, birthing a brand of it that endures at the core of Western society.[29]

Gramsci concocted his ideological *chef d'oeuvre*, his *Prison Notebooks*, out of frustration. European Marxists had looked forward to the Armageddon of 1918, hoping the capitalist-nationalist cocktail that had fueled World War I would give way to socialist uprisings across the continent.

But it did not happen.

The ability of bourgeois democracy to perpetuate itself through democratic means could only be explained, in Gramsci's view, by the enduring sway of religion, tradition, family, and nation among the working class. Replacing economics with culture as the locus of oppression was Gramsci's profound twist to Marxist thought, which had until then identified the power imbalances derived from capital ownership as the ultimate engine of historical change. For

---

[29] Review of Mike Gonzalez's *The Plot to Change America: How Identity Politics Is Dividing the Land of the Free*, published in National Review, June 20, 2022.

Gramsci, workers had compounded their own oppression by espousing the mores of their capitalist overlords.

Gramsci didn't live to see his own writings reach across the Atlantic after 1945. Reprocessing the raw matter of his cultural Marxism to fit Western society was the work of the Frankfurt School, whose leading thinkers spent considerable time in New York as refugees from a Nazified Europe in the 1930s, with Max Horkheimer moving the School's Institute for Social Research from Frankfurt to New York in 1935. In *One Dimensional Man*, Herbert Marcuse, the School's intellectual chief —mentioned above — impugned America's mass consumerism, enabled by the economic bliss of the post-war years and Hollywood's penetration of the American household, as the "dominant culture." The deluded notion of the American dream allowed the country's elite to rule unchallenged, he concluded.

This change of tactics from open Marxist rebellion to Gramscian *gradual* progress towards a *fait accompli* was personified by the German student revolutionary Rudi Dutschke in the 1960s, who called it "the long march through the institutions". His idea was that in societies with a strong capitalist base and infrastructure, the battle for power would be waged by using the institutions and mechanisms of society against itself.

Needless to say, this tactic of stealth Marxism of Stage III. involved a certain degree of duplicity not to say outright lies.

It's main political proponent in America is Barack Obama who managed to keep his relationship with his virulently anti-American pastor, Jeremy Wright, who accused America of state terrorism, out of the headlines; and keep his friendship with a known terrorist, Bill Ayers,who was a co-founder of the Weather Underground, the most violent revolutionary terrorist movement the States had ever seen according to the FBI, which conducted a series of bombings across the U.S.in the 1970s,from hurting his political career; not least with the help of a naïve and compliant press and media that wanted to believe that he was a political moderate rather than a Marxist fellow -traveler.

In Europe it is former German chancellor, Angela Merkel, who for 15 years managed to keep the fact that during the cruel communist reign in East Germany from 1945-89, she was an important part of its indoctrination program.

Culturally, the tactics were wildly successful as documented in detail in the chapters below on gender identity, transgender activism, anti-racism and radical feminism; and politically victorious as demonstrated in the chapters on open borders, globalization and climate change.

Culturally, it was a theme that permeates the Woke narrative: the nagging fear, the Nietzschean angst and the anguish that somewhere out there, there would be a price to pay for throwing thousands of years of civilization, religion, existing norms, customs and traditions to the wind in search of an Utopia whose outcome was as yet uncertain.

For Nietzsche, mankind didn´t have choice because it was an orphan and had to make its choice without its father as its guide.

For the woke it was the Nietzschean dilemma all over again between being weak and being strong, between being the sheep or the shepherd.

And woke decided to be the shepherd.

Psychologically, this had 2 major implications which remain at the core of the psychology of woke: firstly, a self-imposed almost religious vision of *righteousness,* of martyrdom in having the duty of educating and guiding the witless sheep to a better land, a future of happiness devoid of the social strife so characteristic of capitalist society; secondly, the *angst and anguish* that this top-down approach would clash and fail when faced with the ever-growing political democracy in the West based on a belief in the common good sense of the *individual* when it came to making choices that benefitted him.

The psychological price of dishonesty on this scale is richly documented in professional research on the causes of mental illness.

So is the political price in being found out.

For sometimes, inevitably, the mask slips: Barack Obama who at the time his infamous "clinger" statement quoted above was leaked in 2008, was locked in a presidential primary battle in Pennsylvania with Hillary Clinton was speaking to his mostly white and mostly wealthy audience at that most liberal of liberal cities, San Francisco, whom he assumed shared his contempt for the "herd".

One member of the audience didn´t and the leak almost cost him the election, except for the unwillingness of the mostly woke media infatuated by the idea that electing a black President would exorcise the original sin of slavery to hold him to task.

Hillary Clinton was less lucky because she was less liked and her "basket of deplorables" likely cost her the presidency.

Clinton back then accused Barack Obama of elitism. She had a point. But it was the pot calling the kettle black because scorn for the "herd", the "deplorables" and the "clingers" was a sentiment she *shared* with Obama and part and parcel of Woke elitism that as we have seen goes all the way back to Nietzsche.

Politically, the duplicity of the Woke is reflected by the growing chasm in both the EU and the U.S. between the mostly urban elites and rural voters.

When President Joe Biden on August 25, 2022, gave a speech on what his press spokeswoman called The Soul of Our Nation, he didn´t even try to hide the fact that Democrats, the party of Woke, is now officially declaring the survival of democracy a battle between good and evil.,

On that day, while campaigning amid very negative poll ratings, Biden not only called "MAGA Republicans" a threat "to the very soul of this nation" but added: 'It's not just Donald Trump, it's the entire *philosophy* that underpins the — I'm going to say something — it's like semi-fascism.'. (my underline).

More than 74 million Americans, the second highest number of votes ever in U.S. elections, by Biden´s reckoning voted for a semi-fascist system in 2020.

Fascism as an ideology is characterized by collectivist thinking, the belief that the state *is* the nation, that the interest of the state supersedes the rights of any individual and that the real purpose of the state is incorporated by a strong leader.

But, as it happens, those are the very characteristics of the ideology of Woke, an ideology that over the years has hardened into absolute faith that any party or political belief system except its own is illegitimate—impermissible, and a threat to democracy. [30].

EU´s elite, often represented by French President.Emmanuel Macron or members of the European Parliament like the Dutch socialist,Sophie In´t Veldt,discussed in more detail below, routinely decry the democratically elected leaders of Poland and Hungary and their nationalist systems as "authoritarian"; and EU-Commission Vice President, Frans Timmermans, has more than hinted that the former (2016-2023) democratically elected n "nationalist" and "populist" government in Poland was the successor of the "brownshirts "of Nazi Germany in the 1930s.

And, lest we forget, elites on both sides of the ocean are united in their contempt for the universally recognized symbol of the non-woke masses: Donald Trump.

To the extent that otherwise sober political commentators in mainstream media on both sides of the ocean struggle to define Donald Trump other than as deranged.

Yet, they conveniently forget, that before Trump there was the green Party in the U.S. and Victor Orban and Berlusconi in Europe. Both equally hated and reviled by the European Woke.

Demonizing your political opponents, including characterizing them as psychologically unstable, is part and parcel of the political game.

Unsurprisingly, therefore, even his former appointees, including his former attorney general, Bill Barr, try to breach the dilemma of dishing the dirt on him without explaining how they were enticed to work for him in the first place, by assessing him psychologically:

> "He is a consummate narcissist, and he constantly engages in reckless conduct that that puts his political followers at risk and the conservative and Republican agenda at risk,"

and

> "He will always put his own interests and gratifying his own ego ahead of everything else, including the country's interests. There's no question about it. This is a perfect example of that. He's like a 9-year-old — a defiant 9-year-old kid who's always pushing the glass toward the edge of the table, defying his parents to stop him from doing it. It's a means of self-assertion and exerting his dominance over other people. And he's a very petty individual who will always put his interests ahead of the country's, his personal gratification of his ego. But our country can't be a therapy session for a troubled man like this."[31]

Trump, thus, is 1) a narcissist;2) like a 9-year old who has not learned where the boundaries are…yet; 3) a troubled *man* who needs therapy. This is psychologically incoherent: You can´t simultaneously be a narcissist who by definition is a person unable to understand or care about other people´s boundaries, and be looking to learn where the boundaries are while still being unwilling to seek therapy for breaking boundaries .

Nor can Trump by any stretch of the imagination be characterized as troubled by narcissism; a psychological affliction characterized by an inability to relate to others around you.

---

[30] Lance Morrow, WSJ, September 5,2022.
[31] CBS,Interview,Internet.June 23,2020.

He may be full of himself, a braggart, a liar, and the consummate salesman, but you don't get more than 74 million people to vote for you through thousands of rallies and millions of handshakes, by being unable to relate to people.

Trump, in my opinion is the ultimate Nietzschean Ubermensch, who in his own opinion goes where others dare not go, sees what others cannot see and yes breaks all the rules. Only he calls himself and his category of people for people with "killer instincts" and the desire to always win, although even close friends of his doubt that he has ever read Nietzsche or any other philosopher for that matter.

Trump, and this is what aligns him with his "clinger" followers, is an outsider. His voters, despite his wealth, instantly recognize a fellow outsider, a fellow "clinger" a fellow "deplorable".

Trump never got caught in an open mic putting down his voters, because he is, in a word that has otherwise been appropriated by the Woke, genuine. Authentic. He *relates* to ordinary people even though he is not one of them. He speaks *through* them not *for* them.

Unlike Woke leaders, like Merkel and Obama, who constantly have to hide their real selves.

Culturally, the sense of righteousness combined with the fear of the "unwashed masses" illustrate the schism better than any political-science paper however its sophistication.

As exemplified by Easy Rider, a counter-cultural movie from 1969 about two pot-smoking hippies riding their motorbikes across America, looking for authenticity and ending up getting killed by the rednecks who resent the permissiveness and the excesses of their rebellion.

The brilliant soundtrack says, "born to be wild", but, as the movie shows, this, psychologically, is an illusion which when it comes face to face with the rest of society, turns deadly for the Easy Riders.

Southern Comfort (1975) is about a platoon of national guards on military exercise in the Louisiana swamps, who steal the local Cajuns' canoes with disastrous results as the locals pick them off one by one, unseen in the shallow waters of the swamp.

In Deliverance(1972) we do see the locals through the eyes of the main characters and it is not a pretty sight: toothless, backward, sloppy, primitive and mentally handicapped is what Obama's and Clinton's nightmares are made to look like as 4 naturist middle class white men want to take one last trip down the Chattooga river before it is damned up.

The local rednecks insulted by their arrogance and contempt take out their revenge by sabotaging their trip at every turn, sodomizing one and causing the death of another.

On a psychological level, Deliverance- its British director John Boorman was a Catholic and the title is a wordplay on the Lord's Prayer: *Deliver us from evil,* -like Easy Rider is a movie about initiation, the process of growing up and facing reality. Woke critics have interpreted the movie as a protest against civilization's encroachment upon nature.

But the movie is not about nature, but about human nature seen through woke glasses and first and foremost about Woke's existential angst about "clingers", and "deplorables".

The same point permeates the cult series, True Detective (2014) of the second decade of the 21st century, an American anthology crime drama television series about two Louisiana cops, Marty and Rusty,created and written by Nic Pizzolatto, a left-wing college professor of literature..

True Detective, deconstructed, is about Woke´s trip from illusion to power to progressive totalitarianism as illustrated by Rusty´s development in the series from a family man and father of a young girl to disillusioned Nietzschean cynic.

How dare you, Rusty Cohle says, echoing the patronizing sermonizing tone of Obama, who clearly has learned his mesmerizing speechmaking from the very Baptist preachers that are pilloried in the movie, how dare you lowlifes demand an individual right to be heard and seen and be respected? You are beneath contempt.

> "We are things that labor under the illusion of having a self. This accretion of sensory experience and feeling. programmed. with total assurance, that we´re each somebody.When.in fact, everybody's nobody."

This is pure Nietzschean nihilism and contempt for the herd.

It shows Woke´s ill-concealed real attitude to democracy once the masks are off: you losers are too stupid, ignorant, and lazy for your voices to be heard, so please go away and let *us* get on with running things.:

It is rare that members of this underclass take part in the public debate about the Woke system, and criticizes it, but it happens.

In the U.S. J.D.Vance, from a deeply dysphoric redneck family, the son of an alcoholic mother, rose to prominence and a position as a U.S. senator on the back of his memoir about how the underclass lives called Hillbilly Elegy(2016) a touching but brutally honest about lives lived in poverty and on welfare..

Kevin D. Williamson is another white male from a similar background whose Big White Ghetto-Dead Broke,Stone-Cold Stupid,and High On Rage in the Dank Wooly Wilds of the "Real America"(2020),is an indictment not of the Woke system but of the white underclass that "benefits" from it.

The white underclass, Williamson says, suffer from "repeating the mistakes and habits that have left them (or their parents and grandparents, in many cases) in poverty or near poverty to begin with.But they are not and do not see themselves as victims:

> The Left is convinced…of the thesis, that the poor and struggling in the conservative and rural parts of the country are just too besotted with Jesus talk and homosexual panic to understand what actually is at stake for them,and they therefore-the famous phrase-"vote against their own economic interest".

Not so, says Williamson (and J.D.Vance):

> "When …asked,they chose Donald Trump by a very large margin,but then the poor make poor choices all the time-that´s part of why they are poor" …."Progressives preach about- and to-people with whom they have no real connection….If I might be permitted to

address the would-be benefactors of the white underclass from the southerly side of the class line: Ain´t nobody asked you to speak for us."[32]

In the Woke´s binary template of oppressor and oppressed, in spite of their own protestations, the "clingers" are the victims. But they are victims of the *capitalist* system, not their own.

Even more so if they insist on taking what the psychologists call agency, i.e. responsibility for their own actions and mistakes.

That, in the world of Woke, is heresy.

No wonder Paul Krugman, Nobel-prize economist and columnist of the wokest of woke medias, The New York Times, called the book "Truly reprehensible".

A characterization that the book proudly displays on its jacket blurb.

In Europe, Anthony Malcolm Daniels, also known by the pen name Theodore Dalrymple, prison physician and psychiatrist in a slum hospital in East London, used his extensive experience with the British underclass to publicize a much similar analysis, in a series of articles and newspaper columns published collectively in the book, Life at the Bottom: The Worldview That Makes the Underclass.

What is this worldview? In one word: Woke. A review of the book online by the publication, Worthy House,[33] collectively characterizes the "worldview" of the underclass:

> "The chief one is that all of British society, and the underclass most of all, has wholly absorbed to its detriment the philosophy of nonjudgmentalism. Everyone, except benighted reactionary outcasts, recoils from the idea that one thing or action is or can be better, more worthwhile, or more moral than another. From that flow, directly or indirectly, most of the underclass's problems—while the classes above them have retained, to some degree, the structures that permit them to avoid the price of nonjudgmentalism"

> "A final one is that they have wholly absorbed the religion of emancipation, that they have no personal limits, but they instead have unfettered freedom to do exactly as they please, to be funded by others if that freedom needs money. A corollary to this is that no hierarchy of persons or values can be permitted, since everybody is aggressively and always equal (which reinforces lack of aspiration).

Nonjudgmentalism, ignorance of reality, religion of emancipation and lack of personal responsibility: where in the world does the underclass get these ideas from?

Why, from their Woke rulers, Dalrymple says, "who have been feeding leftist claptrap to them through news and entertainment, and through the minions of government, for decades". Most of these habits are....,

> "the liquid in the poisoned chalice of the modern Left, the nasty fruit of the Frankfurt School. The other classes don't pay the penalty for these ideologically driven ideas, but

---

[32] Big White Ghetti, pp.201-02.
[33] Life at the Bottom: The Worldview That Makes the Underclass (Theodore Dalrymple) The Worthy House, September 29, 2018.

they do get to feel smugly superior and righteous, though they keep well away from where the underclass lives."[34]

Part I: Summary.

The Woke anti-authoritarian and rebellious mind-set was formed in its early years of stage I and II, and has remained intact since then, notwithstanding the tactical shift of gradualism since coming to power. Woke may not wear Che Guevara caps anymore, but the burning desire for another fairer, more equitable more just system still burns as brightly as at Woodstock and Thy.

Deconstructed, Woke´s system as it evolves through the Third Stage and becomes *the* system, is clear: like all belief systems, Woke is a system of values with a narrative of "good" versus "evil". The good guys are the Easy Riders, the Freedom Riders, The Black Lives Matters, the Catchers in the Rye, and the #MeToos.

The evil is narrow bigoted nationalists, the populists, the rednecks, the "clingers", the "deplorables" and the White supremacists. Like the rednecks in Deliverance, they not only represent backwardness and degeneracy, but psychologically constitute Woke´s bad conscience, their most atavistic fear.

Christianity has its devil, Islam its Satan, but since Woke abhors all religions, they won´t do.

The devil playing this psychologically important role in Woke´s kabuki theatre are Nazis(in the EU) and white supremacists, racists, "deplorables" and rednecks(in the U.S.). And Trump.

The point of looking at the development of Woke *historically* over three stages, culturally and philosophically, is to make it clear that all 3 stages of Woke's narrative are in fact successive neo-Marxist inspired movements, reflecting the evolution that Marxism itself was undergoing from political protest to revolution and open violence to evolutionary take-over of the West from within.

Woke will argue that this is ascribing far too much importance to an obscure Italian Communist and a few radical student leaders, or conversely, reject it as pure conspiracy theories.

I disagree.

The point of psychoanalyzing the woke mind is to demonstrate that ideas do matter and have real world consequences: the ideas of Nietzsche, Marcuse, the Frankfurt School of Critical Theory, and the Marxist-inspired philosophies of Gramsci over Existentialism ended up the in the hands of a mainly French school of philosophy called Postmodernism, which became the predominant intellectual foundation for theWoke and the West´s collectivist narrative of oppressor vs. oppressed.

Woke leaders from Hayden to Obama know their Gramsci and know what they are doing.'

Their story of gradually transforming the consciousness of society by taking over its institutions, - its " long march through the institutions of the West", is told below.

---

[34] Idem.

Part II: Transforming the Consciousness of Society

Chapter 1: From Individualism to Identity Politics.

Xxxxxxxxxxxxxxxxxxxxxxxxxxxxxxx

Masculine and feminine roles are not biologically fixed but socially constructed.

Judith Butler, American psychologist
Xxxxxxxxxxxxxxxxxxxxxxxxxxxxxxxxxx

Gender is not something that one is, it is something one does, an act... a "doing" rather than a "being". There is no gender identity behind the expressions of gender; that identity is performatively constituted by the very "expressions" that are said to be its results. If the immutable character of sex is contested, perhaps this construct called 'sex' is as culturally constructed as gender; indeed, perhaps it was always already gender, with the consequence that the distinction between sex and gender turns out to be no distinction at all.

Judith Butler
Xxxxxxxxxxxxxxxx

UNDER NYC LAW, EVERYONE HAS THE RIGHT TO USE THE RESTROOMS THAT MOST CLOSELY ALIGNS WITH THEIR GENDER IDENTITY OR EXPRESSION.
Sign on a NYC Restroom door, November 2019.

xxxxxxx

We don't need any more brown faces that don't want to be a brown voice, ",…. "We don't need any black faces that don't want to be a black voice."
Ayanna Pressley, radical Democratic Member of the House of Representatives.

xxxxxx

"If you have a problem figuring out whether you´re for me or Trump, then you ain´t black".
Joe Biden, to black voter,when campaigning to be the Democratic presidential candidate for the U.S. 2020 elections.

xxxxxxx

In his book, The Blank Slate, with the significant subtitle, "The Modern Denial of Human Nature", the Canadian psychologist, Stephen Pinker, argues persuasively and scientifically for the view that biological differences between the sexes do exist and are significant. There´s just too much biological and psychological evidence in our day of DNA and genetic research to argue otherwise. Or, as he said:" Things are not looking good for the theory that boys and girls are born identical except for their genitalia, with all other differences coming from the way society treats them".

Yet, to-day, earnest young people carrying signs of protest around saying "Fuck-The-Binary".

What´s going on?

Gender identity is what´s going on.

The main thing to understand from the perspective of Woke and its march through the cultural institutions of the West, including the now ubiquitous term of gender identity, is that it is new, recent and revolutionary.

Woke, deliberately, revolutionized the relationship between the sexes by changing our age old vocabulary governing the relationship between men and women.

It wasn´t even a *long* march through this particular institution, since the term *gender identity* was coined by psychiatry professor Robert J. Stoller as recently as in 1964 and popularized by psychologist John Money in 1970s.

The Grand Wizard of gender identity is an American philosopher of the Frankfurt School of Critical Theory and a follower of the French Postmodernist, Jaques Lacan, Judith Butler.

[5]

Judith Butler questions the belief that certain gendered behaviors are natural, arguing that what we commonly associate with femininity and masculinity is an act of sorts, a performance, one that is imposed upon us by normative heterosexuality.

Identity itself, for Butler, is an *illusion* retroactively created by our performances:

Int his she rejects the very distinction between gender and sex regularly made in the past by feminists who accepted the fact that certain anatomical differences do exist between men and women and that sex is a biological category; gender is a historical category
.
It´s Woke philosophy at it again.

Its philosophy of viewing everything through the prism of power, oppressor vs. oppressed, has led to a huge wave of sentiment in Woke culture in which it has chosen to deny biological differences between men and women as having any importance.

To complicate matters further, the men-women dichotomy is so old-school that today, depending on who is counting, you have the choice of up to 99 (the BBC´s count) different gender-categories.

Even more confusingly, our gender according to Woke gender identity theory, is open to individual choice since gender, as the theory puts it, is a social construct. The jump from accepting biological differences between men and women as part of our nature to leaving the door open to *choice* of gender identity (the tell-tale marker of the Woke school of thought is that someone "identifies as" trans-sexual or gay, or lesbian) has predictably and inevitably lead to chaos.

Mess with cultural norms that for hundreds if not thousands of years have underpinned civilization, and this is what you get.

But this is my point: for the Woke it never was about social justice for one oppressed group or other but always about sowing enough doubt about capitalist society to transform the consciousness of society from within, to take power and change society in its neo-Marxist image.

Furthermore, it ain´t over yet: if obvious biological differences are optional why stop at gender?

The story of Rachel Dolezal, a white woman passing herself off as African American in order to reach a high position within the National Association for the Advancement of Colored People, NAACP, is an illustrative one. The poor woman misread the culture code completely and when found out was publicly shamed and fired from her job although she loudly protested that she "identified" as black.

No, no, Rachel, you don´t get it: white people cannot be oppressed because under Art. XYZ of the post-modernist Code, white people are the oppressors.

But Dolezal's strategy of lying could have made sense, if only she had done it right: in view of the huge preferential opportunities open to African Americans in admission to colleges, black entrepreneurships, etc. there should logically be ample opportunities for enterprising white folks out there to have a skin pigmentation do-over in order to make a quick buck or make the entry grade for blacks to Harvard.

I mean, if having a penis replaced by a vagina is enough to enter the Women's Tennis Association, shouldn't change of skin pigmentation from white to black be enough to identify as black?

Well…., the thing is, that though these preferential benefits officially are open to all minorities, you really have to be…kind of black to get them, so I don't recommend that Chinese Americans or Hispanics have a do-over just yet.

But wait…. somebody's whispering in my ear that I am already behind the curve. Sure, enough. In the U. K, the University and College Union (UCU) "which represents over 120,000 academics, lecturers, trainers, instructors, researchers, managers, administrators, computer staff, librarians and postgraduates in universities, colleges, prisons, adult education and training organizations across the UK" has recently (Breitbart, November 17, 2019) "declared that *anyone* can "self-identify" as "black, disabled, LGBT+ or women".

To make it obvious to even the most dim-witted, the UCU states that it," supports a social, rather than a medical, model of gender recognition that will help challenge repressive gender stereotypes in the workplace and in society".

But that couldn't happen in real life, could it? That somebody white identifies as black? It just did.

The Miami police department is short on black cops in leading positions, so Captain J. Ortiz saw his chance and told his superiors that although he had earlier indicated on police forms that he was white/Hispanic, he now identified as black. Sgt. Stanley Jean-Poix, president of the Miami Community Police Benevolent Association representing 300 black officers, was unimpressed.

"Black officers are underrepresented as lieutenants and he knew that and lied to get a promotion," Jean-Poix said. "We're insulted and it's disrespectful to the black officers of the police department. "[35]

His superiors, too, failed to see the funny side, and suspended him with pay. But such is Woke's ship of fools my friends, that once you have let this particular cat out of the bag, anything can happen. So, I wouldn't bet the ranch on Ortiz' not winning his case in court.

While we are at repressive gender stereotypes there is, confusingly, one place where repressive stereotypes apparently are OK: politics. Or more specifically the conflation of secondary human characteristics such as skin color, sexual preferences, and gender with collective political choice.

---

[35] The American Mirror, Jan. 23, 2020

In its less sophisticated form, it goes like this: if you are an African American or gay you must vote the same way and have the same political preferences as other African Americans and gays.

Representative Ayanna Pressley, who is black, came out in favor of this somewhat, ahem, racist position when she said:" We don't need any more brown faces that don't want to be a brown voice, ".... "We don't need any more black faces that don't want to be a black voice."

It is unclear whether the "we" is the royal "we" in which case Pressley only speaks for herself, but the somewhat totalitarian message is clear: if you are black and don't vote like I want you to vote, you're not really black.[36]

Pressley's concern for the poor and her own public image was somewhat dented, when it became public knowledge that her main source of income was from being a landlord and that she expanded her portfolio during the pandemic while at the same time introducing a bill that would provide taxpayer-funded relief for landlords.

Joe Biden's message to black voters cited above, makes the same point: if you're black your only choice is to vote for me. Otherwise, you are not black.

Due to Supreme Court Justice Breyer's retirement, there's an open seat on the court. Joe Biden as part of his campaign stated unequivocally stated that it would be filled not just by a woman but by a black woman. Which it was in the spring of 2022: Ketanji Brown Jackson.

Now that's identity politics for you.

Peter Thiel, a successful high-tech gay millionaire, was ostracized from the "Gay Community" for supporting Donald Trump. Trump happens to be in favor of gay marriage, but since everyone knows that Trump is just really an asshole, you lucked out, Peter, so you are out for not reading the Gay Code right.

The black rapper, Kanye West, made the same mistake of getting too friendly with Trump and was pilloried by the African American community for it; although, Trump, despite repeated accusations of racism from the Democrats and their allies in the mainstream media holds no known racist views other than the politically incorrect one that he doesn't suffer any fools, black, tan, white, women, transsexuals, or men, gladly. He will vilify anybody who gets in his way from women, like former Fox reporter Megyn Kelly, over a Spanish judge to the recently departed black Congressman, Elijah Cummings. But that just makes him an equal opportunity supporter not a racist.

Not calling things by their name, in this case not calling people who judge other people by the color of their skin for racists, though that is exactly the textbook definition of racism, distorts reality.

But that is the Woke culture we live in, and it is not about to change anytime soon.

---

[36] Wasington Free Beacon, August 16, 2022

But at least we can take some consolation from the fact that the promoters of this Postmodernist nonsense of wokeness and political correctness constantly get caught out themselves and hoist by their own petard, as it were.

Examples are legion. My personal favorite is the white bi-sexual Congresswoman, Katie Hill, who was in the forefront of the fake allegations of sexual misconduct raised against the nomination of Supreme Court Justice, Ted Kavanaugh.

A "serious serial predator" she called him without a shred of evidence, except a 36-year old episode invoked by a registered Democrat woman that nobody, not even her own friends whom she falsely claimed had been present at the alleged misconduct, could remember.

As a result of her efforts and that of the #MeToo- movement whose motto was "believe women" and screw the age-old principle of presumption of innocence until proven guilty, Congress passed internal rules prohibiting sex between Congressional Members and their staff. Obviously meant to rein in all those horny men using their male privilege to take liberties with their secretaries.

Well, guess what happened? Katie had an affair with a female member of her staff, broke her own rules, and the Democratic leader of the House of Representatives, Nancy Pelosi, dropped her like a hot potato. And she was forced to resign mumbling about a Republican set-up and different sexual standards for men and women.

A hint to Katie and all her fellow travelers and identity-politics apologists: if you want to run with the woke crowd, you had better stay up to scratch on the "rules".

Part II: Transforming the Consciousness of Society

Chapter 2: Transgenderism: Gender as Social Construct on Steroids.

"we're here, we're queer, we're coming for your children."

LGTBQ Activist Chant on New York's annual Drag March on Friday, June 24, 2023.

xxxxxxxxxxxxxxxxxxxxx

"We'll convert your children / Happens bit by bit. / Quietly and subtly. / You will barely notice it."

A YouTube video released two years ago by the San Francisco Gay Men's Chorus.

xxxxxxxxxxxxxxxxxxxxxxxxxxxxx

"In thirty states, LGTBQ people are at risk of being fired, refused housing, or being denied services, simply because of *who we are*".
Human Rights Campaign, HRC.

xxxxxxxx

"Many Genes Influence Same-Sex Sexuality, Not a Single 'Gay Gene'.
New York Times, August 29, 2019, in a piece entitled Many Genes Influence Same-Sex Sexuality, Not a Single 'Gay Gene', reporting on a new study that established that there is no gay gene.

xxxxxxx

"We found *shockingly high levels of sexual harassment and sexual assault.* Around seven out of ten LGBT workers experienced at least one type of sexual harassment at work (68 per cent) and almost one in eight LGBT women (12 per cent) reported being seriously sexually assaulted or raped at work. However, this is a *hidden* problem with *two thirds of those who were harassed not reporting it;* "

Sexual harassment of LGBT people in the workplace, A TUC report published on the UN´s International Day Against Homophobia, May 17, 2019)

xxxxxxx

"Survey finds 70% of LGBT people sexually harassed at work".

The Guardian, May 18, 2019, reporting on the TUC report above.

xxxxxxx

"Today is International #PronounsDay. We all want to be accepted and respected as we are. Make it a practice to ask people for their pronouns and respect them. "
Women's March

✔ @womensmarch Twitter

xxxxxxx

"Puberty suppression "is a *reversible* treatment that decreases the distress of having the wrong puberty.

"The *adolescent* with maturity to understand the consequences of this treatment, can initiate hormone therapy. "
-Pediatric Endocrine Society: Statement quoted in Breitbart, Nov. 5, 2019.

xxxxxxx

Let's be clear: Transgender equality is the civil rights issue of our time. There is no room for compromise when it comes to basic human rights.
Joe Biden, US President

xxxxxxxxxxx

In the U.S., the Diagnostic and Statistical Manual of Mental Disorders, Fifth Edition, Text Revision (DSM-5-TR)[1] under the heading "Diagnosis" provides for one overarching diagnosis of gender dysphoria as "a marked incongruence between one's experienced/expressed gender and their assigned gender".

Recommended "Treatment" may include "pubertal suppression for adolescents with gender dysphoria and gender-affirming hormones like estrogen and testosterone for older adolescents and adults".

Diagnostic and Statistical Manual of Mental Disorders, Fifth Edition, Text Revision (DSM-5-TR)· American Psychiatric Association. 2022.

Xxxxxxxxxxxxxxxx

"If you talk to God, you are praying," "If God talks to you, you are schizophrenic."

Thomas Szasz, Postmodernist philosopher and author of " The Myth of Mental Illness"(1961).

Transgenderism's rise to prominence as a political issue is Woke's greatest accomplishment in transforming society's consciousness in order to bring about social change.

It is also an issue particularly dear to Millennials and Gen Zers heart, a growing and increasingly powerful(Woke) voting demographic.

The driving force behind the rise of transgenderism as a political issue was the writings of French Postmodernist, Michel Foucault, whom we met in the chapter above on "Woke Philosophers", author of <u>Madness and Civilization: A History of Insanity in the Age of Reason</u>, (1961) and Thomas Szasz, Hungarian-American Postmodernist philosopher and author of <u>The Myth of Mental Illness(1961).</u>

Both believed that mental illnesses like gender dysphoria were myths, created by society to enslave those who ignored society's norms. Who could say with assurance that the people locked away in asylums were any more or less insane than the authorities who put them there, they asked?

And society agreed.

Throughout the rest of the century Woke's recipe of deinstitutionalization of the treatment of mental health became the way forward, because it seemed more humane and, at least if one were to believe movies like <u>One Flew Over the Cuckoo's Nest</u> (1975), more likely to succeed.

But Woke psychiatry became so fixated on guarding the patient's civil liberties, that they lost sight of the patient's illness.

And that is why transgenderism is such a divisive subject in the West right now:Woke's fateful and wholesale rejection of traditional mental health prescriptions has come home to roost.

It is literally schizophrenic for any society to have its treatment of transgenderism guided by two mutually incompatible fundamental assumptions: on the one hand that transgenderism is a serious mental health disorder, gender dysphoria[37], requiring strict diagnosis and treatment under the rules of the American Psychiatric Association in the U.S. and similar rules in the E.U.; on the other hand that transgenderism is a political issue grandly proclaimed by the American President and other International leaders as *the* civil and human rights issue of our time.

What is happening?

Firstly, what does LGTBQ even mean? You can be excused for not being totally sure because five years ago, you probably would not even have heard the term; but now you cannot swing a cat without hitting it. Well, it refers to that small part of the general population that "identifies" as Lesbian, Gay, Transgender, Bisexual and Queer. In short, people who don't see themselves as falling into the traditional, biological, bi-nary gender definition of man and woman.

Let's start with the facts: there are no longer any legal discrimination based on same-sex relationships and gender: it's forbidden and if discovered penalized. In the West. Not in the rest of the world where same sex in most countries is outlawed, criminalized, and sometimes, mostly

---

[37] Dysphoria meaning the opposite of euphoria namely," a state of unease or generalized dissatisfaction with life".

in Muslim countries, punished by death. 28 countries, mainly in the West, recognize same-sex *marriage*.

In the U.S. the Supreme Court in 2015 legalized same sex-marriage in Obergefell v.Hodges. To the approval of large majorities of the population.

In 2020 in two cases Bostock v. Clayton County and Harris Funeral Homes extended the antidiscrimination of Title VII of the Civil Rights Act of 1964, to the gay and transgendered, vesting the Equal Employment Opportunity Commission (EEOC) with the power to file lawsuits, conduct investigations and order redress. Effectively drawing parallels between the institution of slavery and modern-day treatment of the transgendered.[38]

Yet, President Biden, says "transgender equality is the *civil rights* issue of our time".

This is absurd. How did Woke get here?

The short answer is that the legalization of homosexuality which until the Supreme Court decision in 2015 already met with general support and had seen homosexual marriage legalized in the majority of U.S. states, was hijacked by Woke and turned into a wider political tool to transform the consciousness of society.

By targeting children.

When activists at New York's annual Drag March chanted "we're here, we're queer, we're coming for your children." and when the San Francisco Gay Men's Chorus released a YouTube video in which 81 of its members sang a song with the refrain: "We'll convert your children / Happens bit by bit. / Quietly and subtly. / You will barely notice it." it was shocking, says Bruce Bawer, gay activist, "But not new. In recent years, such blunt, outrageous rhetoric from the gay left has become pretty familiar. "[39]

"It's disgusting" Bruce Bawer says.". And I know one thing: if anybody is upset more by this sideshow than straight parents, it's gay people who feel that their honorable movement for equal rights has been shanghaied by a gang of psychologically disturbed egomaniacs".[40]

But the ideologues didn't care, Bawer says. They'd hijacked the fate of gay Americans to push their own utopian socialist agenda.

When Bawer appeared on Charlie Rose's show in 1994, to commemorate the 25th anniversary of the modern gay-rights movement, one of the other guests, a radical lesbian, made this agenda clear.

"We don't want a place at the table!" she shouted. "We want to turn the table over!"

---

[38] Boomers, p.187.

[39] Drag queens chanting 'we're coming for your kids' hurt gay rights,Bruce Bawer,New York Post,June 25,2023.

[40] Idem.

Groups like the San Francisco Gay Men's Chorus once played an important role in giving gay Americans a positive image.

The idea of gay people as more or less ordinary people next door was crucial in helping win popular support for gay equality, gays in the military, and, ultimately, same-sex marriage, says Bawer.[41]

Fair enough, but he is still not addressing the elephant-in-the-room question:

Many, if not all countries in the West, celebrate same-sex homosexuality through annual Gay Pride Parades, but the question-Obergefell or not -this raises is why we as a culture are celebrating a lifestyle that in evolutionary reproductive terms, literally, amounts to suicide?

The answer is that Woke is orchestrating, delivering, and celebrating the end of another traditional institution in the West: the end of traditional sexual norms, mainly imposed by Christianity and the Catholic Church.

It is called heteronormativity, and as explained earlier, is a Woke argument mainly propagated by the late, gay, French, Postmodernist philosopher, Michel Foucault: if something is declared normal, such as heterosexual sex, which traditional sexual norms in Western society undeniably does, something else must be abnormal, such as gay sex. That, in the woke perspective, oppresses homosexuality, indeed any other sexual proclivities and in the name of transforming the consciousness of society, must be radically challenged.

Hence Pride and LGTBQ parades long after the "normalization" of gay sex by the U.S Supreme Court in the U.S. and similar mainstreaming in the rest of the West.

Homosexuality, as I said, stopped being illegal decades ago in the West, and that´s a good thing. That´s individual freedom and a right to choose. But it also means that homosexuals can no longer claim victim status. And that those heterosexuals, despite Foucault, are no longer villains.

Why is that not going to happen? The answer, again, is Woke, which will keep flogging that horse as long as it pays off in terms of transforming the consciousness of the society and the culture, we live in. Which is more sexually tolerant, more open than anyone in history. So why this desire to reorder it, to change it?

The answer is that Woke wants *another* society; an anti-capitalist, socialist society, as Herbert Marcuse said, where it runs the show. The Gay Pride and the LGTBQ-crowds are just the useful idiots pulling the wagon.

How do I know? Because many nations in the West are busy passing legislation outlawing gender *identity* discrimination, which is a completely different ball of wax.

Why? Because gender identity is not as innocuous as it sounds: in fact, what it means is that it allows any member of the two sexes to choose, the politically correct word is identify, which gender they want to be, irrespective of their biologically assigned gender.

Not to put too fine appoint on it, the West is passing laws to allow new gender identities, based on people´s lifestyle preferences. I prefer to be a woman, so I must be allowed to use women´s

---

[41] Idem.

restrooms, participate in women´s sports and if sent to jail, go to women´s jail. Even though I am 6 ft. 4 with a beard and a penis. And a rap sheet for multiple rapes. Think I am exaggerating?

IN 2022, the city council of Lincoln, Neb.U.S.A. , passed an ordinance that overhauled its municipal code related to discrimination and the definition of "sex." The council redefined the term to include "sexual orientation and gender identity." And in doing so, it has potentially empowered LGBTQ activists to go after businesses, nonprofits, and citizens with civil penalties and life-ruining fines.

The city council termed the new law a "fairness ordinance." It claimed this ordinance would help protect the LGBTQ community from discrimination. Yet in passing the ordinance, it produced no proof of any discrimination in the city. The new ordinance would, however, make targets out of conservatives and Christians for dissenting from the ever-expanding agenda of radical LGBTQ activists.

The ordinance applies to all public accommodations. Moreover, the city council's definition of public accommodations is so broad as to entail virtually all public spaces outside of someone's private residence.

The broad definitions of sex, public accommodations, and sexual harassment means that activists can target businesses, organizations, churches, private schools, and individuals for virtually any real or perceived threat to the agenda of radical LGBT activists in any public setting.

If it weren't clear enough that the city council is trying to target conservatives, the ordinance spells out that it is illegal for any individual to counsel someone against gender-reassignment surgery. The ordinance also requires businesses, churches, and private schools to allow men to use women's restrooms and locker rooms ("facilities" in its language) if they identify as women. Refusing to do so could force many churches and religious organizations to close their doors, buried under a mountain of recurring fines.[42]

By way of another example, Canada recently introduced legislation that added a category to the forbidden groups of discrimination called "gender identity"; and laid down a series of rules according to which public officials had to address genders by "he" or "she" no more as this was an affront to other genders such as f. ex. transsexuals.

A psychology professor at one of Canada´s universities, Jordan Peterson, refused to address his students with the newly invented personal pronouns on the grounds that it infringed his freedom of speech. And when fined refused to pay the fine. Millions all over the world came out to support him and to this day he has not been prosecuted. On the contrary, the sale of his book <u>12 Rules for Life-an antidote to chaos</u> has made him a ton of money.

The Institute of Art-and Culture Science at the University of Copenhagen, Denmark, did the same thing at the start of the fall semester in 2019 addressing a letter of guidance to its lecturers advising them to avoid such words as "he"," she"," ladies and gentlemen", etc. Not that there had

---

[42] Lincoln, Neb., City Council Votes to Banish Traditional Views from the Public Square, National Review. Nate Grasz, February 25, 2022.

been any complaints from the students: the woke head of the institute just felt it was the *right* thing to do.

Let's follow through on these examples: firstly, this legislation is introduced due to the pressure of an extremely limited group of activists. The number of non-heterosexuals in any society, even in the West where homosexuality is allowed, is small. The number of gays in the West by any serious estimate is about 1.1% of the general population. That of transsexuals about 0.3%. (US National Survey of Men in 1991 and Britain's Office for National Statistics (ONS) 2011, arrive at the same figure two decades apart).

Why are they allowed to lay down the rules and dictate to the majority that gender is in fact no longer biologically determined but a social construct?

The answer, firstly, is that Woke wants the LGTBQ votes. Don't believe me?

Just one example: during the "Brexit" general election campaign, some enterprising journalists discovered that the Liberal Democratic Party on November 22nd had received 100. 000 pounds in campaign contribution from a drug company Ferring Pharmaceuticals, a Swiss company that produces triptorelin, a puberty-blocking drug given to children.

And lo and behold, a few days later, party leader, Jo Swinson, in the Party's election Manifesto came out in support of policies which would make drug treatment of transgendered people much easier or as the manifesto states under the heading, "Demand Equality": the party aims for a "Complete reform of the Gender Recognition Act to remove the requirement for medical reports, scrap the fee and recognize non-binary gender identities"[43]

What does "recognize" non-binary gender identities mean? It means that "we" must accept that the LGTBQ people as a group are entitled to certain rights. Just as affirmative action was put in place for African Americans to help counteract earlier racial discrimination and slavery and various government initiatives are put in place to promote women's careers, or to alleviate alleged sexual discrimination against women, the LGTBQ movement demands measures against alleged discrimination in areas such as housing, and employment, etc. as the quote above shows.

For thousands of years there have been two sexes and X million or billions of individuals. For those of you whose biology knowledge is a bit rusty, a little brush-up: our inherited material, the genes, consists of DNA molecules. These molecules are divided up in so-called chromosomes. Human beings are born with 46 chromosomes in the shape of 23 pairs. Each pair contains one chromosome from each of our biological parents. One pair, called the sex chromosome decide our gender. A sex chromosome can be an X-chromosome or a Y-chromosome. The scientific definition of gender is that a woman has two X-chromosomes that a man has one X-chromosome plus one Y-chromosome.

Certain hormone influences during gestation contribute to developing visible gender characteristics. These genes are basically unchanged throughout life and are not changed no matter how we feel or which operations we undergo.

We also know that same-sex relationships are a part of our culture, sometimes accepted as in ancient Greece, sometimes not as in Victorian England, where it was criminalized. Large parts of the world still don't permit same-sex relations and some still criminalize it as in most Muslim countries. But not the West.

---

[43] Breitbart News, October 24, 2019

Yet, the LGTBQ crowd is screaming shocking discrimination and the transgender crowd insists on their right to self-identify as someone they obviously, biologically, are not. Or as their slogans say:" Fuck the Bi-nary"

And society not only accepts it but applauds it. And complies. I have given a couple of examples already but want to add just one: the Scottish school kid who was thrown out of school for filming his teacher telling him that he could not say in class that there are only two genders because it ran counter to official school policy and was tantamount to discrimination.[44]

And it is. Schools and universities in very left-wing Scotland are per law obliged to teach the non-binary ideology of the left. And since schools per definition teach the truth, tough luck, kid, you are out of here.

How did they do it? Why does Woke promote this nonsense? It is an interesting story of how a small left-wing pressure group can establish itself as an important part of our culture in a truly short time.

And culture drives politics so the demographic of LGTBQs has garnered considerable political power. Remember, even Barack Obama, America's most left-wing president ever, was not in favor of same sex marriage when he took power in 2008. That came 7 years later through a Supreme Court decision.

But today, not just in the US but in countries as different as Protestant Scotland and Catholic Portugal, schoolkids are being taught there are several genders. Facebook enumerates 55 and BBC has produced educational material for children that talks of 99 different genders.

Breitbart London reports that "From September 2020, the British government has made it compulsory for children from the age of four to be given "relationship" lessons which could include teaching children about same-sex relationships, and parents will not have the legal right to take their children out of the classes". (Feb. 25, 2019)

The answer to the question of how this madness happened is: ask Woke. But I will help you out:

Firstly, after the 1968 sexual anything-goes-revolution, we live in an age where.... *almost anything* sexual goes. It is uncool not to be cool about somebody else's sexual preferences, *except*, of course if you're a heterosexual, privileged, white male. Don't believe me? Here's a little story you will like; Scottish Police are investigating a possible "hate speech" crime after signs appeared throughout Perth reading: "It's okay to be white."

The police explained that "Although no complaint has been made to police regarding these posters, they have been brought to our attention and officers are currently looking into the matter".

Peter Barrett, a Perth councilor, said: "This is despicable hate speech. It is covert racism disguising white supremacist views. People should be in no doubt this is no innocuous joke."

"It is the thin end of the wedge and an attempt by racists to get their foot in the door. I don't want a white supremacist racist campaign to be imported from the US on to the streets of Perth," he added.[45]

---

[44] Breitbart, June 24, 2019
[45] Breitbart, Dec. 18, 2019

What are the facts? Fact nr. 1 is that no one has complained. Fact nr. 2 is a question: on what grounds is the police investigating? A local politician says the posters are hate speech, white supremacist, and racist? But, on the face of it they obviously aren´t

Back to the question we asked ourselves about how Woke let this madness happen: an intrinsic part of Postmodernism as we have noted in earlier chapters, is to see people through the prism of oppressor and oppressed. It has worked for radical feminists, and it has worked for the Black Lives Matter movement.

So, the LGTBQ crowd took a page from their playbook and worked hard at establishing themselves as victims. An indispensable part of that campaign was to establish that their lifestyles were not a matter of choice, but a biological necessity. They were so to speak born that way.

So, now we are treated to the spectacle of having woke left-wingers who basically espouse the theory that we are all social constructs not defined by biology, maintaining that LGTBQ cannot help it because their sexual and lifestyle preferences are *biologically* determined.

Or, as the initial quote from the Human Rights Campaign says, we are at risk of being discriminated against because of who we are.

There is just one problem: being LGTBQ is not pre-determined by our genes: it is a choice. The biggest study ever done, focusing not just on male gays as earlier reports, but close to half a million LGBQ people, divided those 774. 000 people up in two groups: those with same sex experiences and those without. It came to the indisputable conclusion: there is no gay gene.

"There is no 'gay gene'," says lead study author Andrea Ganna, a geneticist at the Broad Institute of MIT and Harvard in Cambridge, Massachusetts.[46]

Just as earlier studies have shown that there is no gene for alcoholism. Both are mainly lifestyle choices. Now the radical left crowd had a problem. But not to worry. Their friends in academia and in the media jumped to the rescue. What does Woke do when facts are inconvenient? They lie. The NYT quote above is simply hilarious. Think about it: "Many Genes Influence Same-Sex Sexuality, Not a Single 'Gay Gene'!

That is wildly misleading, because it gives the impression that same-sex behavior is influenced by many genes. But "many "by any definition means 10 or more and according to the journal Science, in which the findings of the study were published:" The researchers found five single points in the genome that seemed to be common among people who had had at least one same-sex experience.

Two of these genetic markers sit close to genes linked to sex hormones and to smell—both factors that may play a role in sexual attraction. But taken together, these five markers explained less than 1 percent of the differences in sexual activity among people in the study." Meaning the two groups. By my reckoning that would mean same sex was overwhelmingly a matter of choice, right?

How can a gene for the sense of smell that the study found may play a role in sexual attraction, together with 4 others that explained less than1 % in choice of sexual activity, become "many genes influence same-sex sexuality"?

---

[46] Nature, 29 August 2019

The answer is that the NYT piece deliberately tells a lie. Note the misdirection, namely that by counterposing "many" and "Not A Single Gay gene" they leave the impression that there are many gay genes. While, in fact, there is none. When Woke must resort to dishonesty on an industrial scale, you know something's up.

But it gets worse: to back up its lies, the NYT doubled down: ...{the} ambitious new study — the largest ever to analyze the genetics of same-sex sexual behavior — found that genetics does play a role, responsible for perhaps a third of the influence on whether someone has same-sex sex. The influence comes not from one gene but *many,* each with a tiny effect — and the rest of the explanation includes social or environmental factors. "[47]

Notice the use of many, when the study actually says that it is five, and underlines "each with a tiny effect". To avoid mentioning the 1% influence which is the conclusion of the study, the NYT wants the inattentive reader to believe the "perhaps a third of the influence" argument.

The problem is that's not what the study says, and the NYT knows it. The line implying that "perhaps a third" of the influence on same-sex relations is genetic, misdirects and lies about what the study says which is:

"When the researchers looked at the overall genetic *similarity* of individuals who had had a same-sex experience, genetics seemed to account for between 8 and 25 percent of the behavior."

Firstly, how does "genetics seemed to account for between 8 and 25 percent of behavior" become "perhaps a third". Which, the last time I looked equals 33%?

Secondly, the 8 and 25% refers to genetic *similarities* of same-sexers, and all it says is that the same-sexers had similarities between 8 and 25%.

"Genetic similarity" is everything from skin-pigmentation to type of hair, but the lie is that the study makes no connection to and no assumption of this influencing same-sex *behavior.*

Because it had already said that genes that may be relevant influence at most 1% of same-sex decisions. The rest, i. e. 99% is socialization, also known as.... choice.

Which Woke really does not want us to know.

But we are still missing the study of what *evolutionary* justification there might or might not be for homosexuality. And that is likely to continue because research questions like "what is the purpose in evolutionary terms of homosexuality" ... "have evaporated in respectable biological debate" because "these are not questions which academics seeking tenure would wish to engage in". In other words, do not mess with the LGTBQ orthodoxy, or activists will harass and hound your employer until he fires you.[48]

Now, don't get me wrong. I don't care who has sex with whom. Have at it and the fact that society doesn't hold you back is a good thing.

But for policy purposes it does matter for society when a group claims and obtains special rights. Especially, when such radical groups succeed in stifling free speech in the process.

---

[47] NYT, 29 August 2019.
[48] Murray, op. cit. p. 33

Maya Forstater, a former tax expert, who was fired from her job at the Centre for Global Development after tweeting that "men cannot change into women", lost her legal challenge against her firing.

The ruling found that the Equality Act 2010 did not protect Ms. Forstater's right to express the philosophical belief that there are only two genders and therefore her firing was legal, Breitbart reports.

The judge in the case doubled down by stating: "If a person has transitioned from male to female and has a Gender Recognition Certificate (GRC), that person is legally a woman. That is not something [Ms. Forstater] is entitled to ignore. [Ms. Forstater's] position is that even if a trans woman has a GRC, she cannot honestly describe herself as a woman. That belief is not worthy of respect in a democratic society," Judge Taylor said.

"Even paying due regard to the qualified right to freedom of expression, people cannot expect to be protected if their core belief involves violating others' dignity and creating an intimidating, hostile, degrading, humiliating, or offensive environment for them," he concluded.[49]

The good judge needs to bone up on his constitutional law. Some rights are more fundamental than others in a democracy and free speech is one of them. He seems to have forgotten that The Bill of Rights is not an American invention but part of the constitutional set-up of his own country, the UK, namely the 1689 Bill of Right Act which states:

"the freedom of speech and debates or proceedings in Parliament ought not to be impeached or questioned in any court or place out of Parliament;".

That, Judge Taylor, means your court, too.

You seem to have less respect for what you call the "qualified right to freedom of expression", a very substantive and very democratic part of the Bill of Rights, than employers' "right" to deny people their livelihood for expressing an opinion that until very recently was uncontested by civilized society.

Here's a memo for you: there is nothing "qualified" (except incitement to civic disturbance) about free speech, which pretty much covers everything, from "hate speech" to pornography) even if your court doesn't like what is being said.

And Judge Taylor-it is not up to you to decide what is a "worthy" belief in a democracy and what is not. In fact, it is the opposite. It was democracy in the U. K. that passed the Bill of Right to force the King to respect other opinions than his own. Democracy is not a set of beliefs about political fads and fashions of the day. It is there to protect people like Maya from the powers that be. You.

The English Parliament passed a nonsensical piece of legislation on GRC which you duly over-interpreted to overrule the constitutional rights of Ms. Forstater to enjoy freedom of speech in favor of the transgender community's "rights" to identify as something they obviously are not.

As mentioned in the chapter on racism, our culture is trying to operate two mutually incompatible belief sets when it comes to civil rights. . Civil rights may have been a concept that started out as a much needed reform to combat racism, but it has evolved into a parallel set of

---

[49] Breitbart, Dec. 19, 2019, UK Judge Rules Belief That 'Men Cannot Change into Women' Is 'Not Worthy of Respect In a Democratic Society'

rights for adjudicating any kind of discrimination or ultimately any kind of difference between groups like women, blacks and transgenders in terms of *outcome*. It is the core concept of the culture of political correctness which dominates the worldview of Woke, but it runs contrary to our traditional Enlightenment values and indeed to our centuries old concepts of democracy.

The truth matters, so Woke is wrong to allow teachers to teach our skids unscientific b. s. and then kick them out of school when they say, "the emperor has no clothing". They are wrong to stand idly by when a woman gets fired from her job because she states the obvious.

Are LGTBQ-people discriminated against? Judging from the TUC study quoted above horribly so. 7 out of 10, the Guardian says according to the quote above.

But take a closer look. The study suffers from several flaws.

Firstly, it conflate discrimination or sexual harassment of LGTBQ people with offences against *heterosexual* men and women. And as mentioned below in the chapter on Feminism these statistics are vastly exaggerated.

Secondly, the statistics are based on people self-reporting, meaning the sample might not be valid because it may be constituted by people who have an axe to grind. Political scientists normally would have a control group of non self-reporters, to double-check, such possible bias in the sample, but I don´t see one. Do you?

Thirdly, the study itself reports that two thirds of the incident of harassment never were reported. Well, how can we know they are true, then? Where is the proof? The answer to that is that in these days of the women´s #MeToo-movement, believing people who feel offended is axiomatic and legal concepts of presumption of innocence are out the window. But as British comedian, Ricky Gervais, says:" Just because you are offended does not mean you are right".

Fourth, what kind of transgression are we talking about here? Rape or attempted rape? The study doesn´t break down the stats, but as was the case with the abovementioned rape studies this study sure casts a very wide net. Here are the categories it uses:

- indecent or suggestive remarks,
- questions, jokes, or suggestions about a colleague's sex life,
- the display of pornography in the workplace,
- the circulation of pornography (by email, for example),
- unwelcome and inappropriate touching, hugging or kissing
- requests or demands for sexual favours,
- any unwelcome behavior of a sexual nature that creates an intimidating, hostile or humiliating working environment."[50]

This, to say it politely, is pretty vague stuff on which to convict someone of discrimination. But the good news is the façade of unity between LGBTQ- groups wanting to do away with the binary is cracking. There are 2 reasons for that: firstly, categorizing LGTBQ as one group doesn´t stand up to scrutiny. Douglas Murray, author of The Madness of Crowds, cited below and himself gay, says about the LGTB community that it "barely exists even within each letter of

---

[50] Sexual harassment of LGBT people in the workplace, A TUC report published on the UN´s International Day Against Homophobia, May 17, 2019, p.3.

its constituent parts"…"Gay men and gay women have almost nothing in common"…. {and they} have a famous amount of suspicion towards people who claim to be "bisexual" …" And there is tremendous dispute over whether the T´s are the same thing as everybody else or an insult to them",

Gays and queers, he claims, remain in conflict, because of the queer contingent, "who mistake exhibitionism for activism, feeling that nobody is free or equal until they have the right to dress in puppy gear and be led on all fours by a "master" down a public street".[51]

The second reason is that that the nefarious consequence of shoving thousands of years of human evolution and experience out the window and letting people self-identify their gender is beginning to show. Transgender males in women´s beds, baths and beyond, such as in women´s sports and prisons, might look progressive and woke on paper, but when women face aggressive advances from trans-males accusing them of homophobia if they don´t accept their sexual advances, when women athletes are crowded out of women´s sports or raped in women´s jails, things start looking a little different even for most fanatical radical left-wing feminists.

Julia Beck, a lesbian activist, who was booted out of the Baltimore, LGBT Commission for describing a male transgender rapist as, ahem, male, and saying that men can´t be lesbians, testified before the US congress, that the draft Equality Act pushed for by the LGTBQ movement group would mean that, "male rapist will go to women´s prisons and likely assault female inmates as has already happened in the U. K. ; female survivors of rape will be unable to contest male presence in women´s shelters; men will dominate women´s sports…. I urge my fellow Democrats to wake up. Please acknowledge biological reality".[52]

"Karen White formerly known as Stephen Wood, 52, a "predatory and controlling" biologically male rapist was jailed for life after attacking vulnerable female inmates in women's prisons whilst claiming to be transgendered and having been convicted of the previous rapes of two other women. "[53]

Two Girl Guides (Scouts) in England were expelled because they opposed the Scouts´ new rules of allowing transgender males joint showers with girl scouts as young as 5 years; and a trans "woman", "Katie Dolatowski, was convicted of sexually assaulting a 10-year-old girl in a supermarket restroom. "Dolatowski, 18, was said to have spent time in the care system growing up and suffer from mental health issues"[54]

The good news is that women, lesbians in particular, are beginning to correct their ways.

Take the case of the sanitary pad producer, Always, which first removed the iconic women´s sign from its products because an 18-year old transgender male, named LGTBQ activist of the year, Ben Saunders, complained that "Not just women use your products".

And then reinstated it when women´s groups, rightly but belatedly, criticized the move from Always and the transgenders as an attack on women´s biology and vowed to boycott its products. Who would have thought radical feminists would ever put the words "women´s biology" in their mouths, but better late than never.

---

[51] Murray, op. cit. pp. 35-39
[52] Breitbart London, Feb. 25, 2019
[53] Breitbart. Oct. 11, 2018. Allegedly Transgender' Prisoner Gets Life After Raping Two Women, Sexually Assaulting Inmates in Female Jail
[54] Breitbart Sept. 2019

If women are increasingly pushing back against aggressive transgender males and not all gay people adhere to the aggressive political posturing of the queer crowd, maybe there's light at the end of the tunnel.

At least one US state has forbidden transsexual males from competing in women's sports and female sports icons from tennis' lesbian, Marina Navratilova to tennis' straight, Chris Evert, are denouncing the take-over of women's sports by aggressive transgender males posing as women.

But the international sports federations have been slow to react, trying to ride the storm by forcing transgender male athletes to take testosterone-reducing medicine, but it is -literally-too little too late. Boys in puberty grow stronger, heavier, and more muscular than girls, through massive inflows of testosterone. Reducing testosterone levels after the fact won't change much.

Change it *before* the fact, and it will. And that is why the transgender movement is targeting pre-puberty and puberty children. Get to them with puberty changing drugs and breast or penis operations-and that will change matters.

And that is why you have drug companies giving obscene amounts of money to any politician that will make it easier to transition for children below the age of consent. All they have to do if the Liberal Democrats and their ilk have their way is to identify as transgender. As it happens, the UK Liberal Democratic Party lost heavily in the December 12, 2019, "Brexit" parliamentary elections, perhaps because that was a bridge too far for voters. And the Swiss Pharmaceutical company lost its bet.

But make no mistake: even though most jurisdictions have laws requiring parental consent, the pressure from corporations and organized transgender groups is on governments to change that; and on parents to let the children decide. A Texas couple had to go to court because the mother consented to her child undergoing sex surgery but the father didn't. Eventually, the court held in favor of the father.

But not everybody is this lucky. A Finnish couple, by court order, was forced to allow their puberty-age daughter to undergo drug therapy to become a male. She had been hanging out with a group of trans-people, and when one of her older friends heard that the parents were refusing, he sued the parents in court. And much to their dismay, he won. They lost a daughter. The T-people won a convert. OK, that's puberty for you, I hear you saying. Kids will do whatever their peer group does.

But the fact is a very high percentage, 70% of transgenders, have mental health problems. And an even higher percentage later in life regrets transitioning and having their breast or penises taken away.

Because being unsure of your gender throughout history has been the norm. It's *normal*.

In fact, as experts claim," There are approximately ten studies in the literature showing that, on average, 85% of children and adolescents with gender dysphoria have resolution or significant lessening of their dysphoria by early adulthood, without hormonal or surgical interventions. "

Furthermore, Dr. Michelle Cretella, executive director of the American College of Pediatricians, says that the Pediatric Endocrine Society's claim that puberty suppressors are a "reversible treatment" is "a bald-faced lie."

"There are no long-term studies of puberty blocker use for gender incongruence in children," …. "Ergo, no one can say blockers are completely reversible and without harm." On the contrary, she says, there is documentation from the Food and Drug Administration that links Lupron, a drug used without FDA approval as a puberty blocker on children and adolescents with gender dysphoria to thousands of deaths.

Dr. Cretella explains:

"Puberty blockers, like Lupron, effectively "castrate" children of both sexes at the level of the pituitary gland in the brain, chemically turning boys into eunuchs and sending girls into a pre-teen menopause. This is why many girls treated for FDA-approved conditions with Lupron have developed osteoporosis in their twenties. Puberty blocking prevents the normal maturation of all organs – including the brain – that depend upon the child's natural sex hormones to develop. Adults treated with Lupron for FDA-approved conditions experience memory deficits. What are we doing to the brains of gender incongruent but physically healthy children?"

Only the Woke do not call it castration. They call it "gender-affirming care." It sounds so nice doesn't it? Who doesn't want to "affirm" people? Especially minors.[55]

I'll tell you who. Any responsible adult.

Because let's remind ourselves what this "gender-affirming care" actually consists of. It consists of telling confused and often deeply unhappy children that their problems can all be sorted out if they decide that they were born in the wrong body and that this is fixable.

How is it fixable? First by easy little things like "puberty blockers" and "hormonal treatment."

Do people realize what these things — also designed to sound simple and innocuous — actually are? Apart from being drugs whose long-term effects we have almost no studies on?

If you are a girl being given "gender-affirming surgery" you will start by being given a "medically necessary" double-mastectomy.

Any woman who has actually had to go through that surgery for serious health reasons will know it is not the fun little procedure the trans lobby call "top surgery." But it is positively breezy compared to the equally cutesy-named "bottom surgery."

I'm sorry for what follows, but people have to know this.

For a girl "bottom surgery" will consist of flaying a young girl's leg or arm to the veins, leaving her with an ugly, unhealable wound on her body while attempting to make something approximating a penis out of it. This skin graft will often not take. When it does the result will neither resemble nor operate like a penis.

That's just the girls. For the boys "gender-affirming bottom surgery" actually means their penis will be cut in half, flayed and partially inverted into their body. This attempt at creating a vagina will cause complications for life. The wound will keep trying to heal up. Urination will almost never be straightforward. Infections will be commonplace, as will painful internal hair growth.

---

[55] The following paragraphs are a paraphrasing of a piece on LGTBQ in National Review of 23 June, 2023.

None of this is about a one-off visit to the hospital. Every child put through "gender-affirming surgery" will be in and out of hospital for the rest of their life. They will have an ongoing relationship with multiple doctors to continue doing the most basic things in life.

When California-based endocrinologist Dr. Michael Laidlaw was asked how the Endocrine Pediatric Society can claim the opposite, he tells us a by now familiar story, of how medical societies have been infiltrated by radical transgender activists with "one of the most insidious child sterilization programs ever devised".[56]

Current NHS rules in the UK, which allow 12 year-olds taking gender transitioning puberty blockers without parental consent have been largely based upon 2012 guidelines issued by the World Professional Association for Transgender Health (WPATH), an organization whose reputation has been called into question by an increasing number of medical experts and analysts because it receives funding from transgender industry and advocacy groups.

Atlanta, Georgia-based pediatric endocrinologist Dr. Quentin Van Meter explained to Breitbart News that WPATH was launched by psychologist John Money and sexologist Alfred Kinsey to push a political agenda for gender ideology.

"This is not a scientifically based organization," Van Meter said. "It's essentially a pseudo-professional group of people who are pushing an agenda and have been since the beginning."

"To be a member in WPATH, you only need to have an interest in transgender issues," he explained. "There is no professional degree required, no training specifically, no certification. If you want to be a member, all you need to do is pay your dues."

What happens to those parents who still won't consent? Well, in a recent article in the Journal of Medical Ethics of the British Medical Journal, "gender-affirming" doctors advised the transgender industry how they can prevail over parents who are reluctant to allow their children to participate in treatments, such as puberty blockers, cross-sex hormones, and surgeries.

"Neglect, as a medico-legal term, can be used to initiate an evaluation by Child Protective Services and remove a parent as a child's legal guardian in the most severe instances, " the authors stated."[57]

So, not only are we obviously being lied to because the drugs used in a process that is likely to prove completely unnecessary are untested. We are also being threatened with having our children taken away from us by the State if we protest this insanity. This is Orwellian. Radical ideologues with the stated goal of doing away with traditional family norms including raising children have taken over supposed "expert" associations to pave the way for implementing their extreme Postmodernist goals.

Think I am exaggerating? A new Scottish draft law will allow anyone in Scotland, including 16-year-old children, to legally change their gender within six months of applying to the government.

---

[56] All quotes from Breitbart, Nov. 5, 2019, <u>Pediatric Endocrine Society Falsely Claims Puberty Blockers Are 'Reversible'</u>
[57] All quotes from Breitbart, 10 Feb. 2020

"We are proposing these reforms because the current system is viewed by many wishing to apply as traumatic and demeaning," said the Scottish Equalities Minister when submitting the draft law.

"Viewed by many wishing to apply as traumatic and demeaning" is politician speak for caving to transgender activists.

And sure enough, the manager of the Scottish Trans Alliance, James Morton, is quoted in the same piece as saying that "The current process to change the sex on a trans person's birth certificate is a humiliating, offensive, and expensive red-tape nightmare which requires them to submit intrusive psychiatric evidence to a faceless tribunal panel years after they transitioned."

But, not to worry. The equalities minister says that:

"Women's rights and protections will be as strong under this Bill as they are today, as we remain committed to protect, respect, and advance the rights of women and girls, " and will… "contain some provisions barring trans women from entering certain jobs, including rape counselors, religious posts as well as from the army if such a person would undermine "combat effectiveness".[58]

Wait a minute, this is incoherent nonsense. If trans women by law are women not males and must be addressed by other people as women, on penalty of losing their job as we saw in the Maya Forstater case above, why must they be excluded from "certain jobs", such as rape counselors?

That can only mean that they really are men, can't it? And if that is true why limit barring women from entering certain jobs to rape counselors? Why not bar them from women's sports, jails, and dressing rooms? Any place where they can harm biological women?

And if the good minister claims women's protection will be as strong under this law as before, why the need to introduce new legislation? The answer is, of course, that this is a pretext; the real purpose of the bill is to make it easier for 16-year old teenagers to transition. Pushed by the transgender movement and the puberty blockers industry.

This is insane. And Woke should be ashamed to let it happen to our gullible kids.

We know that politicians would pander to Pandas if bears had the vote, but this madness has consequences in real life.

Presidential candidate and billionaire Mike Bloomberg released his "vision" for putting in place "a comprehensive policy to ensure LGBTQ+ equality" on Jan. 28, 2020. The vision, according to his website, includes "transgenders' rights to free sex surgery and hormone treatment, rights to shelter based on gender identity, and forcing law enforcement and health care providers to undergo "cultural competency" and "implicit bias" training." (Breitbart, Jan. 29, 2020)

That's us my friends and fellow taxpayers, footing the bill for free sex surgery and hormone treatment for anyone who identifies as transgender and allowing them into battered women's shelters if they so wish.

The quote above on personal pronouns from Women's March is proof of women's support of transgenderism. But in the name of feminism, they are sacrificing young females. That some

---

[58] All quotes from Breitbart, Dec. 18, 2019

mental health plagued adults want to transition is one thing. Let the rules to see a qualified psychiatrist first, self-pay, and long waiting periods run their course. But kids? That's just nuts.

But the biggest flaw in the LTGBQ ideology is the underlying hypothesis that people are to be identified as those groups they share certain racial or sexual characteristics with, not as individuals. For defining groups by a thing, they have had absolutely no influence on, their gender (or race), makes no sense. It is at heart totalitarian. That concept is pure Marxism. And that was supposed to have gone out with the mass murders of Stalin, Mao, and Pol Pot.

Only it obviously hasn't.

Woke has entered dangerous waters when it casually throws away thousands of years of human experience and tries to redefine women out of existence.

Part II: Transforming the Consciousness of Society:

Chapter 3: Race as a Social Construct.

xxxxxxxxxxxxxxxxxxxxxxxxxxx

"The reality of human races is another commonsense "truth" destined to follow the flat Earth into oblivion".

Jared Diamond, geographer, Race Without Color, 1994.

xxxxxxx

"Race is a recent human invention…Race is about *culture*, not biology",

American Anthropological Association.

xxxxxxx

"Human racial classification is of no social value and positively destructive of social and human relations",

Richard Lewontin, population geneticist, The Apportionment Of Human Diversity, 1972.

xxxxxxx

> **"I claim that, unless the contrary can be proved, we must assume that all complex activities are *socially determined*, not hereditary".**
>
> Franz Boas, cultural anthropologist, Culture and Thought, 1911.

"Few ideas have been more harmful than one race or another being inherently superior to others. For this reason, discussion of biological differences between races has been virtually banished from polite academic conversation" says Nicholas Wade in his book, A Troublesome Inheritance-Genes, Race and Human History from 2014.[59]

That social scientists want to exorcize racism from our minds is more than understandable, given the role it played in history including but not limited to the Holocaust.

Woke was at the forefront of fighting not only against the idea of racial hierarchies but against the idea of race itself.

Most prominently the geneticist, Richard Lewontin, quoted above, who is prominent defender of Woke orthodoxy on race, namely that the concept of race is made up, or to put it academically, socially constructed. And that even to question this orthodoxy is tantamount to…racism.

Or as the sociologist Charles Murray puts it, "The orthodox sometime comes surprisingly close (given the obvious cosmetic differences across races) to asserting that biological race is a figment of our imagination."[60]

Unfortunately, just erasing a word from polite speech doesn´t make the concept go away. Franz Boas, in the statement quoted above, tempted fate by saying "unless the contrary can be proved" we have to assume that human minds are a blank slate for society to leave its stamp on; or in other words, all differences between humans are cultural. Well, the contrary *has* been proven. Races *do* exist.

All the quotes above are from before 2003, the year the genome was discovered, and we know better *now* from the mapping of the genome. It is an inconvenient fact and a troublesome inheritance that our human differences are not just based on cultural and social differences acting upon the blank slate of the minds of human beings as documented convincingly by Stephen Pinker in his groundbreaking book, The Blank Slate-The Modern Denial of Human Nature.

What the mapping of the genome shows is that by using the so-called clustering technique, "the genomes of individuals throughout the world cluster together in terms of their genetic similarity. The result is that everyone ends up in the cluster with which they have *the most variations* in common. These clusters always correspond to the five continental races - African, Caucasian (Europe and the Middle East), Asian, Pacific Islander (for example, Australian, New Guinean and Melanesian and Native American"[61]

In other words, if you accept that one can belong to a race without sharing *all* the identifying traits (European skin color is noticeably less white as you move from lily-white Danes to olive-

---

[59] Nicholas Wade, A Troublesome Inheritance-Genes, Race and Human History, Penguin Books,2015, p. 9
[60] Human Diversity, p.132.
[61] Nicholas Wade, A Troublesome Inheritance-Genes, Race and Human History, pp. 96-97

colored Portuguese) you end up with five continental races whose genome for the most important aspects are similar.

Yet the consensus of social scientists still insists that there is no biological foundation for races and that "Race is about culture, not biology" as the American Anthropological Association says.

Let´s test that hypothesis by using Popper´s Falsification Theory, which in simple terms means that if you observe that something is different from what theory claims to be true,f.ex. that all swans are black even though you-or someone else-have seen black swans, it is the *theory* that is wrong, not you.

Firstly, is it *always* true that human behavior does *not* have a genetic, i. e. biological base, as the American Anthropological Association says? In other words, is it true that this statement cannot be falsified? The answer is no. Four examples suffice: Lactose tolerance, high altitude tolerance, the discovery of genes controlling social behavior and the fact that a sub-group of anthropologists, *forensic* anthropologists, use the concept of race in their daily work.

In most populations, lactose tolerance is the ability to digest milk in early childhood weaning, a tolerance which is then switched off in adulthood. But in populations that herd cattle and drink raw milk there was a great selective advantage in keeping the gene that broke down the lactose - the lactase gene - switched on. That´s exactly what happened with the so-called Funnel Beaker Culture that lived in north central Europe between 5-6. 000 years ago.[62]

An even more recent example is from 3. 000 years ago, when Tibetans evolved a genetic variant that let them live at high altitudes.[63]

Furthermore, although much is still to be learned about the genetic basis of human behavior, there are at least two exceptions: First, the discovery of oxytocin, a neural hormone promoting trust, also called the *hormone of trust*, which "dampens down . . distrust …and promotes feelings of solidarity".

The second exception is the discovery of the MAO-A gene and the role it plays in the control of aggression. The role of MAO-A in the control of aggression came to light in 1993 through the study of an unusually violent Dutch family in which the eight affected men all had inherited a *mutated* form of the MAO-A enzyme, the mutation preventing the MAO-A gene from serving its normal function of limiting aggression.[64]

Last, but not least, in an exercise like ours which sets out trying to *falsify* a scientific claim, the fact that not *all* anthropologists agree, falsifies the claim that there are no human races. Forensic anthropologists can and do tell the police with better than 80% accuracy the racial identity of a victim of a crime by using techniques based on clustering techniques.[65]

It is a strong argument, so what are politically correct social scientists and biologists to do? They change the name of the game. Instead of referring to *races t*hey speak of AIMs-Ancestry Informative Markers. And as the Brits say "Bob´s your uncle".

Thus, social scientists can happily go on resisting the notion that human behavior has a genetic basis, stating that race is a cultural concept, a social construct with no base in biology. As

---

[62] Nicholas Wade, A Troublesome Inheritance-Genes, Race and Human History, pp. 60-61
[63] Nicholas Wade, A Troublesome Inheritance-Genes, Race and Human History, p. 3
[64] Nicholas Wade, A Troublesome Inheritance-Genes, Race and Human History, pp. 50-57
[65] Nicholas Wade, A Troublesome Inheritance-Genes, Race and Human History, p. 70

Nicholas Wade says in "A Troublesome Inheritance":" The blank slate notion has been particularly attractive to Marxists, who wish government to mold socialist man in its desired image and who see genetics as an impediment to the power of the state" because Marxists…" see the mind as a blank slate on which only culture can write".[66]

But Woke has to deal with an inconvenient reality, namely that people obviously think racism exists as witnessed by university campuses all across the US A. running courses on racism, Critical Race Theory or organizing themselves in such movements as Black Lives Matter. Can there be racism without races?

The explanation for this obvious contradiction is that racism in the West, but particularly in the US, has been conflated with the institution of slavery. For which white liberals feel continually guilty. As Thomas Sowell (who is black) says in his masterpiece, Black Rednecks and White Liberals, "By projecting a vision of the world in which the *problems of blacks are consequences of the actions of whites,* either immediately or in times past, white liberals have provided a blanket excuse for shortcomings and even crimes by blacks".[67]

But slavery has been around for thousands of years in all continents from Asia to America: whites were enslaved by other whites in higher numbers than blacks as witnessed by the Ottoman Turks capturing central European men women and children in their- almost successful, centuries long conquest of the Christian European world; Africans enslaved other Africans for domestic use long before they started selling them for use in the plantations of the US South. More African slaves died on the journey through the Saharan desert to the Middle East and Muslim North Africa than on the Atlantic crossing.

And slaves in ancient Rome were used as highly respected gladiators and as concubines.

The point being that slavery was not in and by itself a result of racism, but of power and economics. In short, to say that slavery was based on race is as Sowell says," to put the cart before the horse"[68]

Racism as an ideology has historically come *after* enslavement and often as *justification* for slavery, not least in the Deep South. And it came about then because slavery was under intense attack from white people, mainly British religious evangelical conservatives, like William Wilberforce and Henry Thornton, who saw it as contrary to Christian principles and who succeeded in abolishing slavery in England in1807.

Slavery in America has been the subject of much more scholarly research than that of any other region, but in terms of sheer numbers several times as many African slaves were shipped for sale to Portuguese Brazil as the Southern US states.

And indentured servants up until the end of the 17th century outnumbered blacks in the British colonies. They were treated as brutally as blacks, and didn´t, as many people prefer to believe, come voluntarily but consisted mainly of convicts forced onto the ships; and hijacked men, women and children who after the passage which cost huge numbers of them their lives were sold on auctions just like slaves.

---

[66] Nicholas Wade, A Troublesome Inheritance-Genes, Race and Human History, p. 59
[67] Thomas Sowell, Black Rednecks and White Liberals, p. 52
[68] Thomas Sowell, Race and Culture, p. 223

Jim Goad in his book, The Redneck Manifesto - How Hillbillies, Hicks and White Trash Became America's Scapegoats, quotes estimates by a number of respected American scholars on indentured servitude according to which "as many as two thirds of all white colonial immigrants arrived in chains"[69]

So, though slavery is as old as humans and not *per se* the result of racism, someone, somewhere, is always ready to call it America's original sin. The Labour Party in the U. K., like the Democrats in the U. S are now, more than 200 years after slavery was abolished in England and more than 150 years after Abraham Lincoln set the slaves free in the US calling for *reparations* on the basis of the same rationale.

So, racism must be everywhere, right? Indeed, judging from the stories in the media, the constant accusations of racism, you would think racism in the West is worse than ever. Right? You couldn't be more wrong.

First, ask yourself, compared to what? Ante-bellum South and slavery? Nazi-Germany? Hardly. The fact is the West has come a long way since then and there is hardly any racism left to speak of. And it was white people in England who took the lead in abolishing the terrible, age-old institution of slavery. Long before nations on other continents dragged their feet and in some places of the earth, notably in certain parts of the Middle East and Africa, are still dragging.

As Sowell says: "The irony of our times is that the destruction of slavery around the world, which some once considered the supreme moral act in history, is little known and less discussed among intellectuals in either Western or non-Western countries, while the enslavement of Africans by Europeans is treated as unique-and due to unique moral deficiencies in the West".[70]

Sowell may call it ironic but calling it a lie is more appropriate. How do I know? There are 4 reasons apart from the fact that in most parts of the West it is illegal.

Firstly, because the few admitted racists, like David Duke in the US, or small Neo-Nazi parties in the EU, have very, very few followers and absolutely no political impact. You might as well lay awake at night worrying about the survivalist-crowd or the flat-earthers.

But Woke wants you to think otherwise. It is trying to scare you.

Secondly, because the word has become meaningless. When members of the Democratic Party in the US call their own political leader, Nancy Pelosi, a racist, the word has lost its original meaning of African Americans being inferior.[71]

It has become just a slur like asshole or idiot and assigning it to you is really giving the few remaining real racists too much credit.

Thirdly, if racism really were a political force, something a substantial part of the population believes in, the two most important football leagues in the Western World, FIFA and UEFA would not be running ad campaigns against racism. "Say No to Racism" is their slogan as if anybody in their right mind, except a few mentally troubled fanatics would say "yes" to racism.

---

[69] Jim Goad, The Redneck Manifesto-How Hillbillies, Hicks and White Trash Became America's Scapegoats, p. 56
[70] Sowell, Race and Culture, p. 222
[71] Insights and Issues," Pelosi Is Racist On Immigration, Says The Hard Left In Her Caucus", July 9, 2019

Why? Because it would be too controversial; and controversial by definition is avoided in all business because it cuts into profits by turning off potential customers.

If these two organizations would run campaigns for movements like "It's OK To Be White" and support the Oklahoma City University student who was expelled and questioned by police for distributing flyers on campus with that message, I would tip my hat to them. Or if they would campaign against hate speech regulations in the EU which stifle free speech mainly on the right, I would applaud it. But this day and age anti-racism campaigns are a freebie.

Don't be fooled.

The racist abuse in football stadiums? Aren't football fans working class, simpletons and overwhelmingly white?

Football (both of the European soccer-variety and American football) is a contact sport, an aggressive sport, a blood sport where having aggressive supporters, predominantly of the masculine variety in the stands is called home advantage and can make or break a game.

Football fans are supposed to intimidate and rattle the away team, or they are not doing their job. It's not tennis where fans can be told "Quiet please" and where they actually shut up.

And if an effective way to rattle a black star on the away team is making monkey noises, then a few idiots will do it. What FIFA and UEFA forget to tell you is that these idiots more and more frequently are identified by other fans, turned over to the stewards and banned from the stadium for life.

At a recent English Premier League match, between Manchester City and Manchester United, one man making monkey noises were fingered by the fans and arrested by the police for "offences against the public order". There were more than 60.000 people in the stands. And his name was leaked to the press and published with a great deal of moralistic wringing of hands on the sports pages.

Police recently arrested a 13-year old boy for a similar offence at another football match. Liverpool Football Club's captain, Jordan Henderson, called for greater fines and tougher punishment.

At a recent Premier League game between Chelsea and Tottenham, all commentators were up in arms about fans abusing a black player. Six arrests were made because other fans fingered them. What the commentators neglected to say was that fans also abused a player from South Korea.

What commentators also forget to mention is that not every claim of racial harassment from fans is actually true. In the abovementioned Tottenham - Chelsea match, sports commentators and media were in high dudgeon about the claim of serious racial abuse made by a black Chelsea player, Antonio Ruediger. The problem is: he lied. The Football Association could find no evidence of any racial abuse and the matter was quietly shelved.

That isn't endemic racism. That's rough sports and football fans and idiots and kids. But what it does represent is public hysteria over anything racial. The English Football Association is considering jail sentences for racial abuse during football matches, saying that such actions are hate crimes.

And that is deeply troubling because what the woke mob braying for blood is ignoring is that free speech in principle should protect all kinds of speech including hate speech. As I argue in the chapter on free speech, what we are witnessing is social control over all of us.

English Premier League players on a recent match day were wearing rainbow-colored armbands and giant screens were showing support for Gay Pride. What has that got to do with football on a Saturday afternoon, I ask?

Who paid the English Football Association for this stunt? Who among the assembled football journalists even asked the question? None.

It was pure indoctrination in the reigning philosophy of our times: Woke. Free speech has its limits that philosophy says. And we, your political leaders, will tell you what these limits are.

If the police can arrest you for exercising your constitutional right to say obnoxious and stupid things to black or gay players, they can arrest you on other things such as not calling transsexual men who identify as female by their chosen female names. Think I am exaggerating?

Well think again. Remember Jordan Peterson, the Canadian clinical psychologist, I told you about earlier, who was heavily fined for refusing to follow the law on gender identity, on penalty of ending up in jail if he didn´t cough up?

According to Breitbart London, " In the UK, referring to someone as male if they identify as a female can be reported to the police and logged as a "hate incident" with "no evidence" if anyone "perceives" it as offensive".[72]

Beware of what you wish for and don´t give up your freedom of speech, just because the politically correct crowd goads you. They will be coming for you next.

The fourth reason racism is a hoax and a tool used by the Woke to prevent free speech, is that it is selective. Did you ever see the highly rated (and awesome) TV series, the Wire, about black drug dealers in Baltimore or catch one of Dave Chapelle´s stand-up acts? Not least "Sticks and Stones"? These black men use the N-word more often than a slave-trader in the ante-bellum South. But for them it´s all-right. But not for me.

Why?

Any thinking adult knows that using that word and indeed any other word depends on context. There´s a reason American law establishes that just about the only exception to free speech, is crying "fire" in a movie theatre. There´s a reason Western jurisprudence distinguishes between "fighting words", i. e. insults and opinion, i. e. just words. The old saying really is true: "sticks and stones will break your bones, but words will never hurt you".

So, friends, don´t be fooled. Be brave. What´s good for the goose is good for the gander. If everyone is equal before the law and we are all God´s chillun´, then, if African Americans can use nigger, so can you.

That doesn´t mean I´m encouraging you to use the word in talking to your black neighbors at the street party. The *context* won´t be right. Unless you know them really well!

But on a more serious note, we have to ask ourselves: If racism is illegal, socially unacceptable, and rare, why are black studies obligatory at every self-respecting university in the US, why has

---

[72] Breitbart News, October 11, 2018

Black Lives Matter become an important social movement and why is everyone throwing accusations of racism around without abandon?

The answer again lies in the prevalent philosophy of our time: Woke. As in the story of feminism going from a movement against social and legal injustices to a Neo-Marxist revolutionary reordering of society, the same thing is happening to the Civil Rights Movement. It has gone Marxist.

Why? Why is it, as an editorial in The Washington Examiner says, "that 52 years after Martin Luther King Jr. was assassinated, at a time when the ideal of liberty and justice for all is more accessible than it has ever been, when the nation elected the first African American president… and when two have been appointed to the Supreme Court to be carrying on King's struggle and many more sit in Congress, that those who claim for justice in modern times have strayed far from his dream of his children growing up "in a nation where they will not be judged by the color of their skin but by the content of their character. "?

The Editorial answers its own question: the woke Neo-Marxists are at it again:" The cultural Left's intersectionality crusade has separated the country into different corners: White people are not permitted to address racial issues, and men are forbidden from speaking about women's matters (i.e. abortion). Instead, they have embraced an identity politics that veers from merely fighting against all forms of discrimination, to carving people up by race, gender, sexual orientation, and placing those distinctions above all else. "[73]

Martin Luther King would turn in his grave, but the present school of black Woke leaders and ideologues actually consider his famous saying:" We may have all come on different ships, but we're in the same boat now", as…. . ahem… racist. I kid you not. Why? Because, to them it denies the uniqueness of black history; read: slavery.

To these black leaders, Sowell's critique of the left's political use of slavery mentioned above, namely that black culture for the most part was not formed by slavery but by the culture they lived in, the redneck culture of the South, is pure heresy. Coming from a fellow African American, to boot.

For those not familiar with the concept of "redneck", it's a name for a culture formed by the early settlers of America coming from the North of England, Northern Ireland and Scotland, back then a lawless and wild border part of the British Isles, characterized by wild living, loose morals and a tendency to violence, drinking and exaggerated pride.

Sowell's argument, if delicately stated, is that culture matters and that blacks to a large degree have come from a "redneck" culture that put a premium on pride, accepted violence more readily as a means to settle differences than other demographics and responded aggressively to perceived slights.

Sowell is not alone with this theory, which is backed up by Historian David Hackett Fisher in his book, <u>Albion's Seed: 4 British Folkways in America</u>.

For a modern-day description of redneck living, read the excellent book <u>Hillbilly Elegy</u> by J. D. Vance, mentioned above, a man who escaped its clutches to become a Harvard-educated corporate lawyer, but still cannot run away from its influence.

---

[73] Washington Examiner Editorial, Jan. 20, 2020

Sowell criticizes the Woke for using slavery as an ideological vehicle in its attempt to reorder society. Or, as he says somewhat diplomatically:" …what is and is not considered to be a legacy of slavery is too often determined by what advances the ideological visions of today rather than what accords with the record of history".[74]

A glaring example is the crime and incarceration rates of blacks compared to those of whites in the US which routinely are ascribed to the "legacy of slavery" and "institutional racism". But is it true?

First, blacks commit vastly more crimes than whites, mostly on other blacks, which is reflected in their much higher incarceration rates. "Blacks were charged with 62% of all robberies, 57% of all murders and 45% of all assaults in the 75 largest counties in 2009 while constituting roughly 15% of the population in those counties" states an expert on the subject, Heather Mac Donald.[75]

She also convincingly debunks the institutional racism charges from Black Lives Matter and other civil rights organizations.

In a book about Woke, the Black Lives Matter(BLM) story is a particular interesting one: because it, literally, is built on a lie. The organization was founded in 2013 but came into national prominence after the August 2014 police shooting of Michael Brown, in Ferguson, Missouri.

The shooting "spawned a narrative as stubborn as it was false: Ferguson police officer, Darren Wilson (who is white) …allegedly shot the 18-year-old "gentle giant" in cold blood while the latter was pleading for his life, hands raised in surrender" …The facts were that Brown, a budding criminal who weighed nearly 300 pounds had punched Wilson in the face, tried to grab Wilson´s gun and charged at him, leading Wilson to fire in self-defense".[76]

The incident triggered the now iconic "Hands Up, Don´t Shoot" claim which Brown allegedly had said before being shot, which again led to protesters all over the US shouting this slogan while denouncing police brutality against blacks. Including Democratic Congressmen on the step of Capitol Hill, where the US Congress resides.

It was all a lie. The US Department of Justice, led by a black Attorney General, Eric Holder, exonerated Wilson on all charges, including the "Hands Up, Don´t Shoot" hoax.

BLM is also much more than an organization defending the civil rights of African Americans, namely a Neo-Marxist political organization bent on revolutionary change of American society. Just ask BLM leaders Alicia Garza, Patrisse Cullors and Opal Tometi.

In a revealing 2015 interview, Cullors said, " "We actually do have an ideological frame. Alicia and I [Garza] in particular, we're trained organizers. We are trained Marxists. We are super versed on ideological theories." — BLM co-founder Patrisse Cullors, July 22, 2015.

---

[74] Sowell, Culture and Race, p. 222
[75] Heather Mac Donald, The War On Cops-How the New Attack on Law and Order Makes Anyone Less Safe, p. 73
[76] Heather Mac Donald, The War on Cops-How the New Attack on Law and Order Makes Anyone Less Safe, p. 5

Visit the Black Lives Matter website, and the first frame you get is a large crowd with fists raised and in an echo of Gramsci and his call to transform the consciousness of society, the slogan "Now We Transform."

One of its political demands proclaims: "We disrupt the Western-prescribed nuclear-family-structure requirement by supporting each other as extended families and 'villages' that collectively care for one another."

Its ordinary members and activists are brutally honest about their political tactics.

"If this country doesn't give us what we want, then we will burn down this system and replace it. All right? And I could be speaking figuratively. I could be speaking literally. It's a matter of interpretation.... I just want black liberation and black sovereignty, by any means necessary." — BLM activist Hank Newsome, on TV, June 25, 2020.

"We are anti-capitalist. We believe and understand that Black people will never achieve liberation under the current global racialized capitalist system." — Movement for Black Lives (M4BL), of which BLM is a part, in a statement June 5, 2020.[77]

"Trained" Marxists is a particularly revealing turn of phrase. "Trained" to do what exactly? Well as the other quotes reveal," trained" to combat and subvert capitalist society. It evokes Lenin´s concept of, "professional revolutionaries" a strategy whereby the most class-conscious and politically advanced sections of the proletariat or working class, described as the revolutionary vanguard, form organizations in order to draw larger sections of the working class towards revolutionary politics and serve as manifestations of proletarian political power against the bourgeois.[78]

Despite this radicalism a Pew research survey of 2020 found that 2/3 of Americans were supportive of the BLM-movement.

Not anymore.

On January 5, Washington State Attorney General Robert Ferguson issued a "Closure Notice" demanding that BLM "immediately cease" all fundraising activities, because it had failed to file its annual financial disclosure report for tax year 2020, due last November. California Attorney General Rob Bonta followed suit a few weeks later and threatened to hold individual leaders personally liable for late fees. Despite these clear directives, BLMGNF continued fundraising until reports last week exposed their flagrant violations.[79]

According to those reports, the group's charity registration is also out of compliance in Connecticut, Maine, Maryland, New Jersey, New Mexico, North Carolina and Virginia.

---

[77] All quotes from BLM website and internet references.
[78] Thomas Sowell, Marxism-Philosophy and Economics, p.211, William Morrow,1985.
[79] This is a summary of a commentary in Breitbart by Peter Flaherty published February 9,2022, entitled "Where Is the BLM 60 million"?

"It appears that the house of cards may be falling, and this happens eventually with nearly every scam, scheme, or illegal enterprise," Indiana the Republican attorney General, Todd Rokita, told reporters.

BLMGNF founder Patrisse Cullors, the self-avowed Marxist who once called for the "end of Israel" during a 2015 Harvard panel discussion, resigned her post as executive director of the BLM money machine last May 2021, with over $60 million in its coffers, ostensibly to focus on her second book and a television deal with Warner Bros.

But revelations about her personal finances, including the purchase of four homes totaling more than $3 million, were more likely the reasons for her sudden retreat from the spotlight. This news prompted criticism from local black activists, such as one black mother whose son was killed by Los Angeles police: "Black lives don't matter. Your pockets matter," she declared. "Y'all come into our lives and act like y'all got our back and y'all want to say, 'Black Lives Matter.' But after we bury our children, we don't see B, L or M, but y'all out here buying properties."

Speaking of buying properties, we do know where at least some of the $60 million went. It was transferred to BLM Canada to buy a $6 million mansion in Toronto, the former headquarters of Canada's Communist Party. Looks like BLM is returning to its roots.

That will be of little consolation to Heather Mac Donald, who when on the lecture circuit explaining the statistics of black crimes on blacks, is regularly met with fierce sometimes violent protests, when explaining that the reason blacks are more frequently incarcerated is that they commit more crimes, a lot more, than whites.

Thus, Mac Donald, recently had to be escorted by police fearing for her safety from the stage at Claremont McKenna College, a top California college where the admissions data tells us that most of Claremont McKenna's admitted students in terms of income fall within the top 5% nationally: Her crime? Giving a presentation, while being called, you guessed it, a "racist", presenting the abovementioned facts on policing in the US which essentially undermine the whole "institutional racism" crime theory.

But facts are facts, and it is a fact that 95% of black murder victims are killed by…blacks.[80]

But then what would explain the large differences in criminal behavior between blacks and whites?

We know from experience and science that there are no innate reasons blacks should not be as successful in schools, universities and in society as other ethnicities. In 2016, a chain of public charter schools that overwhelmingly serves poor black and Latino students, Success Academy in New York City, outperformed state averages on standardized tests. Chicago's Urban prep Academy has spent years sending all its mostly minority graduates to four-year colleges and universities.

Jerome Hudson, himself black, blames "affirmative action", the policy of racial preferences instituted by white left-wing Postmodernists.

His basic argument is that reverse discrimination cannot cure discrimination. Two wrongs don't make a right, he says: "Today, two mutually exclusive Americas cannot exist. We are either an affirmative action America, where some of us are held to a lower standard based on skin color,

---

[80] Jerome Hudson, <u>50 Things They Don't Want You to Know</u>, p. 19

or we are all equal under the law, free to fail or succeed no matter what group we happen to be born into. Both cannot be true."[81]

He is right. Not just on affirmative action but on all the cultural problems identified in this book as polarizing or dividing the West as illustrated by what this book calls the ongoing cultural war between Metropolitan Elites and the average voter.

The larger problem is that our culture lives according to two different set of rules on liberties: the old ones as exemplified by the U.S. Constitution of 1789 and the French Constitution of that same year, incorporating basic freedoms of speech, religion, assembly, the classic Enlightenment freedoms.

And the second one which arose in the 1960s and which I define as Woke which tries to replace the old liberties with new, incompatible ones based on *group identities*. Christopher Caldwell, for many years a columnist for the *Financial Times* and senior editor of the *Weekly Standard*, says, "Much of what we have called 'polarization' or 'incivility' in recent years is something more grave," he writes. "[I]t is the disagreement over which of the two constitutions shall prevail."

In the U.S. for example, the battle between opponents of affirmative action like Hudson and its proponents really is a question of which definition of freedom to live by politically and legally: that of the Enlightenment or that of Woke.

So far, Woke has won the day. So much indeed, that the logical conclusion to Jerome Hudson's analysis of affirmative action, i.e. the repeal of the 1964 and 1968 Civil Rights Act, is a distinct outlier.

Although Woke suffered a temporary setback when the U.S. Supreme Court on June 28,2023, declared the use of race as a criterium for college admission for unconstitutional in the above mentioned case of Asian Students v. Harvard.[82]

In Europe, the elevation of human rights, to a privileged position that no one disputes, mirrors that of civil rights in the States.

But here the code word to look for is not racism but diversity. You might be excused for thinking that diversity would mean a battle to have new immigrant groups represented at all levels of power, but you'd be wrong: it's about *women* breaking the "glass ceiling". Which as we shall discover in the next chapter is already a done deal.

But not, as in the Harvard case, without bending justice a little bit on the way.

The problem with affirmative action both in questions of race or women's rights is that in the real world resources are not unlimited. So trade-offs have to be made.

Harvard doesn't have unlimited space at the table so if blacks are admitted ahead of better qualified white candidates, the white candidate loses out. And sues. And wins, because in the West according to our various constitutions all men[meaning people]are created equal.

As luck would have it this message was driven home in Europe on the very same date of June 28,2023: An inquiry found that the British Airforce, the RAF, had illegally discriminated against *men* in recruiting new candidates in favor of....women.

---

[81] Jerome Hudson, <u>50 Things They Don't Want You to Know</u>, p. 19
[82] Students for Fair Admission v.Harvard.

The American Declaration of Independence that most classic expression of Enlightenment thought on human freedom says" We hold these truths to be self-evident, that *all men* are created equal, that they are endowed by their Creator with certain unalienable Rights, that among these are Life, Liberty, and the pursuit of Happiness.". That means individuals, we as human beings as opposed to other species. It doesn´t mean certain groups of color, race, religion, or gender preferences.

Racism is a good example of how Enlightenment morals got it right. They believed that all men are created equal and that therefore slavery was wrong. Woke claims the opposite and that society is racist. But they are lying on the facts. Enlightenment moralists and Christians abolished slavery. In 1807 in the British empire which spanned the globe and in 1863 in the States. Yet, here we are today, facing the same b.s. about institutional racism and ubiquitous racism in the body politic. Why? Because of Postmodernism.

Because progressive left-wingers and other Neo-Marxists took over the civil rights battle and used it to bring about revolutionary change.

It is in this way, says Helen Andrews, prominent American writer and journalist, that civil rights, as embodied in the Civil Rights Acts of 1964 and 1968 have evolved from a specific response to a specific emergency problem to "new grounds for overruling and overriding legislatures and voters on any question that could be cast as a matter of discrimination. That was coming to mean *all* questions."[83]

As Helen Andrews goes on to say, "This metastasis was contrary to the explicit assurances of the original sponsors of the 1964 law. Senator Hubert Humphrey famously promised to eat the paper on which the bill was printed if it were found to require anything as ambitious as *racial preferences in hiring*. He also promised that it would create only "about 400 permanent new Federal jobs."

Within ten years the Justice Department's Civil Rights Division alone had more than twice that number. "The bill does not permit the Federal Government to interfere with the day-to-day operations of a business," promised Representative William McCulloch of Ohio, ranking Republican on the House Judiciary Committee. It did not tell a bank "to whom it may or may not make a loan" or a landlord "to whom he must sell, rent, lease, or otherwise use his real estate."

Of course, the Civil Rights Act did just that and more. Part of the problem is that civil rights law is fundamentally vague, even self-contradictory. Just two examples:[84] Affirmative action at professional schools is defended on the grounds that minority populations are better served if they have doctors and lawyers who look like them.

But when Walgreens was found to be assigning black managers to stores in certain neighborhoods on the logic that black customers are better served by managers who look like them, the resulting anti-discrimination case cost the company $24 million to settle. Last year,before being overturned by a Supreme Court decision in the summer of '23, a judge upheld Harvard's admissions policy against the lawsuit brought on behalf of rejected Asian applicants

---

[83] THE LAW THAT ATE THE CONSTITUTION-*The United States now has two constitutions. Which of the two constitutions shall prevail?*

Helen Andrews reviewing Christopher Caldwells´s Book,The Age of Entitlement,Claremont Book Review, Winter 2020.

[84] Helen Andrews,op.cit.

because she found that Harvard *must* be allowed to ignore *objective* criteria, like test scores, in favor of *subjective* measures like personality.

The Civil Rights Acts were trying to resolve sometimes mutually contradictory purposes, avoid racial preferences in hiring but facilitating employment opportunities for blacks, advancing educational progress for blacks but avoiding admission quotas, etc., etc.

But to be race-conscious but colorblind, is like being subjective and objective at the same time: it is not possible. Only the courts say it is. As Walmart and the Asian applicants to Harvard found out the hard way.

Who drove this process? Woke.

As Caldwell says, "The less consistent the law is, the more power left-wing activists have to define what the rules really are";[85] and thus the rise of civil rights legislation to promote liberties fundamentally at odds with Enlightenment values did not come about by accident but is the crowning work of the Woke seeing an opening in the way of thinking of the West-and taking it.

Both the late Thomas Sowell, Jerome Hudson and, as shown above, Heather Mac Donald, have met with furious backlash.

My personal favorite is a senior lecturer at an English, University, Wolverhampton, Adrian Byrne, who when reviewing Sowell´s ideas about the relative unimportance of slavery as compared with the influence of redneck culture, was unfortunate - or dumb- enough to write that such nonsense "was easy for a rich white man to say".[86]

Sowell is black and I don´t know how rich he is, and neither does Byrne. But the error is understandable: to the Woke ideologues according to their oppressor-oppressed prism only white people could be dumb enough and racist enough to hold views different from their own.

Whatever you do, tread very carefully when you enter the world of racism and even more, racism and biology.

So how did we end up at a point where racism though being rarer than any time in history in the West, is still one of the most hotly debated, political issues? Despite the fact, that slavery was common, legal and existed everywhere all over the world until fairly recently, was not specific to the US, and owes its abolition solely to the West in general and white men in particular?

There are two main culprits for this crazy turn of events: Critical Race Theory (CRT) and Implicit Bias Theory.

According to the first one, Critical Race Theory," recognizes that racism is engrained in the fabric and system of the American society. The individual racist need not exist to note that institutional racism is pervasive in the dominant culture. This is the analytical lens that CRT uses in examining existing power structures. CRT identifies that these power structures are based on white privilege and white supremacy, which perpetuates the marginalization of people of color"[87]

Though the theory admits up front that individual racists actually do not exist, we are asked to believe that American society though practically devoid of racists is still racist to the bone

---

[85] Helen Andrews, op.cit.
[86] Douglas Murray, The Madness of Crowds, p. 154
[87] UCLA School of Public Affairs on CRT

because of "institutional racism" which in turn is based on "white privilege" and "white supremacy".

This is incoherent gobbledygook.

Left-leaning judge Richard Posner of the United States Seventh Circuit Court of Appeals is a little bit more diplomatic, but still makes the same point when he labels "critical race theorists as the 'lunatic core' of 'radical legal egalitarianism. '" He writes,

"What is most arresting about critical race theory is that ". . . it turns its back on the Western tradition of rational inquiry, forswearing analysis for narrative. Rather than marshal logical arguments and empirical data, critical race theorists tell stories — fictional, science-fictional, quasi-fictional, autobiographical, anecdotal—designed to expose the pervasive and debilitating racism of America today. "[88]

White privilege" and "white supremacy". Critical race theorists tell stories, fictional, science-fictional, quasi-fictional, autobiographical, anecdotal.

Do you see the pattern? It´s Woke´s dualism at it again: Oppressor vs. Oppressed. And it is Woke´s disdain of facts again: any narrative, even those completely untethered to truth and reality will do, if it serves the goal of undermining present-day society.

And Posner´s analysis of CRT as a child of Postmodernism is about as clever a criticism you will ever find.

But Woke thinking is predominant in the world you live in so now you´re prepared and next time somebody throws the words "White privilege" and "White supremacy" at you, throw this book or Posner´s quote at them.

But it gets worse. If explicit racism has by all accounts diminished if not vanished in the West, how do we account for racial disparities in income, job, crime etc.?

Racism, the "Implicit bias" theory says. Only now it is unconscious.

If the bias is only implicit, i. e. invisible, how do the social psychologists know? Because they invented a test called the Implicit Association Test (IAT) to determine a person's level of subconscious racism. How does that work? The test, which can now be taken online, asks participants to respond to a series of photos of human faces. As words flash on the screen, participants are then asked to categorize them as "positive" or "negative." The test analyzes the participant's responses and tells them whether they carry subconscious biases.

The "implicit bias" test is a test designed by psychologists Anthony Greenwald, Debbie McGhee, and Jordan Schwartz to determine a person's subconscious racism. Mahzarin Banaji, who has served as the chair of the psychology department at Harvard University, also contributed to the project. The test has received much fanfare from progressives since its introduction in 1998.

"Project Implicit," the organization that is in charge of maintaining the online test, has partnered with Harvard University to expand its reach. The test is currently hosted on Harvard's website.

However, there is a problem with the test:researchers across the political spectrum have questioned its accuracy. One study conducted of the "implicit association test" revealed that it

---

[88] Posner, on Critical Race Theory,Internet.

had a test-retest reliability of 0.60, meaning that individual participants would likely receive a different test result after taking the test for a second time.

New York Magazine published a column detailing the trials and tribulations of the "implicit association" test.

"The IAT, it turns out, has serious issues on both the reliability and validity fronts, which is surprising given its popularity and the very exciting claims that have been made about its potential to address racism, " columnist Jesse Singal wrote. "That's what the research says, at least, and it raises serious questions about how the IAT became such a social-science darling in the first place".

Breitbart News reported in July that the researchers behind the "implicit association test" still defend the project despite concerns about its accuracy.

The test is currently being used by corporations, universities and even police departments to first test the implicit bias levels of their staff; and then, of course, ask the same psychologists who invented the IAT to run seminars to help the poor unconscious racists get rid of their implicit basis. Sweet gig, but it is a scam.

There are several problems with the IAT approach, the obvious one being that many blacks fail the test.

Furthermore, it´s unreliable, meaning it doesn´t get the same results each time, a key concept in scientific research.

When a VOX journalist, Senior Correspondent, German Lopez, first took the test, it told him that he carried no preference for white or black people. But Lopez took the test again to confirm its consistency. To Lopez's surprise, he received a different result each additional time he took the test. "I took the IAT again a few days later. This time, I wasn't so happy with my results: It turns out I had a slight automatic preference for white people. According to this, I was a little racist at the subconscious level — against black people.

Then I took the test again later on. This time, my results genuinely surprised me: It found once again that I had a slight automatic preference — only now it was in favor of black people. I was racist, but against white people, according to the test. "[89]

But even worse is the premise that anyone in their right mind would use response-time methodology to conclude "that any differences in sorting times for black and white faces flow from unconscious prejudice against blacks" …. or even worse…," that such unconscious practice, as measured by the IAT predicts discriminatory behavior"[90]

Recent psychometrical studies have, unsurprisingly, debunked the tests; but the damage has been done; and IATs are still widely used in hiring new staff not only by big corporations and large universities but also small police departments.

There are many reasons, including cultural and biological ones for disparities, economic and social, between races, but implicit bias is not one of them.

So, what are the reasons for this racism hysteria?

---

[89] Breitbart, Jan. 22, 2020
[90] Heather Mac Donald, The Diversity Delusion, p. 89

The answer to this is a good deal less flattering to Woke than it would like.

John McWhorter, who is black and teaches linguistics and American studies at Columbia University in New York, thinks that the anti-racism of white people that claims to "dismantle racist structures" is actually harming his fellow black Americans by infantilizing black people, setting black students up for failure and promoting policies that disproportionately damage black communities".[91]

He calls it woke racism.

What motivates woke racists?

To get around to it we must go back to a more than hundred year old theory first formulated by the Norwegian-American economist, Thorstein Veblen, in The Theory of the Leisure Class, in which Veblen argued that the leisure class were characterized by their nonproductive consumption of goods; put simply, their display of what they could afford was a means of expressing social superiority.

"In the past, upper-class Americans used to display their social status with luxury goods. But, today, as trendy clothes and other products become more accessible and affordable, there is increasingly less status attached to luxury goods.

The upper classes have found a clever solution to this problem: luxury beliefs. These are ideas and opinions that confer status on the rich at very little cost, while taking a toll on the lower class.

McWhorter is right: woke racism is not an example of virtue signaling; it's a marker of class which confer status on entitled whites but takes a toll on the people, black African Americans, it purports to defend.

Others are less kind to Woke leaders, like Jesse Jackson whom a prominent critic has characterized as "No one in civil rights is better at extracting large sums from big corporations" or Al Sharpton, the who have turned anti-racism into a richly rewarding racket and a stint as a MSNBC host.[92]

Woke was naïve, to say the least, in underestimating the vast changes in cultural attitudes, its radical transformation of society´s consciousness would entail.

As Claremont Review of Books has it in an article in 2023 called The Anti Racist Racket:

> ….. civil rights leaders were too optimistic in thinking that the mere opening of opportunity would ensure black success. As it turned out, the vast changes in wider cultural attitudes that were dissolving racism in the 1960s were also harming the worst-off blacks by removing the stigma from self-destructive habits that blacks had long shunned, notwithstanding the history of slavery. Going on welfare became no longer shameful but rather reparations for oppression, nor was not working a personal failing but instead the result of job discrimination. Society, by excluding, oppressing, and impoverishing the criminal, argued social critics in the '60s and '70s, was to blame for black crime, not the outlaw himself. Perhaps he was even a

---

[91] John McWhorter, Woke Racism, from the jacket blurb, Portfolio Penguin, 2021.
[92] Boomers, Helen Andrews, p.141-50.

manly rebel against an unjust society, and to imprison him was only to redouble the victimization society inflicts on him. And as that era's whole culture was having its fling with sex and drugs, the stigma against drug use and unwed childbearing tottered.[93]

Woke completely ignored the danger of these attitudes filtering down the social scale, with the tragic result of entrenching a black underclass in the urban ghettoes, held down by non-work, welfare dependence, drug use, dropping out of school, crime, and weak, single-parent families. Too many poorly educated single mothers proved ill-equipped to train children in the virtues and cognitive skills that make for success, or to discipline them in a way that didn't leave sons with the contempt for women and for authority that is a main theme of today's rap music. In place of the work ethic and the deferral of gratification an inner-city culture of victimology, grievance, and opposition to a society blamed for failings that would otherwise seem personal.

As the Claremont article says: "With what dismay must Americans of all races view the consequences today!

Indeed!

. According to official statistics:

> "In 2018, seven out of ten black children were born out of wedlock, compared to 28% of white babies (and, in 1965, 24% of black babies). The rate of homicide offenses among blacks is eight times higher than among whites, and black men, 6% of the U.S. population, are 40% of the nation's cop killers, the FBI reports. Urban police departments pile up their own dismal statistics. In 2019, the 9% of Los Angelenos who are black committed 44% of their city's violent crime, while St. Louis blacks, just under half the population, committed most of that city's. The 23% of New Yorkers who are black accounted for 72% of the shootings and 63% of the murders in 2020, and black Chicagoans, less than a third of the population, committed 71% of the murders."[94]

Woke's anti-racist social engineering policies have had almost 60 years to prove their worth and by any reasonable standard have failed both blacks and whites miserably. When it comes to race, Woke is not working.

xxxxxxxxxxxxxxxxxxxxxxxxxxx

---

[93] Claremont Review of Books, Winter 2022/23, The Anti Racist Racket
[94] Idem.

Part II: Transforming the Consciousness of Society

Chapter 4: Feminism: The Identity Politics of Moral Superiority.

xxxxxxxxxxxxxxxxxxxxxxxxxxxxxxx

"... women who 'adjust' as housewives, who grow up wanting to be 'just a housewife, ' are in as much danger as the millions who walked to their own death in the concentration camps. . . they are suffering a slow death of mind and spirit. "
Betty Friedan, The Feminine Mystique, 1963.

Xxxxxxx

"A woman needs a man like a fish needs a bicycle",

Irina Dunn, a distinguished Australian educator, journalist and politician.

xxxxxxxx

Feminism is about fairness, redistribution of wealth and power and influence; it´s about changing the old order whereby men have had most of those things for most of human history.

Laurie Penny, Bitch Doctrine: Essays for Dissenting Adults, 2017.

xxxxxxx

"Women are better leaders than men. " "I'm absolutely confident that for two years if every nation on earth was run by women, you would see a significant improvement across the board on just about everything. . . living standards and outcomes. "
Barack Obama, at a conference in Singapore, BBC News, Singapore, 16 December 2019.

xxxxxxx

"I know those opposed to quotas will ask: "Why choose women just because they are women?" I don't know, but for generations men have been chosen because they are men, so is it a problem? Let's just try the opposite."

Marlène Schiappa, France's secretary of state for gender equality and the fight against discrimination, Financial Times, Nov. 20, 2019.

xxxxxxx

"**If #MeToo has made men feel vulnerable, panicked, unsure, and fearful as a result of women finally, collectively, saying "Enough!" so be it. If they wonder how their every word and action will be judged and used against them, Welcome to our world. If they feel that everything they do will reflect on other men and be misrepresented and misunderstood, take a seat. You are now honorary women.** "
Soraya Chemaly, Rage Becomes Her: The Power of Women's Anger

<u>Xxxxxxx</u>

Society for the past 100 years has moved aggressively to abolish legal impediments to the equality of the sexes. Men were at the forefront together with women and largely succeeded in doing away with *legal* barriers to equality between the sexes.

The fact that men, indeed white men, were instrumental in the successes of women's emancipation movements is an unwelcome circumstance that Woke progressive history writing mostly leaves out: without white men's efforts and sacrifice there would not have been the progress we have seen. 32 men (and 68 women) signed the Seneca Falls Declaration of Women's Rights in 1848, at a congress in N.Y. State organized by white men taking place at a white church at the invitation of a white male pastor, but you would have to look long and hard to find that out.

Why do they leave it out? Because it does not fit with the Woke bi-nary perspective of the struggle for power being between oppressor and oppressed, because it would mean that the oppressor would actually be helping the oppressed, cooperating as it were with the oppressed and then they wouldn't be oppressed any more, would they? Furthermore, by the 1980s by and large this revolution had been accomplished. But this is not the story you are being told.

It's bad enough that women for quite a few decades now have claimed that it was their *turn* at the wheel and that they would do a better job than men. But it is worse if when asked to prove it they claim to be offended. I remember an episode during a trip I took with my then political party's foreign policy committee to our sister party in Bolivia, where we met various political actors and activist movement in what was then still Evo Morales' de facto one-party state.

The women's organizations were constantly griping about how the men didn't let them take up any real influential role in their organizations, how macho they were, etc. and after a couple of hours of this, I about had my fill of this b. s. and politely suggested that they form a women's political party.

Talk about a faux pas. The women strongly objected to this "preposterous" idea and the leader of our little group, a feminist later to go on to become Minister of Culture in Denmark, let everyone around the table know she didn't share this opinion and that I was speaking out of turn.

But to have the narcissistic and ridiculously self-absorbed former President of The United States, Barack Obama, (that was former U. K. Prime Minister David Cameron's leaked characterization of Obama) spout the same politically correct line on a paying gig in Singapore that probably netted him well north of 200 grand is too much to bear.

For one, why didn´t Obama say so when he was in power? Or, even better, if this is the way he feels, why didn´t he step down and let one of the capable women in his cabinet take over? The answer is, of course, that he is not serious. What has gender got to do with leadership? Nothing. Furthermore, Obama´s statement is completely incoherent: leaders are individuals with the ability to persuade a big number of followers to... *follow*. Logically, not *all* women can be better leaders.

But we have *tools* to deal with this kind of political correctness. So, let us put his statement to the *falsification test*. Political science rarely finds itself in a situation where it can actually put a theory like Obama´s to the test, because critics usually can argue that the historical situations are different when comparing great women leaders like Margaret Thatcher or Angela Merkel or Queen Victoria with Winston Churchill or Roosevelt or illustrious male kings and male political leaders.

But we do have one recent example where we have perfect laboratory conditions, where the surrounding factors are in fact constant, with the only variable in question being who did a better job of leadership, the woman, or the man in question: Brexit.

Theresa May and Boris Johnson both faced the same EU negotiators on the other side of the table, led by the same chief negotiator, Michel Barnier; and both had to placate the same fractious Conservative Party MPs in Parliament. They faced the same Northern Ireland impasse over the Irish border and the same lack of a working majority.

Theresa May called an early general election despite having promised she would not do so and lost it so badly that she had to depend for her political survival on a handful of MPs from.... Northern Ireland. She then managed to present the *same* withdrawal agreement proposal negotiated with the EU to the British Parliament three times in more than 2 years of Parliamentary chaos and was voted down with such large number *each time* that she eventually was forced by her *own* party to step down in disgrace.

Her successor, Boris Johnson, in less than three months managed to renegotiate an agreement with the EU, not least by showing who´s boss by firing 21 of his own Conservative Party members, some of them very influential within the Party, who didn´t vote the party line; and, when Parliament still tried to block Brexit, also called an early election, in which he campaigned so successfully that the Conservatives won their largest victory since 1935. On this evidence, the women-are-better-leaders theory collapses like an overdone soufflé.

But the falsification test just shows how silly the whole thing is: the fact is that the UK has had one of the most successful political leaders of all time in Margaret Thatcher. And one of the worst in Theresa May and, incidentally, thereafter, Boris Johnson. And none of it had anything to do with being a woman or a man, but everything to do with classic leadership abilities like knowing your voters, having a game plan and executing it and getting a good team around you, and yes, when things went wrong, not stubbornly trying the same failed plan again and again.

The nonsense of identity politics is nowhere clearer than in fatuous platitudes about women being better than men.

But feminists obviously didn´t get the memo. For the flip side of the "women are better leaders" trope seems to be: if they *aren´t*, they can always blame men.

I have chosen the quotes above to make two points:

The first point is, of course, that our radical feminist parents clearly are the daughters of Woke Marxist Postmodernists as witnessed by their world view of oppressor vs. oppressed. They are also truly angry ideologues out to "exercise power for the purpose of social change" as the Postmodernists have it. Betty Friedan, according to Helen Andrews, was a "self-obsessed malcontent who deliberately concealed her past as a fellow traveler of the Communist Party USA" and Gloria Steinem "had good reasons for considering the nuclear family a trap" namely that her father was "ne´er do-well hustler practically a con man" and her mother spent most of her life institutionalized.[95]

The second point is that all radicalized women directly or indirectly blame men. The old joke that "it is never too late to blame your parents" is being re-enacted; only this time women don´t blame their parents but *me*.

It´s the combination of these two aspects of radical feminism that gives me the right to be slightly suspicious about women´s real motives in presenting themselves as victims of men. Could it be their real purpose to use their victimhood to re-arrange society according to their political ideology?

I think so: when Ms. Penney´s reason for wanting to get her hands on "power and influence" and "changing the old order" is that "men have had most of those things for most of human history", her point is not only that women feel it´s their turn, but also that men have made a hash of it and therefore women are convinced they can do a better job. Not to put too fine a point on it, they clearly feel morally superior. Historically, putting people in power who feel morally superior to others has not worked well.

On the substance, the claim that men have been in power for most of human history is ahistorical, a lie. *Most* men, historically, until *recently* have not been anywhere near power and influence; in fact, most nations of the world until very recently, and indeed even to-day in the world´s most populous nation, China, have been run by a small clique of powerful men or sometimes by *one* absolute ruler with the rest of us being indentured servants if we were *white* and lived in the U. S and *slaves,* if were black and lived in the US ,and *serfs* if we lived in Russia and large parts of central Europe. '

Peasants, until recently even in now democratic Scandinavia, were legally not allowed to move from where they lived, often on the land of wealthy landlords, had to work part of the week for him for free and allow him his "jus prima noctis", meaning the right of the first night with your wife after marriage.

Denmark was an absolute monarchy until 1849 with strict censorship laws and no freedom of speech or association and even after that, the King basically picked the people who should run Government according to his preferences. *Most* men only got the right to vote without restrictions such as owning property about 50 or 60 years *before* all women did.

"Most of human history". Give me a break.

But it gets worse.

The #MeToo movement further confirms my suspicions: when a #MeToo feminist like Soraya Chemaly, in the quote above from her book, <u>Rage Becomes Her: The Power of Women's Anger</u>, with a straight face argues that it is only fair that men now get a little bit of their own medicine,

---

[95] Boomers,op.cit. p.4-5.

she is not presenting an argument: she is venting her anger at men as a collective a group, exacting revenge. For what?

I think I know why: the main purpose of #MeToo according to its founder, a black civil rights activist called Tarana Burke, is to help women come forward and report sexual assault and harassment. The main assumption being that woman coming forward has not happened in the past including our recent past.

Why? Because women allegedly have been afraid to. Afraid of what? Men, and society's reaction in general, she claims. And she is credible, because her own story is a powerful one of overcoming sexual abuse living in a housing project in New York City.

But the problem is she does not leave it at that, as the following quote shows. She says, "as I have said repeatedly …. the #metooMVMT is for all of us, including these brave young men who are now coming forward. Sexual violence is about *power and privilege*"[96]

So, that lets the cat out of the bag, doesn't it? We are back in Woke territory, aren't we? It's not about sexual harassment and rape anymore but about the powerful and privileged using sexual violence to dominate weak and vulnerable people: women. The sex is incidental. It's the old Woke binary prism of oppressor v. oppressed. #MeToo is a political operation. And the politics are Woke.

Concrete radical politics at that. By way of example, the 2018 nomination to the Supreme Court of Ted Kavanaugh, was almost scuppered by supporters of the #MeToo movement who argued that Christine Blasey Ford, Kavanaugh's main accuser of sexual harassment against all evidence, including that of her best friend who could not confirm any part of the accusations, which she alleged happened more than 20 years ago and never reported to the police, should be believed simply because she was a woman.

What happened to the centuries old principle of presumed innocence, I ask?

And, thankfully, I am not the only one who doesn't buy it. Camille Paglia, cultural critic and famously politically incorrect professor at the University of the Arts in Philadelphia, PA, says: "the feminist obsession with rape as a symbol of male-female relations is irrational and delusional.[97] And she goes on to say:" By defining rape in exclusively social terms -as an attack by the powerful against the powerless-feminism has missed the point. It is woman, as mistress of birth, who has the real power".[98]

With freedom comes responsibility, she argues, and women can't turn around now and blame men and men's society for a sexual freedom they themselves wanted and promoted:

" Feminist ideology" Paglia says," began by claiming to give women freedom, enlightenment, and self-determination, but it has ended by alienating professional women {not working- class women who have fewer illusions about sex}, from their own bodies. "[99]

When she was a college student in the sixties, Paglia recalls, the college police locked the door to her dorm to keep the horny boys out. And female nurses couldn't marry *and* keep their job. There's been a lot of condoms washed under the bridge since then, but if women want equality

---

[96] #MeToo founder Tarana Burke quotes from internet.
[97] Camille Paglia, <u>Vamps and Tramps</u>, p. 24
[98] Camille Paglia, <u>Vamps and Tramps</u>, p. 27
[99] Camille Paglia, <u>Vamps and Tramps</u>, p. 29

they are going to have to stop crying to Mama and the authorities about how unfair the world is every time they go to a party, get drunk and wake up the next morning regretting it. Guess what? So, do men.

On top of that it is based on a statistical lie.

Christina Hoff Sommers has done more than anyone to undercut the statistics behind the charges that 1 out of every 4 women have been raped and shown that it is a lie. The real figure, she says, is likely much, much lower. To back it up she points out that of those classified by studies as having been raped, 73% said they hadn't been.[100] She also points out that *male* rape figures if they are to be trusted are higher than those of female rapes.[101]

Rape against anyone is inexcusable and a crime. But Hoff Sommers' debunking of the stats does weaken the accusations by radical feminists of an existing rape culture among men, not out for sexual satisfaction, but *dominance* of women.

But it is Paglia who puts the final nail in the coffin of the rape culture and toxic masculinity accusations against men, by putting them in the cultural context where they belong, namely the sexual revolution of the '60s and its "anything-goes culture".

Feminists and women in general supported this revolutionary change of behavior between the sexes and bought into the myth that women's sexual nature is just like men's: women are just as randy as men and just as sexually aggressive-once society allows it- as men.

For feminist Sue Ellen Browder it was a fatal mistake.

"The most destructive, divisive, media-perpetuated fantasy is the delusion that anything-goes sex with no commitment from the man somehow 'liberates' a woman," she writes. And later, "The reduction of a woman's full personhood to her sexual desirability and sexual desires is the real injustice we're fighting."

It may be a media-perpetuated fantasy and a delusion, but mainly it's a lie. Women's sexuality is shaped by the biological facts of carrying the baby and having to nurse their offspring for quite some considerable time.

As Camille Paglia says:" Women's discontent and confusion are being worsened by the postmodernist rhetoric of academe, which asserts that gender is a social construct and that biological sex differences don't exist or don't matter. Speaking from my lifelong transgender perspective, I find such claims absurd. That most men and women on the planet experience and process sexuality differently, in both mind and body, is blatantly obvious to any sensible person".[102]

But unfortunately, it wasn't blatantly obvious to the Woke wing of the feminist movement who saw an opening and took it.

Sue Ellen Browder tells the story:" The second-wave feminist commitment to "liberated" sexuality soon morphed into a demand for free abortion.

---

[100] Christina Hoff Sommers, Who Stole Feminism? How women Have Betrayed Women, p. 213
[101] Christina Hoff Sommers, Who Stole Feminism? How women Have Betrayed Women, p. 25
[102] "Provocations-Collective Essays" by Camille Paglia, p.201

"In November 1967 at a meeting of the National Organization for Women, a bare majority of its members voted to include in the group's bill of rights a demand to repeal all abortion laws. After the vote, one-third of the members resigned, feminists who were committed to women's rights but who opposed abortion."

"Literally overnight, due to the vote of a mere fifty-seven people . . . 'reproductive rights' had become synonymous with women's fight for equality in education and the workforce," Browder concludes. [103]

Why did they do it? I think the answer is that our radical feminist parents bought into the oppressed v. oppressor worldview of the Woke; and too many other women, especially, as Paglia says, college-educated, professional ones, followed.

By way of example women´s movements like #MeToo have supported LGTBQ activists on the assumption that they all were in the same boat, that of the oppressed.

Well, now that transgender females with beards, muscles and penises are taking over their bathrooms and sports and raping them in their jails, perhaps it is time for women to realize that they have been naïve. They have been had. There is no "rape culture". Men are not your enemies. And to combat those few men that are, learn to say no unequivocally, no more Miss Nice Girl; and while we are at it, be prepared to defend yourselves verbally and, if need be, physically.

And if someone *does* go too far in the workplace: press charges.

Unsurprisingly, there´s already research showing a social backlash. In fact, good evidence, that if the #MeToo movement really sets out to help women, it is failing.

Men, since #MeToo, are *less* likely to hire attractive women. And have them go along or go with them on business trips. And *more* likely to follow the much ridiculed but highly sensible (former US Vice-President) Mike Pence Rule: never have dinner with a female without your wife present.

Sexual harassment is illegal and unacceptable. But men and women have different sexualities and sexual communication and signals between men and women are not always straightforward.

And not always provable in court. It´s often a case of "she said-he said".

But that, too, is changing.

Several men accused of sexual harassment have already lost everything, jobs, family, and social status. Sometimes on flimsy evidence.

Like the infamous Hollywood producer, Harvey Weinstein, whose wife has left him and whose career is cancelled because he in the spring of 2020 was convicted of non-consensual rape in a NYC court room.

Which he strenuously denies, pleading consensual sex between women looking for what *he* could offer: a career in Hollywood.

---

[103] "Reclaiming the 'F Word', National Review, March 28,2020, Aleandra de Sanctis interviewing Sue Ellen Browder.

He thought he had a strong case, not least because the two women who accused him of rape continued to have sexual relations with him after the alleged rapes.

But he miscalculated and is now serving a 23-year prison sentence at New York's notorious Riker Island prison.

#MeToo said "believe women" and the jury believed them. As did mainstream media which uncritically repeated the #MeToo spin.

But relations between the sexes are more complex and the power dynamics more complicated than #MeToo is willing to admit.

For Harvey Weinstein's conviction on the contrary provided yet another nail in the coffin of the "sexist society" trope. Why? Because a society cannot be both sexist and convict a man for what in any other age would have been dismissed for lack of evidence?

Any other age? Take the case of Alfred Hitchcock, major American filmmaker in the 1950s and early 60s, but like Weinstein with an ambivalent and politically incorrect view of women as both objets d'art and suffocating dominatrices. the Madonna/whore complex. He reportedly made "crude overtures" to Tippie Hedren, the star of two of his masterpieces, Marnie, and The Birds, and when she refused him in no uncertain terms "maliciously sabotaged her career".[104]

Without any consequences to *his* reputation and career.... back then. Hedren knew refusing Hitchcock's advances would torpedo *her* career but slapped him down anyway. Unlike Weinstein's accusers who continued dating him long after the alleged rapes.

Fast forward 60 years: Weinstein, too, was a famous filmmaker, had a reputation as a feminist and was a producer of one of the major films coming out of Hollywood in recent years, "Good Will Hunting". But that didn't save him. What has changed?

Radical feminists and their woke male followers are crowing about a victory for rape "survivors", but facts are stubborn: Weinstein was not convicted of rape in any traditional legal sense of using coercion to have sex. In fact, he was acquitted on exactly those counts that implied coercion. But he *was* convicted of being every feminist woman's nightmare of toxic masculinity. ugly, fat, white, horny, and powerful, *a political* verdict in total alignment with the main theme of this book, namely the decaying of our culture under the onslaught of Woke.

Why was the verdict *political*?

Because "MeToo has been strangely silent on an eerily similar case concerning the claims of a former staffer of President, Joe Biden, Tara Reade, who claims Biden digitally raped her in 1993.

Biden is a staunch #MeToo supporter who publicly backed #MeToo in its campaign against the nomination to the Supreme Court in the summer of 2018 of Ted Kavanaugh. And #MeToo is suddenly as stumm as a Trappist monk.

Clearly, #MeToo was up against the wall. It proudly and publicly supported the "believe women" meme when trying to block a Republican candidate for the U.S. Supreme Court but held back when a Democratic presidential candidate, Joe Biden, was charged by a woman in almost exactly similar circumstances of the same crime.

---

[104] Camille Paglia in "Women and Magic in Alfred Hitchcock" published in Provocations,2018.

But the truth dawned on even the most woke women when New York governor, Andrew Cuomo, was forced by his own female attorney general to step down, And when she revealed that Cuomo's policy of smearing his female accusers had been devised by none other than the leaders of the local chapter of "MeToo.

"MeToo clearly is a Front for the Democratic Party

To advocate that women qua being women must be *believed* in cases of alleged sexual crimes is one thing. Dubious at best and a departure from the Enlightenment and modern legal principle of "innocent until proven guilty".

But to apply that principle *selectively* undermines its very rationale and makes it…political.

The mainstream media's cover-up of the Joe Biden case leaves what our reigning political philosophy, Woke to which our journalistic elites wholeheartedly subscribe, unmasked: reporting for them never was to seek out the truth but an attempt to exercise power for the purpose of social change.

For the truth is that sexual harassment is not *always* a one-way street. A British woman in Cyprus was recently convicted of falsely accusing 12 Israeli male youths of rape.

Is it only men that abuse power? Apparently not. Female schoolteachers all over the West are regularly sent to jail for sex with their under-age students.

The Joe Biden case illustrates that the most worrying sign of the Woke nature of the #MeToo movement is its all too apparent readiness to wave away the relevance of the centuries old legal principle of "innocent until proven guilty"; and, conversely, its insistence on its mantra of a priori *believing* women. I would argue that believing a member of your own sex a priori is sexist and a serious departure from the rights of everyone, including white powerful men, to a fair hearing.

Furthermore, the case was political for a much more trivial reason: the D.A. bringing the case, Cyrus Vance, had a lot at stake. He had been severely criticized for not bringing charges against Mr. Weinstein *five years earlier*, before the producer became a symbol of sexual harassment and ended up in the crosshairs of the #MeToo movement. What changed his mind? He was up for re-election next year and #MeToo was giving him a hard time.

So, when the jury found Mr. Weinstein guilty of two *lesser* felony sex crimes, even though it acquitted him of the three major charges the DA's office had filed against him, it was not just a legal victory for Mr. Vance but a shot at re-election. He even adopted the language of "MeToo, declaring "This is the new landscape for *survivors of sexual assault* in America," … "This is a new day."[105]

Why is it a *new* day? Had the law changed in the past 5 years? No. But the prevailing political winds had- and Cyrus Vance bowed to them. That's not unusual for our democratically elected political leaders, but it does show that the case was driven by *politics*. The identity politics of Woke.

But don't take my word for it. Men, including white men like me, in general are not, indeed cannot, under the Woke logic of group identity, be considered credible on #MeToo matters.

---

[105] Cyrus Vance on Weinstein, internet search, NYT.

Toni Messina an experienced *female* criminal lawyer, who followed the Weinstein case and reported on it for Thomson Reuter, asks the same question:" Will the sweeping impact of the #MeToo movement and its imprint on popular consciousness overpower a clear-headed analysis of the law? Will the Weinstein trial become the case that sets the standard for defining rape in much broader and more general terms?".

Her answer: "I hope not".[106]

Her argument? "I haven't heard much evidence of "forcible compulsion," the key element in the charges against him. "Forcible compulsion" means to "*intentionally compel* either by use of physical force, or by a threat which places the person in fear of immediate death or that she will immediately be kidnapped."

Furthermore, she says, "Generally, the victim does not continue a loving or sexual relationship with the aggressor, accepting gifts, signing off on emails with hearts and hugs, or appearing with him the next morning at breakfast as though nothing occurred."[107]

Indeed.

Instead of champagne and red caviar there should be red ears at #MeToo headquarters right now.

How could two adult women press charges of rape against a man they continued dating and having consensual sex with long after the alleged rape?

The answer: by pretending to be adolescents.

Psychologists were brought in to explain why the women did not file charges when it happened and how, psychologically, the women felt obliged to cover up the rapes.

But the fact remains: both women did two mutually inconsistent things, namely accusing a man of rape while continuing to have sex with him. Tippi Hedren, 60 years ago, was made of sterner stuff.

For, any way you slice it, that is not taking responsibility for your actions. The very definition of.... adolescence.

You don't agree? Well, how about hearing the same take on #MeToo adolescence from a *woman* feminist? Will that get your attention?

In a piece entitled 'Grow Up' vs. 'Me Too', Meghan Daum, author of <u>The Problem with Everything: My Journey Through the New Culture Wars</u>, is asked what her advice is to today's "trembling and triggered young feminists" in the wake of the Harvey Weinstein case.

" Grow up", she says." Being a woman carries with it certain costs, she agrees, but also a great many counterbalancing benefits. Toxic femininity exists as surely as does masculine variety.

---

[106] My Prediction on The Harvey Weinstein Verdict, And Why The Prosecution Already Won Even If There's An Acquittal-The case may well shape a new definition of rape and determine which cases prosecutors pursue in the future. Toni Messina, Thomson Reuter, Feb 18, 2020.

[107] Ibid.

Negotiating awkward or unpleasant sexual situations is something grownups must learn to do, she holds, and it's hardly the case that only women emerge from such situations with regrets."

"Very often the self-styled badass woman will tell us that some quotidian male infraction rendered her short of breath, or bereft of speech, or nauseated in the tummy, or unable to work. Why do today's "strong, confident" women so often make very public displays of weakness and an inability to cope?"

Daum obviously doesn´t buy into the #MeToo credo of *believing* women." The feminist vision of male conquerors and female vassals forced to do their bidding or endure their abuse is not even close to the truth", she says.

And she is adult enough to quote an example from her own life:" She used to have lunches with an older man (she doesn't supply his name) who she thought might be able to advance her career. Lunches turned into dinners and dinners turned into something resembling dates. Things never turned sexual, but the possibility hung in the air and at one point he invited her to his house for a weekend. She declined, and he apologized for asking. Daum today (she is now 40) understands she was leveraging her sexual power, teasing the older man, to aid her career prospects. If there was an imbalance of power here, it's not obvious who held the advantage.

She cites the "countless ways that women frequently have power over men: in the use of sex as a tool for manipulation, in parenting dynamics, in the ability nowadays to shut down a conversation by citing male privilege. . ... Power dynamics shift among all kinds of people all the time." Funny how gaslighting is, these days, a supposed masculine specialty. "In my lived experience," Daum says, "women's gaslighting skills generally far exceed those of most men."[108]

Predictably, the #MeToo movement´s fanatical obsession with regulating any and every indication of sexual harassment has led to a series of public authorities adopting guidelines on how to avoid giving offense, ranging from "unwanted jokes" to-I kid you not- "facial expressions":

In the UK, Rebecca Hilsenrath, who chairs the Equality and Human Rights Commission, outlined sexual harassment concerns in a letter to 400 major firms which called for stringent anti-harassment policies in light of the 'Me Too' scandal, says The Daily Mail.

Pub banter and jokes with colleagues can amount to sexual harassment even if unintended and businesses must train staff to be aware of risks at after-work events, the equality watchdog has warned.

Unwanted jokes and even *facial expressions* can also amount to unacceptable behavior even if 'that is not how it was intended'[109]

That is Woke gender Stalinism, pure and simple.

---

[108] All quotes from "Grow Up vs. #MeToo", National Review, March 9, 2020.
[109] Daily Mail, Jan. 15, 2020

You will argue that I am reading too much into the personal opinion of some members of radical feminist movements; but the opinion that women somehow deserve special treatment because they have been treated unfairly by men throughout history has gone mainstream and is even widespread among female *political* leaders, too.

Just two examples: Christine Lagarde, head of the European Central Bank, famously claimed that if the mis-managed bank that set off the financial crisis in 2008, Lehman Brothers, had been called Lehman *Sisters*, the financial crisis would never have happened.

Her underlying and completely unproven thesis, later called the Lehman Sisters Theory, was that testosterone-driven macho men took too many risks. Lagarde in all seriousness, in the 21st century, is blaming men as a group for a serious financial calamity. Really? Men like her father who gave her half of the chromosomes that has made her one of the most powerful women in the world, are to blame for the financial crisis?

What was the reason for the financial crisis of 2008-9, I hear you ask? Fraud. Financial fraud. Committed not just by Lehman brother but many others in the financial sector. Or as Niall Ferguson says, "There will always be greedy people in and around banks. After all, they are where the money is -or is supposed to be. But greedy people will commit fraud or negligence only if they feel that their misdemeanor is unlikely to be noticed or severely punished".

The real scandal was the failure to hold these people accountable, to apply the law, says Ferguson. The laws were simply ill-adapted to the purpose.

The French Minister, Marlene Schiappa, goes one worse: she directly says when answering the question of why people should be put in position of power uniquely on the basis of their gender, that since *that* is what *men* have been doing for ever, why not try the opposite?

This is completely incoherent. Two wrongs do not make a right, and what she is upset about is precisely that, according to her, men have done women wrong in the past. So, how can she propose to make up for what she obviously considers an historical injustice by *another* wrong?

How can two of the most powerful women in the world, Lagarde and Schiappa, without embarrassment, spout this obvious nonsense? Because Woke has brainwashed even highly intelligent and successful women -our mothers 'generation-into buying a worldview of seeing everything through the prism of oppressor v. oppressed.

To get to the point of demonizing white men, feminists have had to do everything from jump through some linguistic hoops to outright lies. To compare housewives to concentration camp prisoners was absurd back in the 1970s when Margaret Thatcher was revolutionizing Britain and even more so today where women take up all kinds of prominent positions in society from Head of the European Central Bank to French Minister for Equality.

The truth is: there is no gender pay gap, no inequality nor glass-ceilings once one corrects for the difference in men's and women's *nature*: most women simply have different *priorities* than men. Their choice of professions is not as driven by money as men, they negotiate less aggressively for pay, they prefer content jobs with human contact, etc. etc. Pay discrimination, by the way, has been outlawed in the West since the sixties.

Wage differences are not proof of discrimination but proof that men and women don't think alike when it comes to prioritizing the important things in life.[110]

By way of example, the famous 77 cents to the dollar "wage gap" that former and insufferably woke President Obama, always quoted, is a phony, says Mona Charen, an American feminist and writer. "It is derived by adding the total earnings of men and comparing them with the total earnings of women, and that's a meaningless comparison. The "wage gap" doesn't account for hours worked, job tenure, skills, or education…. [In fact} If you compare childless women and men under the age of thirty, not only does the so-called wage gap disappear, but women *out earn* men".[111]

Woke feminism has led women into another dead end: the destigmatization of abortion which has gone from being safe, legal, and rare and socially unacceptable to being safe, legal and unlimited and a matter of women's "choice" up until and sometimes after birth. All that matters is that abortion is a woman's choice, say the radical feminists. She decides and everyone else, including the husband, the family, and the rights of the fetus, does not matter.

But it is not that straightforward in real life; abortion is and always has been traumatic for women. So why lie about it? The story of Planned Parenthood shows why.

According to its website, Planned Parenthood (PP) is a Federal Government funded organization providing *reproductive* health services.

But what it really is becomes clear when reading its 2018-19 Annual Report: it is a pro-abortion, pro-choice lobby organization. You think I am exaggerating?

Well, Planned Parenthood itself claims that only 3% of its business is abortions. As if by implication Planned Parenthood is a disinterested provider of a public services and has no role in the "women's right to choose" political campaign that every Democratic presidential candidate subscribes to. A slogan that may seem anodyne, but which has seen abortion taking on the role of contraception decades after the birth control pill has become ubiquitous. Or as Jerome Hudson says, a practice that has become "appallingly pervasive to the point of infanticide"[112]

The stats of 3% have been debunked even by the left-wing press: it turns out Planned Parenthood inflates its total number of services by counting *services* rather than patients." For example, one patient coming through its doors for an abortion may also leave with a pack of pregnancy tests and a prescription for birth control. This one patient is counted as three separate services"[113]

It's a focus of this book to deconstruct the Woke narrative. So why is Planned Parenthood lying? And what are the real figures?

---

[110] Mona Charen, Sex Matters-How Modern feminism Lost Touch with Science, Love and Common Sense, p. 210
[111] Mona Charen, Sex Matters-How Modern feminism Lost Touch with Science, Love and Common Sense, p. 211
[112] Jerome Hudson, 50 Things They Don't Want You to Know, p. 7
[113] Jerome Hudson, 50 Things They Don't Want You to Know, p. 6

The real figures first: In 2018, Planned Parenthood facilities performed 345, 672 abortions, an increase of more than 13, 000 abortions from what the group reported for the previous fiscal year. That is also the highest number of abortions that the group has ever performed in a single year since it began reporting its abortion data.

This statistic reveals that, as the abortion rate in the United States has declined steadily over the last several decades, Planned Parenthood's share of the annual abortions in the nation has continued to increase.

Late last year, the Centers for Disease Control released its data for 2016, showing about 623, 000 abortions for the year.

Based on the CDC statistics, then, Planned Parenthood clinics perform more than *half of the total reported abortions* in the US

Why lie about it? Because, in reality Planned Parenthood is a lobby for the abortion industry and as this is incompatible with receiving federal funding, it has to hide this fact. But don´t just take my word for it.

Planned Parenthood in its *own* Annual Report says:

"Though we *weren't able to stop the confirmation of Supreme Court Justice Brett Kavanaugh*, Planned Parenthood supporters across the country — including abortion patients and sexual assault survivors who courageously shared their stories — mobilized a movement that will continue to change our culture for years to come. • Planned Parenthood engaged more than 60 *storytellers* to participate in ads, rallies, press interviews, and more. • More than *1,000 people showed up each day* of Kavanaugh's original Senate Judiciary Committee hearings. • Hours before Kavanaugh's confirmation, Planned Parenthood and coalition partners organized people in "No Justice, No Seat" marches in 75 communities across the country, including a massive rally on the steps of the Supreme Court. "[114]

Ted Kavanaugh was the Supreme Court judge mentioned above who was almost prevented from being nominated on the basis of unsubstantiated accusations from a woman supported by the #MeToo movement; and Planned Parenthood now openly admits to being an active part of that plan.

Protesting or advocating for a certain policy is part of democracy. But PP is doing it on the taxpayers' dime. Taxpayer support for PP is at a record high of more than $616 million in 2018. Over the past 10 years taxpayer support of Planned Parenthood has increased by almost 70%, including those taxpayers who are *against* free abortion anytime anywhere.

Furthermore, PP enjoys tax-exempt status, despite the fact under U.S. law such status can be terminated," when an organization devotes "a substantial part of its activities to attempting to

---

[114] Real Clear Politics, Kristina Hawkins, Why Does Planned Parenthood Get to Avoid Paying Taxes?, Jan. 8, 2020

influence legislation, " "participate or *intervene in any political campaign* on behalf of, or in opposition to, *any candidate for public office*"[115]

Planned Parenthood, on its *own* admission, is guilty on both accounts. Hence the lies.

I am offering this analysis because, although all this is public knowledge, nobody has dared lay a glove on PP. Why? Because women are an important voting demographic, not least professional women, and they are overwhelmingly pro-choice, pro-abortion, pro PP and pro-Democratic Party. Taking them on would be risky for the Republicans but suicidal for the Democrats. But that doesn´t relieve women of responsibility for the policies the organization is supporting.

Furthermore, in a further blow to the organization´s credibility, Planned Parenthood executives were caught on secret video admitting to *illegally* altering abortion procedures to provide fresher, more intact fetal parts. To research institutions. For *sale*. Talk about a conflict of interest for an organization allegedly helping mainly vulnerable women handle *parent*hood.

Obstetrician-gynecologist Dr. Forrest Smith, who has administered thousands of abortions, testified about the video:

"There's no question in my mind that at least some of these fetuses were live births."[116]

Mona Charen, in "Sex Matters", says that "Abortions at any stage are violent acts on a living child but late term abortions are particularly disturbing". ….. . with partial-birth abortions, the cervix is artificially dilated. The abortionist pulls the baby out of the birth canal up to his or her shoulders. Before the head is pulled through, he inserts the sharp point of scissors into the base of the fetus´ skull to make a hole. He then inserts a small hose, vacuums out the brain (collapsing the skull) and pulls the head out."[117]

Furthermore, a new study in British Medical Journal has concluded that unborn babies can feel pain before 24 weeks and possibly as early as 12 weeks' gestation.

Two medical researchers, including one who claims to be a "pro-choice" pain expert, assert that recent investigations strongly suggest unborn babies who are aborted prior to the 24-week legal limit that exists in Britain could be experiencing pain as they are being *terminated*.

"Overall, the evidence, and a balanced reading of that evidence, points towards an immediate and unreflective pain experience mediated by the developing function of the nervous system from as early as 12 weeks," the authors conclude. (Breitbart, Jan. 22, 2020)

To alleviate this problem, the authors somewhat casually suggest analgesics for the fetus before it is *terminated*.

On top of that, women having abortions have risks of bleeding and exposure to disease, as well as higher risks of mental health issues, higher rates of suicide, infections, further surgeries

---

[115] Planned Parenthood Annual Report, www.plannedparenthood.org
[116] National Review, November 12, 2019
[117] Charen, op. cit, p. 99

(including hysterectomies) and infertility. Breast cancer rates are higher for women whose first pregnancy ended in abortion.[118]

There is another statistic that PP is rather coy about:"79% of Planned Parenthood's surgical abortion facilities are strategically located within walking distance of African and/ or Hispanic communities"[119]

Could there be a connection with the fact that black women make up more than 36% nationally of all abortions and in some states more, like Michigan, where they account for 14% of the population but represent 50% of all abortions?

Are we witnessing a complicit relationship between what is effectively an abortion industry that preys on vulnerable minority women and the biomedical industry that uses the fetuses for research? The US Congress seems to think so and has investigated the matter, so far without major repercussions for PP for the political reasons I mentioned above.

It would come as a surprise to no one if "you know the eugenic origins of Planned Parenthood" as Hudson says. Eugenics is the belief that human beings can improve the *qualities* of the human species, especially by such means as discouraging reproduction by persons having genetic defects or presumed to have inheritable undesirable traits, by using forced sterilization or forced abortions.

Margaret Sanger, the woman that founded the organization, was a known eugenicist, campaigning for "racial betterment" by stopping the reproduction of the unfit, targeting blacks in particular with her 1940, "Negro Program", Better Health For 13,000,000" which promoted "family planning".

Or even worse, are we witnessing a feminist movement that has taken the mantra of a "woman's right to choose" into infanticide territory? And neglected to take into consideration, the considerable price minorities, especially African Americans have had to pay?

Radical feminism's mantra that "men are bad news" had another predictable consequence: it has led to the breakdown of the "traditional" family and the rapid increase in single mothers. But the "women need men like a fish needs a bicycle" meme has serious social consequences for men; for while single mothers may be just as good at raising daughters as traditional families, that is not true for boys. Boys raised by single mothers start life with a serious handicap and are much more likely to have behavioral and mental problems, get in trouble with the law and having trouble finding employment.[120]

Focus has been on the *absence* of men in single mothers' lives, leading some politicians to blaming men for not taking responsibility for their offspring-with particular emphasis on African Americans where single motherhood is most prevalent (70 % of all African American households are run by single mothers). But is that fair? African Americans in the 1950s had higher marriage rates than whites, so if we apply a little falsification theory that cannot be the explanation. Why not blame women for deciding to get pregnant without wanting the fathers to

---

[118] Real Clear Politics, op. cit.
[119] Hudson, op. cit., p. 2
[120] Charen, op. cit. p. 197

be around? And why not blame radical feminists (and the media and Hollywood) for telling single mothers a lie, namely that they are just as good as traditional families in raising boys?

The turn of women´s movements into mendacity is a reality of our time. These organizations and their defenders in the media have been running stories about the horrors women faced back in the day when confronted with unwanted pregnancies: coat-hangers, Lysol-a cleaning detergent-used to induce miscarriages- and all that. But these are yesterday´s dilemmas not present days´ realities. Anti-conception means are omnipresent and easily accessible, and women know it. Furthermore, adoption agencies are crying for more women to allow other women, unable to have a child of their own, to adopt their babies. A recent Supreme Court decision overturning an earlier decision, Roe v.Wade,which allowed abortion up until birth, in spite of the Armageddon-like protests of radical feminists, does not change this reality, but simply leaves the question of legislation on abortion to the individual U.S. federal states.

In-womb photos allow us to know the reality of life in the womb -from unborn babies reacting to light and pain to movement from the tender ages of 7-8 weeks. There´s just no excuse anymore for women closing their eyes to the truth: we are at it again practicing infanticide. Without having the excuse of unavoidable biology in the form of unwanted pregnancies as did our ancestors.

It was women´s organizations like PP that pressured Vermont to pass a law on abortion guaranteeing women this right 8 months and thirty days into gestation. That would be 9 months or more brutally, *live birth* abortion, wouldn´t it? New York State passed a similar law and PP in its Annual Report considers it one of its prime political goals to lobby for similar legislation in *all* US states.

Camille Paglia in her essay "Women and Law" says that "Today, the major issues facing feminism are these: is woman a *victim*, mutilated by the horrors of history, or is she a capable and resilient agent, responsible for her actions and desires? To what degree should the state act to further the crucial advance of women in society. Are legally enforced quotas and other preferential remedies authentically progressive, or are they reactionary, paternalistic, and infantilizing? Should women having escaped control by fathers and husbands, now transfer that humiliating dependency onto the labyrinthine bureaucracy of the state?[121]

We now know the answer and it is not the one Paglia would have chosen: Women, both the silent majority and the Woke have gone down a blind alley. As Mona Charen says," If feminists had stuck to lobbying for equal pay, opening more job opportunities to women, serving on juries…. they would have made significant contributions to social advancement. Instead, they *chose* to become revolutionaries howling at the nature of femininity, love, marriage, and motherhood".[122]

And we now know *why*. All the leading feminists from Betty Friedan over Gloria Steinem to Germaine Greer and Laurey Penny are Postmodernist Woke Marxists. Their turn towards revolution did not come about by mistake or accident. It was the other way around: they deliberately chose feminism as a vehicle "to exercise power for the purpose of social change".[123]

The mystery is why so many non-Woke women bought into it. And still do.

---

[121] " Women and Law" by Camille Paglia in "Provocations-Collected Essays", p.159-60.
[122] Charen, op. cit. p. 28
[123] Stephen R. C. Hicks, Explaining Postmodernism, p. 12

Summary: Part II:

It is axiomatic for Woke to claim authorship and ownership of all cultural liberation movements in the West, including gender identity, transgenderism, anti-racism, and feminism.

The truth is radically different.

The West was on a trajectory of liberalization of social norms in all the above areas long before Woke: the first movement for homosexual rights arose in Berlin in the 1890s, the emancipation of slaves in the early 1800s, Brown vs. board of Education in which the Supreme Court declared the "separate but equal doctrine" governing race relations in the U.S. for unconstitutional came out 10 years *before* the first Freedom Riders, and abolitionists in England abolished slavery in what was then the world's only superpower in 1808.

The feminist movements were started in the early 1900s, the political suffragettes in the U.S. and the Blue Stockings in the U.K. at the same time and it was Denmark which long before the Youth Rebellion of the late '60s and '70s, in 1924 nominated the first female minister in the World.

As our deconstruction of the Woke narrative shows, the fact is that Woke captured political and cultural movements *already* implementing rapid social and democratic liberalization, and *radicalized* them.

BLM, Black Panthers and their leaders like Stokely Carmichael; Judith Butler, identity politics, #MeToo, Simone de Beauvoir, Planned Parenthood, live birth abortion activists, and radical transgender activist like the San Francisco Gay Men's Choir, were movements *captured* by Woke in order not to promote their original message of which society largely approved, but to transform the consciousness of society and pave the way by stealth for a different kind of system of which society did not approve: Socialism.

Where did the Woke leaders get this idea of seeing themselves as an elite vanguard? From Lenin, who got it from Nietzsche and his theory of the Ubermensch. In <u>What Is To Be Done?</u> (1902), Lenin said that "a revolutionary vanguard party, recruited from the working class, should lead the political campaign because only in that way would the proletariat successfully realise their revolution; unlike the economic campaign of trade-union-struggle advocated by other socialist and social democratic parties."[124]

And Lenin passed this somewhat …ahem,…elitist idea on to Woke and its leaders in the West, like Macron and Merkel and Obama and Hillary Clinton who have no compunction about disregarding the voice of the masses if it stands in the way of "progress".

---

[124] From Internet search: Lenin quotes on vanguard.

Part III: Woke´s Long March Through the Institutions

Chapter 1: Woke´s One World Internationalism: the EU.

xxxxxxxxxxxxxxxxxxxxxxxxxxxx

Imagine there's no countries
It isn't hard to do
Nothing to kill or die for
And no religion, too.

Imagine all the people
Livin' life in peace.

You may say I'm a dreamer
But I'm not the only one
I hope someday you'll join us
And the world will be as one.

John Lennon in his song, Imagine.

xxxxxxxxxxxxxxxxxx

Imagine there´s no countries-it was the mantra first of the hippies, now of the globalist Davoisie. Their humanitarian universalism argues that a person who limits his loyalties to a single nation will only become narrow-minded and chauvinistic.[125]
    Helen Andrews in Boomers.

xxxxxxxx

At the entrance to the Visitors´ Centre of the European Parliament there is a plaque which reads: "…national sovereignty is the root cause of the most crying evils of our time… The only final remedy for this supreme and catastrophic evil of our time is a federal union of the peoples…".

xxxxxx

The Brussels veteran and former Belgian prime minister, Guy Verhofstadt, called nationalists for "**a populist nightmare**" and a "**cancer**" on the EU.

xxxxxxx

"The word 'nationalism,' as it exists in today's political lexicon, connotes xenophobia and white supremacy",
New York University´s student-run newspaper, Washington Square Times, [126]

xxxxxxx.

"**Centenary of Armistice Day 1918:**

Millions killed by nationalism.

---

[125] Boomers, p.37
[126] Breitbart, October 24, 2019

Our future: A strong and peaceful Europe".
<u>Vox, a European Commission Newsletter introducing the French President, Emmanuel Macron´s speech on the centenary of Armistice Day, the armistice that ended WWI.</u>

Xxxxxxxxxxxx

" We need to remind ourselves why the United Nations was established in the first place, why NATO, why the World Trade Organization and other international institutions…it was because of the lessons that were drawn out of the Second World War and *excessive nationalism".*
<u>Angela Merkel, the former German Chancellor, in an award speech on January 29, 2019, praised the EU as an arbiter of order and peace in a post-WWII world</u>

xxxxxxx

On September 1, 1939, nationalism in the shape of Nazi-Germany started the bloodiest war in human history, WWII, by invading Poland, so the woke narrative goes. There is just one problem.

It isn´t true.

On September 1,1939, Nazi-Germany *and* (2 weeks later)communist Russia invaded Poland and started WWII.

Describing the event otherwise is like a rape victim reporting to the police that she was raped by two men one of whom pinned her down while the other penetrated her.

And the police reporting that there was only one assailant.

But *why* that part of the history is underreported and undertold is more interesting for our purposes. Sure, historians know the truth, but why don´t you?

There are 2 main reasons: firstly, winners always write the story and the history-not the losers. Secondly, the EU has been shopping a narrative to us of how it was born on the ashes of WWII, which was started by bad, bad nationalism that is prone to always start wars and commit crimes against humanity. That would be Nazi-Germany, right? Absolutely. But Stalin´s Communist Russia was nationalist, too, and committed worse crimes in sheer numbers against humanity than Nazi-Germany ever did. But the EU cannot admit the truth now, can it? It´s too late.

But think about it for just a second: why is nationalism so bad when it *starts* WWII, but wonderful when it *wins* WWII as the 2 very nationalistic world powers, the USSR, and the USA, did in 1945? Logically both narratives cannot simultaneously be true.

The answer, of course, is that Nationalism is bad only because Woke has adopted *inter*nationalism as its go- to remedy for all the ills of the world: "nothin` to kill or die for-and no religion,too" ,as John Lennon says.

Unless there is something wrong with the facts, I have given you. And there isn´t. Therefore, there must be another real explanation other than nationalism.

So, if it doesn´t make sense to blame nationalism for WWI and II who is to blame?

Appeasement. The policy of the West world including the USA which was responsible for making Germany respect its commitments imposed by the Versailles Treaty of 1919 after Germany allegedly had started the *first* world war, was one of appeasement towards Hitler´s repeated breaches of Germany´s commitments.

The problem is that by singling out nationalism as the cause of WWI and WWII, Woke sowed the seeds of present- day storms.

It all started with a lie: History, is of course open to various interpretations, but to blame nationalism as the cause of WWI as President Macron does in the quote above is a falsification of history, since WWI was mainly a power struggle between 6 *empires* with many different nationalities: the British, the French, the Austro-Hungarian, the Russian, the Ottoman and indeed, the German empires (yes, Germany, too, had its colonies mainly in West-Africa).

Even that hot bed of political correctness, the European Parliament, in a recent resolution concluded that Germany was not solely responsible for the start of WWI, but that other countries contributed in equal measure. [127]

But it was too little too late: the nationalism- is -evil quote above, "that national sovereignty is the root cause of the most crying evils of our time… The only final remedy for this supreme and catastrophic evil of our time is a federal union of the peoples…" had taken root.

Furthermore, the end of the Cold War, in 1991, engendered a newly potent *trans*nationalism, contemptuous of national boundaries and supportive of institutions of global governance. To quote National Review editor, Rich Lowry, in a piece called the Treason of the Elites, in this view, old *national* loyalties were not just anachronistic but morally unsupportable. Lowry quoted the social critic Richard Sennett who wrote of "the evil of a shared national identity" and Professor of law and ethics Martha Nussbaum, who warned of the "morally dangerous" dictates of "patriotic pride, recommending instead a commitment to the "worldwide community of human beings."

Brexit supporter, and British MEP, Anne Widdecomb, hit the nail on its head, when she warned Eurocrats to "learn the lessons" from Brexit and scale back on federalism, or else the European Union will not survive.

Addressing fellow MEPs and senior EU bureaucrats in the European Parliament in Strasbourg, France, Ms. Widdecombe said: "The European Union started with six *countries*. The vision then was that it would be a loose alliance of sovereign *nations* in a trading agreement with some sort of political co-operation with a totally noble ideal that that would somehow promote peace.

"If that had remained… and was still the vision, I venture to say that I don't believe that Britain would now be leaving.

"That didn't happen. Co-operation morphed into *domination*. Sovereignty morphed into a *superstate*. That is why Britain is going. "[128]

---

[127] RC-B9-0097/2019, Sept.18,2019.

Indeed.

It wasn't supposed to be like this. As Ms. Widdecomb says, the European Union was started not as a union but as a European *market*, an economic idea: let's rebuild Europe after 2 devastating world wars that started in Europe.

When did it all go wrong for the EU? It all started with my fellow countrymen-the Danes. In 1992 in a referendum, this small country of 5 million plus inhabitants on the cusp of winning the European Soccer Championships in Sweden, on a wave of nationalism, rejected a proposal to change the course of the three European *Communities* and turn them into a European *Union*.

The European elite was in shock. This was the first serious set-back since it all started back in 1958.

What to do? Go back to the drawing-board or ignore the voters?

Woke political leaders chose the latter. A fateful choice but one that was to be played out again and again when voters in referenda in Holland, Ireland and France in the succeeding years voted no to the idea of an ever-increasing European empire. Why?

The EU at the time of the Danish "nej" in 1992 just came off the back of a huge success: the implementation of the Single Market. Eurocrats, were proud after having tussled with a project that surpassed all hitherto undertaken efforts in harmonizing national EU legislations into a huge European market.

But the Danish referendum, and subsequent referenda in Holland and France, should have shown Woke that voters did not care.

Instead, once the project of a single market was successfully finished, Europhiles had to find other ways of justifying their existence and salaries.

Some political analysts of the EU have called it the "bicycle principle": you either keep on pushing the pedals or the bike falls over.

And that was the reason that the European *Economic* Community, in those years after the Single market went from being a market to becoming a Union, the EU. The success of building the Single Market went to the heads of the EU's political class who started dreaming of a monetary union, a European currency, enlarging the EU by taking in new member states and becoming, you know, an empire.

So, alas, the truth is, the European Union came about *despite* the rejections by national electorates. And what could not be passed with the consent of the governed was passed through back-door deals in Amsterdam, Dublin, and Lisbon.

And the EU grew bigger and bigger. All Central Europe's former Soviet satellite-countries, like Poland, Hungary, Romania, Bulgaria, the Czech Republic, Slovakia, Slovenia and the 3 Baltic States who had been subjugated by a totalitarian non-democratic regime, the *Soviet* Union, for almost 60 years were included without anybody asking the voters in the EU for their consent.

The excuse of the EU was that these new member states wanted so badly to join the EU's project of peace after so many years of Soviet subjugation, that we had no choice but to let them in. Which we did in 2004. Paradoxically it is some of those very same member states, like Hungary,

---

[128] Breitbart, Jan. 16, 2020

Poland, and the Czech Republic, who *now* do not want to give up the national identities they fought so hard to keep under Soviet occupation and *now* are complaining that the *European* Union sure is beginning to act and look like their old, totalitarian and arrogant headmaster, the *Soviet* Union. Without the Gulags, the show trials, mass executions and KBG, of course, but similar, nevertheless.

But the EU continued to pay no attention to the "nationalists" and the original rhetoric of the founding years of the Common Market continued undiminished by reality: nationalism was still the big bug bear which had caused 2 World Wars. And the rhetoric still was, that from the ashes of the disaster caused by nationalism the EU had single-handedly saved Europe through a project of European co-operation, of soft power, internationalism, and globalism, of peace, of healing of old wounds, of justice and above all of democracy and diversity.

The former Soviet satellites begged to disagree but it wasn´t until the fateful years of 2015, 2016 and 2020 when 4 events rocked the ordinary man in the street that the masks came off our political class:

The first one was when former German Chancellor, Angela Merkel´s Open Door immigration policy let 1 million *economic* refugees jump the external borders of the EU in Greece and Italy; and block the motorways and train station and border crossings all over the EU heading for the nirvana of northern EU-countries with their open doors and welfare handouts.

It was chaos and a huge set-back for everything the EU thought it stood for: multi-culturalism, diversity, open borders and tolerance. And it split the EU down the middle.

But Merkel drunk with hubris after the successes of the Single Market, the introduction of the Euro as the EU´s single currency and Eastern Enlargement, in a phrase whose arrogance more than anything symbolized the leader of a Woke political class that had lost its head, said:" Wir schaffen das"(We can do it).

Only she couldn´t and her fellow Europeans wouldn´t. As they said, mockingly:" Wir schaffen das… nicht".

After that came Brexit in June 2016, another big shock to the EU Establishment who were so full of themselves that they had confidently predicted that no one in their right mind would voluntarily leave their paradise on earth.

And after that the third whammy: the election of a nationalist, Make America Great Again, Donald Trump as U. S. President. And after *that* the Covid19-crisis with its subsequent loss of trust in the system Woke had set up. And their self-serving narrative about it.

And that´s the reason the EU is in the crisis that it is now.

Only, the truth is: the EU elite *created* the crisis by closing their eyes and ears to reality and refusing to recognize, let alone acknowledge, what was happening: that by not listening they had lost the trust of ordinary voters. To this day the EU political class *still* don´t acknowledge that they have failed their own people.

All mainstream parties in Northern Europe with the sole exception of Denmark (which has the toughest immigration laws in this region) have lost ground; indeed, sometimes been wholly wiped out by voters fed up with bullshit and lies about everything from mass immigration to political correctness.

Yet, the EU´s political class *still* refuses to recognize, let alone work together, with EU-sceptic parties that have garnered 20% or more of the support of the voters; as witnessed by the treatment of the AfD (Alternative fur Deutschland) in Germany which has arisen to be the 2nd biggest political party in several federal states and the Sweden-Democrats (Sverigesdemokraterne), presently (summer of 2023) the biggest political party in Sweden.

In Germany, all parties in the German Bundestag in Berlin in 2019 voted out the duly democratically elected AfD head of the Legal Affairs Committee, Stefan Brandner, because of a few fairly innocuous political tweets, an event that has *never* happened before in German history; and in Sweden, though losing the last parliamentary elections badly, the leader of the Swedish Social Democrats leader was approved as head of a minority government because none of the center-right parties, as in Germany, would touch co-operating with the Sweden-Democrats with a 10-foot pole.

Predictably, these anti-democratic maneuvers have led to even more of a surge in the popularity ratings of these two parties.

In Spain which everyone thought was immune to the siren song of nationalism because of Franco´s dictatorship and the Spanish civil war from 1936-39, in recent Spanish parliamentary elections, a nationalist party, VOX, went from 0, 2 % to 15% of the votes and a status as third biggest party in Spain on a platform of nationalism and anti-immigrations similar to those of AfD and the Sweden-Democrats.

Nevertheless, the Spanish socialists, still nominally the biggest party though having seen their vote tally go *down* decided to form a minority government with a far-left party, PODEMOS, styled on the platform of the late Hugo Chavez´ Venezuelan government.

In Portugal, the Chega("Enough") Party went from under 1 % to 7 percent of all votes in the February 2022 elections. Yet the winning Socialist party refused to cooperate with them.

What was Woke thinking?

1 in 4 Europeans voted for Euro-sceptic parties in May 2019 elections to the European Parliament and the mainstream political groupings that had run the EP for 40 years lost badly.

Yet the political class composed of heads of states and government gathered in the European Council in June 2019, and in back-door deals closed to the press and the public, went ahead and nominated people that were all in favor of *more* EU-integration to fill the top 3 posts in the EU, i. e. the President of the European Commission, the President of the European Council and the head of the European Central Bank. It was as if only they mattered and democratic rules were for losers.

In this process they overrode the choices of the European Parliament. And on top of *that* they simply picked out of thin air three people, none of whom prior to the selection had even been *candidates* for the job.

So after an election that without any doubt showed an increase in euro-skepticism and disgust with the political class, the very same political class got together and ignored the voters and selected as top leaders people who wanted an EU-army, a Euro-zone budget, a common EU frontier agency, Frontex, whose job was to wrestle away the control by individual member states´ of their external borders which hitherto had been a national prerogative, in order to slip in *more* economic refugees into the EU; and last but not least an UN Global Compact on

Immigration Pact that would all but guarantee even more economic immigrants from Muslim North Africa and the Middle East.

And lied to us about it by passing it off as if this were the logical outcome of the EP elections.

The story of the U.N. serves up the same hype of uniting a world torn apart by war and devastation into a peace-loving *inter*-national community, *the* International Community, whose very presence is a guarantee that war is now no longer an option: "ain´t gonna study war no more" as a popular refrain of a popular song from those early post-war days stated it.

If the EU´s main bug bear is nationalism, the U. N. ´s main culprit is race. It was the ideologies of the superiority of *races* as in Nazi Germany and Japan that had led the world astray and from now on everyone, all peoples all cultures were equal:" Yankee, Russian, white, or tan, Lord a man is just a man, we´re all brothers and we are only passing through" as in another popular ditty from that same period had it.

But the U. N., too, lost its shine after failing to intervene in Srebrenica, while Christian Orthodox Bosnian Serbs in 1995 slaughtered 8000 young Muslim Bosnian men under U. N. protection in a U. N. -designated "safe area". And after failing miserably, despite repeated warnings, to prevent the Rwandan genocide of more than 800. 000 Tutsis in 1995, murdered by their fellow countrymen, the Hutus. Obviously, we weren´t *all* brothers.

But this is not the standard narrative we are being told by the International Community, neither by the EU nor the UN. Their rhetoric of international Kumbaya continues unabated.

So, what *is* the source of war, I hear you ask? Depends. It´s complicated and many theories have been advanced by political scientists over the years. What we do know is what is *not* a source of war: democracy. If people have a say they never vote to go to war, *provided* they are not being filled with a bunch of lies by their government, their elites and their media. In Russia the Communists took power in 1917 through a coup d´état, without a doubt. But your teachers will have told you that I´m wrong because Hitler took power in Germany by democratic means. They are lying.

So, what really happened? You have to look at the timeline. Hitler, in 1932, twice ran for President of Germany and twice was defeated.

Furthermore, Hitler and his Nazi-party, never in a free and fair election got more than 40% of the votes. In fact, in democratic elections in July and November 1932, the Nazi-party never got more than 38% and 32 % respectively.

But, despite suffering a set-back in the November 1932 elections, they finally did win the Chancellorship for Hitler in 1933, in a back-room deal, when the ageing and senile German Chancellor, Hindenburg, was persuaded not only to nominate Hitler German Chancellor but also to dissolve the Reichstag.

This allowed Hitler to harass political opponents and intimidate the electorate, inter alia by setting fire to the German Parliament, the Reichstag, two weeks before the March 5, 1933, election. Even more importantly, Hitler´s private Nazi regiments, the SA and Stahlhelm, were ordered by the acting Minister of the Interior, Hermann Goering, a prominent Nazi, to" monitor" the vote process all across Germany and it was his Ministry that "counted" the final votes.

Even *then*, the Nazis only "got" 43, 9 % of the votes. So how anyone can say as the New York Times did on the 75th anniversary of the March 5, 1933, elections, that "democracy produced a monster", is yet more proof of the main theme of this book: we are being duped by fake narratives.

Hitler did eventually take power, but it was through a parliamentary coup d'état in the German Reichstag (Parliament), not through democratic means. Historians like Allan Bullock and William L.Shirer disagree: Shirer says "Thus was parliamentary democracy finally interred in Germany. Except for the arrests of the Communists and some of the social Democratic deputies, it was all done quite legally, though accompanied by terror".[129]

Not so fast. Hitler manages to dissolve Parliament, institutes a reign of terror against his political opponents, sets fire to the Reichstag and jails all Communist deputies and some of the Social-Democratic ones, and it's all "legal"?

He intimidates deputies from other parties by lining the wall of the building where the German Parliament meets with his storm-troopers. He makes false promises to the Reichstag that no laws would be allowed to "affect the position of the Reichstag and swears to the leader of the Centre Party, which was to give him the extra votes needed to pass the law abolishing democracy in Germany, that he would respect the President's power of veto, a statement he promises to deliver in writing but never does, and Shirer and other can still claim that "The Germans had no one to blame but themselves"? I don't think so.

The German *people* when directly asked, twice rejected Hitler in two presidential elections in 1932 by wide margins and his party in free and fair elections never manages to win more 'than 38% of the popular votes. Their elected representatives let them down and allowed themselves to be duped into abolishing the parliamentary democracy a majority of voters still wanted is closer to the truth. Yet, we are still served Hitler's own oft-repeated propaganda line, that he came to power "legally" and told by the NYT that this is proof that democracy ain't what it's cracked up to be?

Why do the preachers of woke internationalism (and the NYT is at the forefront of politically correct internationalism believe you me) lie to us?

The answer is that the Left historically has an ambivalent relationship with democracy. Lenin called democracy "a useless and harmless toy" while, like Hitler, creating many of the outward appearance of democracy such as a constitution, elections, and legislative bodies.

David Horowitz was right on the money when he said: "Every progressive has a totalitarian inside screaming to get out".[130]

The NYT infamously covered up the atrocities of early Communist rule. The truth that woke ideology is hiding is that the "democracy" they are using to justify their internationalism is not real.

Democracy is inextricably linked with *communities*, with *people*, and most recently with the democracy of the *nation* state. Democracy literally means choice of the people, which in Greek is called "demos".

---

[129] William L. Shirer, The Rise and Fall of the Third Reich, Pan Books,1964,p.249.
[130] From internet search on David Horowitz.

But the EU and the UN and all the other international institutions do not have a "demos". There are no demos who voted for the dictatorial decisions of the European Council, I mentioned above.

Guy Verhofstadt, the former Belgian Premier and Brexit coordinator for the European Parliament, screaming for the EU to become an empire to fight off competition from China, Russia and-you read it right, the United States, on whom the EU's military security is totally dependent through NATO, has no *mandate*, no *demos* for these mad ravings which only serve to illustrate what happens when a politician cannot be controlled by the voters.

I know you will say that the European Parliament to-day is elected via direct democratic elections. True. And that the EP has the power to reject the new Commission.True.But only en bloc,which means a rejection will mean institutional paralysis and starting all over again.

That is not a real choice and member states know it.

Which is why the candidates EP originally selected for President of the EU-Commission were completely ignored by the real power in the EU, the European Council, composed of heads of governments-and state, who met in secret and picked candidates unknown to the voters. And when the European Parliament whose candidates had been rejected met to vote on the candidate *imposed on them* by the European Council, *their* vote was also *secret* so nobody could hold *them* accountable.

So, we got screwed. Again.

And if you wonder why nationalism is such an object of hate and derision, the simple explanation is: nationalism with its democracy and its voters' power *and* incentive to hold politicians accountable is a threat to the One World Orthodoxy of woke ideology.

Part III: Woke´s Long March Through the Institutions

Chapter 2: The European Union and the Soviet Union: Woke´s March from Idealism to Authoritarianism

---

"Inside every progressive there is totalitarian screaming to get out."
David Horowitz, American writer who moved from Marxism to Conservatism.
xxxxxxxxxxxxxxxx

" We are building the first ever non-militaristic empire".
Manuel Barroso, former Portuguese President of the European Commission, about the EU.
xxxxxxx

" Let´s create a single Euro-African economic area. It would have an enormous potential that remains untapped. 1. 5 billion consumers, 20 trillion in value, able to rival with China".
Guy Verhofstad, former Belgian Prime Minister and President of one of the biggest political groups in the European Parliament, in an (in)famous twitter tweet.
xxxxxxx

" The Franco-German partnership has an obligation not to let the world fall into chaos and to lead Europe to peace.... It is for this reason that Europe must be stronger... [and become] a more sovereign European super state with one army, one immigration law and one budgetary policy".
French President Macron in a speech to the German Bundestag
xxxxxxx

" Europe is not a secondary nation. Europe in its entirety is a vanguard: it has always defined the standards of progress".
Macron in an open letter to the Citizens of Europe
xxxxxxx

Oh, really, two world wars started in Europe, and Europe has always "defined the standards of progress"?

"A single Euro-African economic area", where the EU would partner up with the world's poorest continent, still overwhelmingly tribal and more often than not run by totalitarian leaders with no concept nor knowledge of modern-day democracies, whose economic contribution would be close to nil and whose very different, and as far as North African populations go, mainly Muslim populations are already fleeing their homelands for the social welfare benefits of Northern Europe?

A European superstate?

Those are *good* ideas?

You may shrug Macron's and Verhofstad's bullshit off as empty bluster but the facts are clear: woke politicians are beginning to talk of matters that 10 years ago were no-go and non-starters: An EU army? A common Euro-budget and a common external borders and immigration policy? All the hallmarks of something much bigger than an Economic Community in Europe, something akin to an…. European Empire.

But notice the misdirection: the quotes above are talking about a *European* army, a *European* budget when what they really mean is an *EU*-army. an *EU*-budget etc.

Large parts of Europe, including post-Brexit UK, Norway, Serbia, Bosnia, Albania, Switzerland, and more are not even members of the EU. And 8 EU-countries, including my own, Denmark, are not even members of the Eurozone.

And wrap your heads around this; despite the incessant talk of the *massive* EU-bureaucracy, the EU is a *small* place, a very small place, with about 45,000 eurocrats most of whom are employed as drivers, secretaries, and translators. That's about the size of the city administration of one of the smallest EU-capitals, Copenhagen, and *it* doesn't even need translators. The EU, obviously, doesn't have the capacity to run Europe, even if it wanted to, which it doubtlessly does. In fact, it doesn't even run the EU, which in purely technical terms is still being run by its national administrations, although admittedly often based on laws passed by the EU.

So, what are we being told here? Firstly, we are being lied to plain and simple: the EU is not synonymous with Europe and woke knows it. But it also knows that most of us are sympathetically inclined towards the idea of Europe, where we have travelled, have friendships, family, lovers, whereas a good deal of us are somewhat skeptical about the fairly recent political phenomenon of the European *Union*, with its rules, regulations, red-tape and yes, *anti*-nationalistic rhetoric and *inter*nationalist hyperbole.

Secondly, there is much more truth, indeed it *is* the truth, in Macron's statement about the Franco-German couple. Not in its ability to prevent the world from "falling into chaos" which is, of course, absolute mad megalomania, but about Germany and France essentially *being t*he EU.

Without their "partnership" there would be no EU. And this has become clearer to everyone involved because of two recent events: Brexit and the election of Donald Trump as US President. Why? Because it has changed the game plan of the EU's biggest and economically strongest player: Germany.

Germany, traditionally, has been the strongest ally of the U. S on the continent together with the U. K. But Donald Trump's criticism of the EU for its meagre contributions to its own defense in NATO and its protectionist tariff-barriers towards the US has singled out Germany as the main culprit.

Furthermore, Germany because of the lost two world wars has become more pacifist and has moved further to the left than any other EU member state. In his book, Wir Verstehen Die Welt Nicht Mehr, (We Don´t Understand the World Anymore), German historian, Christoph von Marschall, explains how the German worldview has moved from the aggressive militarism of the first half of the 20th century to a kind of preachy, internationalist, globalist and above all pacifistic, "Moralischer Groessenwahn", moralistic megalomania, as he calls it.

With Angela Merkel as its woke figurehead.

The former head of the German conservative party, CDU, Annegret Kramp-Karrenbauer, who was installed in her job post of Defense Minister by Merkel was widely ridiculed when she proposed that the EU send a peacekeeping force to the Turkish-Syrian border where Turkey had set up a buffer-zone against all international law, only to admit that Germany itself actually ….ahem, wouldn´t be able to provide any troops.

There is no popular support for increasing Germany´s contribution to NATO, i. e. increasing its own military budget; and nowhere in the EU is Donald Trump more loathed than in Germany. It is not hard to understand why: when the world view of Germany, the world´s 4th biggest economy is that of appeasement, internationalism and open borders, Orange Man isn´t your man, is he?

What with Brexit and Donald Trump, Germany was left with either revising its foreign policy to align more with the Western alliance, in particular the US, a policy alien to the appeasement instincts of both its leader, Angela Merkel, a former communist born and raised in East Germany, and the German voters, or a closer alignment with France.

And France has always, whether under right-wing presidents, like, Charles de Gaulle, or socialist ones, like Francois Mitterrand, favored the restoration of French hegemony in Europe and has always had a strong anti-Americanism as part of its culture. It is France that´s pushing for the EU to become an empire; and it is Germany, whose political power is wholly bound up with anti-nationalism because of its two lost world wars which *needs* the internationalist bona fides of the European Union more than any other country, which is getting dragged kicking and screaming into the new European Union Empire.

The transition to empire is the result of a process that as indicated above has led the EU from being an *idea*, a project for peace in a part of the world torn by horrendous wars, to an *ideology*, with all the hallmarks of a quasi-secular religion.

Surely, I am exaggerating? Maybe, I am, but others seem to agree. Let me give you just three examples of quite different political philosophers from three very different countries that all independently of each other have come to the same conclusion:

The Polish political philosopher and former Chairman of the European Parliamentary Group of European Conservatives and Reformists, Ryszard Legutko, in "The Demon In Democracy-Totalitarian Temptations In Free Societies" whose main, indeed only theme, is a description of the similarities between the Communism of the Soviet Union and its satellites and the liberal democracy of the EU. I use his book´s main chapters as a template.

David Gress, Danish political philosopher, and historian, in "EU-Europe´s Enemy" and last but not least, the Israeli political philosopher, Yovram Hazony, in "The Virtues of Nationalism".

All three authors ask the same question: is the European Union on the way towards falling for the same totalitarian temptation as he Soviet Union?

My take is: yes, it is and even if there are no KGBs, no Stalins and no Gulags in the EU it is high time to admit it.

History: the similarities are evident in the two systems' perceptions of their place in history. Both systems consider and considered themselves the end-station of progress, or as Legutko says in The Demon In Democracy: "Communism and liberal democracy are believed to be the ultimate stages of the history of political transformations"[131]

Communism saw itself as historically bound to prevail everywhere. Macron and the EU, as the quotes above illustrate, are convinced that the EU has a mission "not to let the world fall into chaos". All the world needs to do to avoid "chaos" is to follow the EU's example of peaceful cooperation between former enemies.

Utopia: Both systems by claiming to be *final* meet the definition of Utopias. I know you will argue that Utopias are unrealistic fantasies and that both the EU and the Soviet Union are and were very real. But, in fact, historically, utopias have been very practical, sometimes pedantic, blueprints for the *good* society.

Dualism: Both systems, despite their propaganda of being open and inclusive, see the political world in terms of them and us. You will object and mention the multi-party nature of the countries making up the EU and its insistence on diversity, democracy, and inclusion, but as the harsh treatment of the governing nationalist parties in Poland and Hungary shows, the EU's tolerance only stretches so far; and has proven unable to cope with political philosophies wedded to the idea of the nation state, never mind nation-states based on religion and patriotism. The EU's *them and us* dualism, thus, is between mainstream (EU) and non-mainstream (EU-critical countries) the latter often characterized as extremist, illiberal or even downright fascist.

The EU's criticism of the two above-mentioned countries has as its main component the claim that they don´t observe and respect *European* values. But what the EU really means is that they don´t respect the *EU*'s woke, progressive and leftist values, such as diversity, open-borders, anti-traditional family policies, anti-religious sentiments, pro same-sex marriages, LGTBQ rights, etc.

However, contrary to the EU's claims, these "values" are far from traditional but in fact *newly* adopted and have only very recently come into the mainstream, as exemplified by the very recent legalization of same-sex marriage in our time. On the contrary, they constitute the EU's *deviation* from traditional European values like church, religion, family, and the nation and represent the EU's adoption of woke neo-Marxist values which in turn are a reaction *against* traditional European values.

As an example, the often-cited statement from the Hungarian leader, Victor Orbán, about Hungary constituting an "illiberal" democracy is erroneously used to claim that he is a totalitarian or authoritarian despot in the making. When, in reality, he is referring to the fact that Hungary under his leadership will not go down the "liberal", woke road of the above-mentioned diversity, open-borders, same-sex marriage, anti-nationalism and anti-patriotism progressive EU values. The misdirection about European as opposed to EU "values" is intentional on the EU's part. But it is a lie.

---

[131] Legutko, p. 43

Historically no value has been more important to European values than Christianity; yet, the EU has done nothing but fight to remove Christianity from the public square as witnessed by the European Court of Human Right forbidding religious Christian symbols in public schools in Italy and the EU fighting and winning the battle to delete any references to Christianity in its, ultimately failed, attempt of pushing through a US style EU Constitution.

There is certainly no traditional value, either, about the EU's criticism of the nation state. Historically, the main reason behind the ascendance of the West and Western European civilization is the nation-state. It is exemplified by the historian, Niall Ferguson's seminal book, Civilization-The West and the *Rest,* which convincingly argues that it was small Western European *nations* like Renaissance Italy and Industrialism's England that 500 years ago made Europe leave China and other ancient hitherto powerful empires in the dust through a combination of individualism, democracy and free enterprise.

Ideology: Both Communism and woke democracy have morphed into *ideologies*. Ideologies are the enemies of ideas and of freedom of thought. They are so to speak the ossification of ideas.

Examples in Communism are its dualist practice of them vs. us, which in Communism is the *proletariat vs. the rich*. Opponents' views are stigmatized as being a function of their *rich* class, f. ex. the wealthier peasants, the Kulaks, who though by no means rich were persecuted on charges such as "capitalist lackey" or "bourgeois".

The ideology of woke liberal democracy is characterized by the dualism of Woke's paradigm of *oppressor vs. oppressed*. But the purpose is the same: to defend supporters of the system and defeat opponents. It follows that oppressed people whether sexual, racial, women or even religious minorities like Muslims in the West, qua being oppressed must be protected, f. ex. through "hate speech" laws, and cannot legitimately be allowed to be criticized.

Conversely, the oppressor, identified by woke ideology as men, is allowed to be the constant subject of derision and scorn. In particular, the sky is the limit for criticism of *white* men of the masculine soccer fan variety whose "toxic masculinity" is stigmatized, whereas criticism of black men is verboten because black men are a minority and oppressed to boot.

People of Asian background, on the other hand, though they seem to fit the bill of oppressed people-of-color, are not really to be considered oppressed even in such cases as the admission quotas to Harvard where Harvard officials demonstrably and self-admittedly weighted the SAT - scores of Asian candidates below those of African Americans to avoid the embarrassment of seeing half of their student body consisting of Asian-American students.

They *do*, however, have higher I. Q. s than white folks.

So, could white people by this standard not rightly consider themselves as being discriminated against, too? This the intellectual and moral mess that woke ideological thinking gets you into; but at least we are being treated to the highly entertaining spectacle of seeing woke democracy defending that blacks are given preferential treatment perhaps even reparations because of the oppression of earlier days and slavery, whereas Asian-American minorities, who have suffered similar discrimination in the US for centuries and are also people-of-color, somehow don't qualify for the same preferential treatment.

Art: Another ideological marker is *art:* in Communism as well as in woke democracies, artists that followed the cultural codes of the day, and produced respectively Soviet Realism, i. e. art positively portraying Soviet workers; or, since woke ideology is decidedly anti-Christianity, suitably anti-religious work of art like the "Piss Christ", a 1987 photograph by the American artist and photographer Andres Serrano which depicts a plastic crucifix submerged in a small glass tank of the artist's urine, will be hailed as woke beacons of truth.

Religion: Both Communism and woke ideology are hostile to religion but mask it through an official policy of neutrality or equal protection of *all* religions and an alleged policy of protecting their citizens´ right to exercise them. This is, however, in both cases an obvious lie: there can be no equality of treatment between religions such as the Russian Orthodox Church that just as the Catholic and Protestant Churches has been around for centuries, at times have competed with the secular state for power and are interwoven with the very fabric of Russian and European civilizations and other more marginal religions. The reality is that Communism as well as woke ideology both understand that religion is a powerful competing force for their stated goal of reorganizing society and an obstacle to their creation of a *new*, Communist or EU, *man*.

The clash between Woke ideology and Enlightenment human rights, such as freedom of speech and religion, is an everyday occurrence within the EU, most recently observed when a former Finnish Interior Minister, Ms. Paivi Rasanen, was charged with hate speech for having pointed out that when the Finnish Lutheran Church celebrates Pride Day it is contrary to the Bible, which condemns homosexual acts,[132]

This illustrates that totalitarian temptations are not limited to anti-democratic or non-democratic countries like Russia, China, or Cuba. It is the other way around. Totalitarianism is a *human* temptation for all of us. And a warning signal to all of us: those countries and others like them, from Vietnam to Venezuela are not totalitarian by *accident* but because their *citizen*s didn´t insist on their right and indeed their responsibility to hold their political leaders accountable. They preferred to believe their lies.

The quote from Juvenal: "Who will guard the guards"? has an answer: we the people. We cannot delegate it to someone else. The problem with internationalism in general and the EU and the UN, as all the above examples of lack of democratic accountability show, is that there is no one to guard the guards. No one to hold responsible.

It is in reaction to this situation that nationalism and populism is on the rise. Not because normal people like the voters in Spain, Portugal, Sweden, and Germany suddenly have become more racist or xenophobic than before. But because woke ideology in its infatuation with the utopian vision of One World Internationalism have neglected to take their concerns seriously, or even worse have vilified those that dare question their narrative.

---

[132] BBC News,24 january,2022.

Part III: Woke´s Long March Through the Institutions

Chapter 3: Woke´s One World Internationalism: the UN and Open Borders

xxxxxxxxxxxxx

"WE THE PEOPLES OF THE UNITED NATIONS DETERMINED

- to save succeeding generations from the scourge of war, which twice in our lifetime has brought untold sorrow to mankind."
- to employ international machinery for the promotion of the economic and social advancement of all peoples,"

> Bullet points of the Preamble of the Charter of United Nations.

xxxxxxxx

"London's greatest strength is our diversity"

> Sadiq Khan, Mayor of London, after an Islamic terrorist, Usman Khan, killed three U.K. citizens at London Bridge.

xxxxxxxx

"The world of tomorrow is a world of empires in which we Europeans, and you British, can only defend your interests, your way of life, by doing it together, in a European framework and in the European Union. "

> Guy Verhofstadt, MEP, trying to convince the U. K. to stay in the EU.

xxxxxxxxxxxxxxxxx

If "excessive" nationalism is the root of all evil and was the cause of two world wars as Angela Merkel and the U. N. seem to believe, it is indeed logical that *inter*nationalism might be the way to a better future.

Internationalism has had more than 75 years to prove its case, but has it? Well, let's look at the track-record of some of the most prominent international organizations and judge them by their actions rather than rhetoric.

The United Nations was created immediately after W.W.II in the belief that only a multilateral institution could guarantee world peace.

The United Nations was primarily a security institution with the task of *preventing* wars by offering a forum for talks rather than conflict, summed up in the adage that "jaw-jaw is better than war-war".

But that did not go well. In fact, the U.N. presided over of two of the worst atrocities in our time: the 1994 Rwandan genocide where the majority population of Hutus killed almost a million of its minority citizens, the Tutsis, with the U.N., though it had been amply warned, failing to intervene; and the Srebrenica massacre in July 1995, where 8.000 men and boys, Bosniaks (Bosnian Muslims) were killed by the Bosnian Serbs (Serbian Orthodox). The U.N. totally underestimated the religious components of the civil war and the massacre but should have seen it coming as the leader of the Bosnian Serbs was shown on video saying:" The time has come to take revenge on the Muslims."

The United Nations accepted the blame for having failed to protect the Bosniaks in Srebrenica, which in 1993 the UN Security Council had formally designated a "safe area. " In a critical internal review in 1999, UN Secretary-General, Kofi Annan, wrote, "Through error, misjudgment and an inability to recognize the scope of the evil confronting us, we failed to do our part to help save the people of Srebrenica from the [Bosnian] Serb campaign of mass murder. "

Inexplicably, this had no repercussions; in fact, since then, the United Nations' role has been *expanded* to include refugees, climate change, weapons, health, and even global criminal justice.

Let's take refugees first see if the U. N has done any better in terms of its stated goals of helping make the world get together and solve its problems.

The International Organization for Migration, IOM, which calls itself an U. N. organization on its website proudly displays its political philosophy:

> Migration is
>
> - Desirable
> - Inevitable
> - Necessary

You would therefore expect that woke's narrative would focus heavily on denying facts that undermine the immigrations is desirable, necessary and inevitable meme. And you would be right.

Let's take our deconstruction tools to these three arguments and see if they stand up to scrutiny.

The desirability argument first. At the core of this argument is the concept that diversity is desirable and that therefore immigration from people from all over the world is a good thing, something to be proud of as London´s Mayor says in the quote.

However, what some woke people consider desirable, f. ex. diversity is not falsifiable: it´s just an opinion.

But as opinions go, the IOM cannot reasonably be in any doubt that this opinion increasingly is one not shared by large parts of the voters in the West. The proof is in the rise of anti-immigration political parties in all EU-countries without exception. And the resistance to President Biden´s open borders policy in the U.S.

In fact, according to a recent study of European populist parties, in 31 European countries commissioned by The Guardian, populist parties have gone mainstream and more than tripled their support in Europe over the past 20 years.

Matthijs Rooduin, a political sociologist at the University of Amsterdam, who led the research project, says" Not so long ago populism was a phenomenon of the political fringes". . . " Today it has become increasingly mainstream: some of the most significant recent political developments like the Brexit referendum and the election of Donald Trump cannot be understood without taking into account the rise of populism"[133]

Pro-immigration politicians claim that immigration is the European way of life, but according to Byron Roth, the "most salient fact about the history of immigration in Europe is that prior to the mid-twentieth century, immigration was *limited* and consisted almost exclusively of people moving from one {European} country to another". In fact, throughout the 1800s Europe was a major *exporter* of people; millions of Irish, English, Italians and Germans left their homelands to settle in the United States"[134]

Byron Roth´s more important point is a psychological one, namely that woke ideology has adopted a *multicultural* philosophy on immigration that is ill suited to accommodate present day immigration from very different cultures and countries. And in doing so have ignored human *nature.* Human beings are not by their nature in favor of diversity. In fact, he says "The Us-Them dichotomy is so pervasive among hunters and gatherers, and indeed among all human groups, that it hard to deny that it is a fundamental feature of human nature. "[135]

It is a point of view shared by the left-wing Israeli historian, Benny Morris, who in a new book, co-authored with another historian, Dror Ze´evi, on the Turkish genocide of Armenians, The Thirty Year Genocide, argues that ethnically homogenous societies are more stable." When the minority wishes to defeat the majority, demographically or militarily, the liberal majority is confronted with a dilemma. They either have to jettison their liberalism or accept their defeat", he says.

---

[133] Revealed: one in four Europeans vote populist, The Guardian, Nov. 20, 2018
[134] Byron M. Roth, The Perils of Diversity, Immigration and Human Nature, p. 385
[135] Byron M. Roth, The Perils of Diversity, Immigration and Human Nature, p. 106

Not surprisingly, his stance has met a furious backlash and when asked why, he says: "Because people in Paris and London like multi-culturalism, and they say that in an ideal world we all live together in peace and harmony and so on. It may be the ideal world, it is at any rate an anti-nationalist perspective, I respect. But in the real world …..it doesn´t look like multi-culturalism works. I'm not even sure it will work in Europe. "[136]

Indeed. The working-class people, who are experiencing woke ideology´s multi-cultural experiment with mass-scale immigration will, because the new immigrants are their new neighbors, know what Roth and Morris are talking about.

So, no. Immigration isn´t desirable, per se.

But that´s not the way Woke sees it. By way of example, incoming EU-Commission President, Ursula von der Leyen, created a portfolio for" Protecting the European Way of Life" which in its mission statement called for its commissioner, to" address and allay legitimate fears and concerns about the impact of irregular migration on our economy and society.".

That created a furious backlash. Dutch social democrat and insufferably politically correct MEP, Sophie in´t Veldt in an op-ed piece in Politico Europe joined the shitstorm and rejected that our "way of life" is being threatened by people seeking asylum, or simply seeking a better life, in Europe. " Nothing could be further from the truth she said. " The real threats to our European Way of Life come from…. populists:"

"National governments within the EU's borders are chipping away at women's rights, LGTBTQ rights, freedom of the press and the independence of the judiciary. They want to replace democracy, diversity, and the rule of law with "traditional values" and "illiberal" democracy", she says.

Ms. in't Veldt forgets to note that the portfolio was about "irregular" migration, irregular being the politically correct word for illegal, and covers up her lie of omission by calling the illegal immigrants "people seeking asylum, or simply seeking a better life in Europe."

The references to "National governments" are to Poland and Hungary with whom the EU is in a bitter fight over their refusal to accept refugees under the EU´s proposed settlement scheme. As a consequence, the EU has taken Poland to the European Court of Justice over new legislation lowering the retirement age for certain judges; and the EP passed a resolution condemning Hungary for its attack on European values, i.e. its opposition to same-sex marriage and transgender ideology.

The "illiberal democracy" meme, as discussed above, stems from a speech Hungary´s PM, Victor Orban, gave a few years back in which he said that if the EU´s liberal democratic values were based on anti-family, anti-religion, same sex-marriage and the relativism of an anything-goes sexual culture, then Hungary would be proud to call itself an "illiberal" democracy.

---

[136] All quotes from The Logic of Ethnic Cleansing, Weekendavisen, June 24, 2019 translated from Danish.

Wokers, since then, have jumped on this statement, and implied that Orban was in fact a quasi-dictator, but it is a lie: no-one has put a finger on the Hungarian electoral system, though it, to their great regret has led to ever recurring elections of …Mr. Orban.

What in the world is Ms. in't Veldt smoking?

First, she lies about the kind of immigration we are talking about, namely illegal immigrants, immigrants that break the law by entering a country illegally. They're not asylum seekers, in fact they're avoiding the asylum process.

Secondly, what has national governments allegedly chipping away at women's rights and LGTBQ rights got to do with the claim that national governments "want to replace democracy, diversity and the rule of law with traditional values and illiberal democracy"?

The short answer is nothing. Democracy literally means that people choose: It is government of the people, by the people for the people. And if they choose to be skeptical about identity politics, #MeToo, or transgenderism, that is their right.

But these "rights" are the main building blocks of woke internationalism, and Ms. in't Veldt is a fully paid-up member.

Are women's rights and LGTBQ rights and diversity part of the European Way of Life.

Not really.

Same sex-marriage is a very *new* phenomenon in the culture of the West. So is the acceptance of homosexuality as an acceptable way of living out your sexuality. Diversity is a code word for immigration, and historically diversity has been considered a *risk* to the social cohesion of communities, rather than a benefit.

I am all for same-sex marriage and women's rights but don't tell me they are examples of the European Way of Life.

They are, in fact, new *deviations* from the traditional European Way of Life, which for hundreds of years has been based on family and Christianity. The traditional values that Poland and Hungary defend.

But the real kicker is that Sophie is hiding something from you. Recent immigration into the EU has overwhelmingly been coming from Muslim Middle Eastern and North African countries.

The thing she is hiding from you, is that Muslim immigrants don't integrate well. Ruud Koopmans, a Dutch professor in immigration at the Humboldt University in Berlin has studied Muslim integration in the EU for more than 20 years and is pretty unequivocal about his conclusion: there are no examples of successful Muslim integration in the EU. Zero, nada, zilch, aucun, ninguno, nul.

The reason? Religion, he says. No matter how you slice it, Islam. Even if you correct for socio-economic and demographic variables, the data show the same.

It's the same reason that the countries of origin of Muslim immigration are doing poorly. It's about conservative views on women's role in society, women not participating in the labor market, high fertility, and low investment in children's education. Furthermore, the rise of Islamic fundamentalism is a factor because immigrants carry this fundamentalist interpretation with them when they migrate. [137]

Ruud Koopmanns might have added that homosexuality is punishable by death in many fundamentalist Muslim societies and as for LGTBQ, literally, don't even go there.

Koopmanns ́research shows that 2/3 of his Muslim respondents consider religious rules as more important than the national legislations under which they are living. Read they prefer Sharia law.

About 60% could never be friends with a homosexual person, while 45% rejected friendships with a Jew. This just to anticipate Sophie in't Veldt's objection that these fundamentalist views are not mainstream in the Muslim world. Sorry, Sophie. They are.

You are lying to us. Muslim immigration into the EU is a threat to the very values that are so dear to you and that you accuse the "populists" of "chipping away at, namely tolerance of diversity, and non-mainstream sexual norms, women's rights, etc. These are, but exactly, the norms Islam does *not* respect.

It's quite absurd to listen to a female, left-of-center MEP, criticizing "populist" governments for their attacks on their narratives, i.e. women's rights, LGTBQ -rights and diversity while arguing in favor of opening the West's borders to those very forces that will do their utmost to destroy it.

And Koopmanns isn't alone.

My favorite example is the story of the woke left-wing British Labour politician credited with popularizing the word "Islamophobia, Trevor Phillips, the former head of Britain's Equalities and Human Rights Commission (EHRC), who just got expelled from his party on the grounds of being an "islamophobe" because of telling the truth about Muslim integration.

Talk about being hoist by one's own petard as Shakespeare has it. They don't come anymore woke than Trevor Phillips so what went wrong? Phillips had a change of heart, or as he says:

"For a long time, I too thought that Europe's Muslims would become like previous waves of migrants, gradually abandoning their ancestral ways, wearing their religious and cultural baggage lightly, and gradually blending into Britain's diverse identity landscape. I should have known better,". [138]

So, no. Immigration isn't desirable, per se.

---

[137] Translation from Danish of interview with Dr. Koopmanns, Weekendavisen, Jan. 2, 2019, on the basis of in his recently published book, »Het vervallen huis van de islam. Over de crisis van de islamitische wereld« (Islam's Crumbling House. About the crisis in the Islamic World)
[138] Breitbart, March.9,2020.

Apart from the difficulties of Muslims' integrating into Western society, the multi-culturalism, diversity-is-good-meme, suffers from a number of fallacies.[139]

The first fallacy is its claim that the best way to learn about the world and its culture is not to travel around the world but to encourage the world to come to you-and then stay.

The second is that the value of migrants continues to increase as their numbers increase.... but it isn't true. Every 100,000 extra Somalis, Eritreans or Pakistani who enter Europe do *not* magnify the resulting cultural enrichment 100,000 times.

The third one, is, that just as all cultures have positive things going for them, they also have negative aspects.

The Muslim culture of *protection* of women by keeping them at home, which is charitable interpretation of women's status as second-class citizens in Muslim countries, has as a flip side the lack of respect for women that don't respect Muslim norms.

The surge of rape in Sweden and the story of the Rotherham gangs of Muslim men from Pakistan and North Africa grooming often underage girls for prostitution, are cases in point. In both cases, U. K. and Swedish authorities tried to cover up the truth for fear of stirring up racial tensions, i. e. intimidation from Muslims and Muslim organizations.

And for fear of being called Islamophobes and racists.

Is it inevitable, as the IMO, claims? Nothing is inevitable, except death and taxes.

The last time we heard this kind of talk about the inevitability of certain historic events, were in the first half of the 20th century from the two main totalitarian competitors, the Nazis and their 1000 Year Reich and the Communists about the victory of the proletariat.

That didn't work then and it won't work now. It is a rhetorical trick, to make us believe, that we are powerless to change the course of history.

But we're not. It is a lie and a highly falsifiable one, because countries from Poland to Hungary, the latter by building a wall on its Southern borders, have prevented mass immigration into their countries. As has Israel. As has Australia. And Donald Trump was working on it.

Is immigration necessary?

This is an area where factual claims and counter claims are flying. This is where your analytical tools will be indispensable.

There are two main arguments that the pro-immigration crowd in the EU deploys: changing demographics means Europe is getting older, so we need immigrants to take up the slack, or economic decline will set in; and immigrants are a net benefit to the host countries. Both are falsifiable:

---

[139] cp. as Douglas Murray points out in his book, The Strange Death of Europe.

The pro-immigration crowd argues that demographic patterns are changing. Which is true: It is a fact that Europe's population is getting older and declining.

But it is not a fact that *therefore* more immigration is necessary as the U. N. argues. Immigrants get old too and their birth rates, as happens in all societies in the world, will decline as their prosperity increases.

The real problem is declining birth rates in Europe. The reason they are declining: economic insecurity. More women especially in Southern Europe feel they have to forego having more children than 1 or max 2, because having more children will be a financial burden on the family. The problem is that the so-called replacement ratio, where we replace those dying with new generations is 2. 1 child per couple.

Reversing this pattern is a matter of political choice, and new mass immigration is the preferred solution of woke ideology.

But that is obviously just postponing the problem. It's a pyramid scheme. Think about it: Woke wants us to import large numbers of young immigrants, to solve our "graying" problem. But *they* get "grey" as well, and then we will have to import ever larger numbers of immigrants in order to keep the welfare we-and they-have come to expect.

Therefore, if Europe wants to reverse its population decline *without* increasing migration it will need to lift birth rates. The obvious one is tackling the problem at its roots: give incentives to women for having more kids.

Hungary is the latest to adopt radical measures to try to tackle the problem. The alleged "populist" Prime Minister, Viktor Orban, has declared fertility clinics to be a strategic sector. Young families are already offered a loan that they do not need to pay back if they have a third child. Women who have four children will be exempt from income taxes for life.

Poland's conservative Law and Justice government introduced payments to encourage larger families. Its Family 500+ program hands out 500 zloty (€118) a month to low income families for their first child and to every family for subsequent children.

Woke hates this. It wants *the State* to run the show, so it throws in the feminist argument: when forced to choose between raising children or having a career, women have traditionally opted to work…and therefore the most successful measures are for *the State* to take over child-rearing to make life easier for working mothers: more kindergartens, creches, etc. Essentially women paying *other* women to raise their kids. [140]

To back up this policy choice, it argues that Europe's highest fertility rates are in secularist places, like France, thanks to its generous welfare spending and cheap childcare. Or Sweden which comes in second, also thanks to generous family policies as well as encouragement for men to do more childcare. Successive *governments* have successfully provided crèches rather than the government-owned fertility clinics Mr. Orban wants in Hungary, Woke says.

---

[140] FT editorial, How best to boost Europe's birth rates. Working mothers need government support, not traditional values, Jan.13,2020.

Boy, those woke elites really hate that guy, so let us take the falsification tool to their argument, meaning that if parts of their arguments can be proven to be false the whole argument is untrue. If someone says <u>*all swans are white*</u> and you know that someone somewhere demonstrably has seen a black swan, that statement is false.

Firstly, these two exemplary countries only enjoy the relatively highest fertility rates because of the massive influx of *Muslim* immigrants from the Middle East and North Africa, who traditionally favor large families, into both countries.

Secondly, the pro-state intervention crowd omits to mention that the fertility rates of France and Sweden are *still* substantially below the replacement ratio of 2. 1 child per couple: France had the highest total fertility rate, in 2017 among EU countries at 1. 90, followed by Sweden (1. 78), Ireland (1. 77), Denmark (1. 77), the UK (1. 74) and Romania (1. 71). [141]

So, the demographic argument won´t work: importing huge numbers of immigrants from North Africa and the Middle East will cause huge social problems due to our cultural differences, huge political problems because normal people won´t accept new waves of immigrants; and it won´t work because immigrants get old, too, and less fertile as they benefit from increasing prosperity.

The second part of the immigrants-are -necessary- argument, claims immigrants are a net benefit to their host countries.

This, although it is a highly falsifiable argument, is probably the one area where Woke has lied to us the most.

It works like this: Governments commission a report on the net effects of immigration and comes up with a conclusion which the media then runs with, that immigrants are a net benefit to the economy or at worst net neutral.

How can it be true that an immigrant family arriving in its adopted home country is a net benefit to that country without ever having paid into that country´s welfare system *before,* while enjoying the benefits of the welfare states such as free schooling, health care, etc, from day one?

As Murray says," Because such things are so obvious it requires a concerted effort to pretend they are untrue ". How does woke do it then?

Easy! They conflate *high-skilled* immigration from the non-EU countries in Europe, from other parts of the West and the richest Asian countries with the mass *low skilled* immigration from the poorer parts of the Middle East and North Africa.

To give a couple of examples: a 2013 study from the University College of London concluded that "far from being a "drain" on the system, the financial contribution of "recent immigrants" to the country had instead been remarkably strong"[142]

---

[141] Eurostat (March 2019), "Fertility Statistics"
[142] Murray, The Strange Death of Europe, p. 40

"But the study had performed the usual sleight of hand", says Murray. " It had presented the best and least culturally strange immigrants {from the EEA, the European Economic Area}, as in fact being typical immigrants". When he delved into the study, he found that non-EEA migrants during the study's reference period had actually taken around 95 billion pounds *more* in services than they had paid in taxes.[143]

A recent French parliamentary report has suggested that mass migration into France does not actually help boost the economy, as frequently claimed, but is only net neutral. (Breitbart, Jan. 26, 2020)

But the OECD recently stated that Mass Migration Costs France 10 billion Euros a Year.

Both cannot be true. Somebody's lying to us and we know it's not the OECD, who has no political reason to deny the facts.

Denmark publishes stats broken down into categories of immigrants and these stats confirm what Murray claims: only by conflating migrants from the West and from non-Muslim nations like China and India can the woke arrive at such deception: for 2015, Syrians, Somalis, and Iraqis together with Pakistanis were the heaviest burden on the Danish state budget. Syrians cost 3. 9 billion DKK, 224. 000(Euros 29.000) per person. Somalis, 1. 8 billion, 158. 000(Euros 20.500) per person, etc.[144]

So, Woke lies to us about the cultural and social impact of immigration, and it lies to us about the cost of immigration.

Nowhere more blatantly than in the UN itself.

On refugees, the UN has become the world's number one promoter of Open Borders, touting the benefits of immigration-legal and illegal. Through its Global Compact on Immigration, adopted over the protests of the U.S. and many EU-countries in December 2018, it has effectively erased the distinction between political refugees, whom countries under international rules must accept, and economic migrants-whom they must not.

In the process it makes absolutely no bones about its political advocacy on an issue that splits voters in the US and the EU (which is where the economic migrants want to go) down the middle and perhaps more than anything undermines social cohesion and agreement in the West.

Hungary's foreign minister, Péter Szijjártó, crystallized the criticisms of the UN Migration Pact by calling it an attempt to "legalize illegal immigration".

The UN in its response maintained somewhat feebly that the document was non-binding.

To which the Hungarian sarcastically retorted that "in view of the fact that the document contains the word 'obligation' on eighty occasions, the claim that it only includes recommendations is a false one. A legally not binding document would not prescribe the

---

[143] Murray, op. cit. p. 42
[144] Danish Ministry of Finance, www.fm.dk

establishment of national action plans, and accordingly it is 'clearer than day' that, just like the originally voluntary mandatory quota, the Global Compact for Migration will become a point of reference, mandatory, and the basis for international judicial decisions,"[145]

Indeed. The non-binding issue was a lie and a red herring as the EU-Commission's own Legal Service confirmed in a leaked memo two months after the adoption of the Compact, in February,2019.

Why weren't we told this *before* the formal adoption of the UN Compact? Why was the EU-Commission withholding crucial legal information as to the real scope of the Compact, to the extent that someone felt compelled to actually leak the memo? It doesn't take much brainwork to see why: the memo was damaging because it undercut the U. N's main argument that the Compact was really just a paper-exercise of a non-binding nature.

What did the memo say? It stated clearly that while the Global Compact might or might not be binding for *other* countries, EU-countries were bound to implement its provisions under the EU-Treaty.

So how did the EU political class respond to that fairly damning memo? By another lie, claiming that the EU's Legal Service memo was just the Legal Service's opinion and not that of the whole EU-Commission. Absolutely untrue. The Legal Service is the main arbiter within the EU-Commission of what the EU-Treaties mean and what they stand for. My father, who worked for the EU for 33 years, is very clear: The Legal Service's opinion is an order, not an option. When the Legal Service says the Compact 's binding for EU countries, it's binding for EU-countries.

The only institution that can overturn that legal memo is the European Court of Justice. And we haven't heard from them, have we?

But the Hungarians weren't the only ones to smell a rat. Dutch MEP and Co-President of the Europe of Nations and Freedom (ENF) group, Marcel de Graaff, in a similar vein has called the compact "a legalization of mass migration," by declaring migration" a human right", which it manifestly does.

Adding insult to injury, legal analysts warned that the document could be used as a basis for making criticism of mass migration illegal, since one basic element of the new agreement was the extension of the definition of hate speech. There is therefore a real danger of criticism of migration becoming a criminal offence and that media outlets that give room to criticism of migration can be shut down.

Like it? The U. N obviously has its own agenda which is to be the promoter of any issue that is global in nature and therefore, most logically, should be dealt with by the one international body whose reach and jurisdiction is global.... namely itself.

And those of us who are asking the question of whom we hold responsible for this dangerous nonsense, are left without answers. We know German diplomats were behind the initiative, but we are powerless to hold anyone accountable, except of course our national politicians, who run

---

[145] Breitbart October 16, 2018

for cover behind the now obvious lie that the Compact is non-binding and that the "international community" wants it adopted.

Next time someone accuses you of harboring irrational fears of mass-immigration, tell them the story of the UN Global Compact on Immigration.

But it gets worse: In 1946, the UN *Commission* on Human Rights assembled for its first meeting. Its principal objective: after the atrocities of the Nazi regime was to reaffirm the principle of human dignity, and guarantee fundamental freedoms for all, or in the bureaucratese language of the UN, " to weave the international legal fabric that protects our fundamental rights and freedoms and to allow it to respond to the whole range of human rights problems…including setting the standards to govern the conduct of States…. and acting as a forum where countries large and small, non-governmental groups and human rights defenders from around the world voiced their concerns. "[146]

Wait a minute! Aren´t we talking about the UN´s Human Rights *Council*?

Well, yes, but the problem is things didn´t exactly turn out as planned, so the UN decided to change its name. What happened? Well, according to UN Watch, a Geneva-based non-governmental organization whose stated mission is "to monitor the performance of the United Nations by the yardstick of its own Charter", …" things turned ugly. Dictatorships hijacked the Council. In 2003, they elected the murderous regime of Libya's Muammar Qaddafi as chair.

This final straw prompted UN Secretary-General Annan to call for scrapping the Council, which he said was plagued with "politicization", "selectivity", and a "credibility deficit"—all of which "cast a shadow on the reputation of the United Nations system as a whole. "[147]

So, what is an international organization to do when things "turn ugly"? Change its name, of course, and that´s how the Human Rights *Commission* became the Human Right *Council*. Like it?

Did it change its behavior? Eh, not really.

Consider its record in responding to gross violations. Over 50 sessions, only 14 of 193 countries have been condemned, less than what even the discredited Commission accomplished.

The majority of abusers enjoy impunity. In China, 1.3 billion people are denied freedoms of speech, assembly, and religion. Tibetans are tortured, Muslim Uighurs put in re-education camps. The Council's response? Silence. But, in violation of the criteria guaranteed in the Council's 2006 charter, China was elected as a member.

In Russia, dissidents are harassed, arrested, even assassinated. Vladimir Putin's regime launches bloody wars, invading Ukraine and swallowing up Crimea. The Council's response? Silence.

---

[146] UN Human Rights Council, www.ohchr.org
[147] Jerusalem Post, May 16, 2016

In Saudi Arabia, women are subjugated, and beheadings are at an all-time high. The Council's response? Silence. A recent attempt to investigate Saudi Arabia's carpet bombing of Yemeni civilians was quashed. Saudi Arabia, too, was elected a member.

So, what did the HRC do to defend the principles of its own Charter? Absolutely nothing. On the contrary: the UN elected every single one of the above abusers as a Council member. With more than 50% non-democracies, the Council's membership is the worst ever.[148]

How do you explain that a body whose mandate is to advance human rights worldwide would count among its members Saudi Arabia, China, Egypt, Democratic Republic of the Congo, Cuba, Bahrain, Eritrea, and Somalia?

According to Freedom House "Some of these states are leading authoritarian regimes that have set out to eviscerate political opposition and crush all dissent at home while subverting democracy beyond their borders, including by taking aim at multilateral institutions. All eight feature systematic violations of fundamental rights whose perpetrators enjoy domestic impunity and far too little international accountability."[149]

But there is one place where the Council is very active: Israel.

In fact, it has adopted almost as many resolutions condemning Israel, (45, 9%) as for the rest of the world combined.

Speaking of Israel, the Human Rights Council is not the only international organization singling it out for special criticism: The WHO, The World´s Health Organization is joining the crowd.

In May, 2019, at its annual assembly, it voted for a UN resolution, co-sponsored by the Arab group of states and the *Palestinian delegation*, that singled out Israel as the only violator of "mental, physical and environmental health, " and commissioned a WHO delegation to investigate and report on "the health conditions in the occupied Palestinian territory" and in "the occupied Syrian Golan, " and to place it on the agenda again at next year's meeting.

Out of 24 items on the meeting's agenda, only Item No. 19 against Israel, focused on a specific country.

"The UN reached new heights of absurdity today, " said UN Watch executive director Hillel Neuer, "by enacting a resolution which accuses Israel of violating the health rights of Syrians in the Golan, even as in reality Israeli hospitals continue their life-saving treatment for Syrians fleeing to the Golan from the Assad regime's barbaric attacks."[150]

Wow! Israel, must be a real bad ass when it comes to human rights, to be singled out like that, so perhaps it is a good time for you to ask: compared to whom?

---

[148] UN Watch, www.unwatch.org
[149] Freedom House, With New Members, the UN Human Rights Council Goes from Bad to Worse, November 19, 2018
[150] UN Watch, May 25, 2019

The answer is, of course, that Israel, though it has its problems and is certainly not perfect, is doing all right, thank you very much: the 2013 Freedom in the World annual survey and a report by US-based Freedom House, which attempts to measure the degree of democracy and political freedom in every nation, ranked Israel along with Tunisia as the Middle East and North Africa's *only* free countries.

Which leads to the conclusion that there must be another reason why Israel is being singled out, and that we are being lied to about what is the truth is.

I will give you a couple of hints, though: Did you notice that the Palestinian Authority was behind the attacks on Israel. I emphasized hoping you'd notice.

That Arab states which are political enemies of Israel, support the PA is unsurprising.

But why would the EU back such a resolution. The answer is that we know that woke ideology is consumed with viewing the world through the prism of oppressed and oppressor.

So, sorry, no prizes for guessing who the woke ideology thinks is the villain and who the victim in the Israeli-Palestinian conflict.

Furthermore, the politicization of our international bodies, like WHO, is not just a harmless game of politics.

During the Coronavirus pandemic, China, rightly, came in for a lot of international criticism for muffling Chinese doctors who warned against the human-to-humans transmission of the virus and being slow in transmitting this information to the international community.

But what did the WHO do which after all has a platform for sharing this kind of information among international health authorities, called The International Health Regulations (IHR), a framework for exchange of epidemic prevention and response data between 196 countries?

It is a legitimate question since Taiwan reported the danger of person-to-person transmission to IHR on December 31,2019. Where did their info come from? Chinese colleagues in China.

Only, the WHO never put up this information on the IHR.

Taiwanese government officials told the Financial Times the warning was not shared with other countries. "While the IHR's internal website provides a platform for all countries to share information on the epidemic and their response, none of the information shared by our country's [Centers for Disease Control] is being put up there," said Chen Chien-jen, Taiwan's vice-president.[151]

Why? As FT puts it, "Taiwan is excluded from the WHO because China, which claims it as part of its territory, demands that third countries and international bodies do not treat it in any way that resembles how independent states are treated. The WHO's relationship with China has been criticized in the past, with some accusing the organization of overly praising Beijing's handling of the coronavirus outbreak despite allegations local officials had initially covered it up."

---

[151] FT, March 20,2020.

As if further proof of the shenanigans of our international organizations was needed, a tweet from the World Health Organization, January 14,2020,said : "Preliminary investigations conducted by the Chinese authorities have found *no clear evidence* of human-to-human transmission of the novel #coronavirus (2019-nCoV) identified in Wuhan, China."

This happened in spite of the fact that WHO *knew* that Chinese doctors had known since late December that the virus could spread from human to human. And knew that on January 3, China arrested eight people for "publishing or forwarding false information on the internet without verification and subsequently had issued a warning that anyone caught using social media to share coronavirus information obtained from anywhere but state-run media or organizations would face between three and seven years in jail."

WHO, unbelievably, *continued* the cover-up of Chinese misconduct with another tweet on January 23,2020,: "For the moment, WHO does not recommend any broader restrictions on travel or trade. We recommend exit screening at airports as part of a comprehensive set of containment measures." Obviously, considering how many carriers were asymptomatic, this amounted to recommending contagious people be allowed to travel across borders.[152]

Well, I hear you say, that's just a couple of international committees gone rogue.

OK, how about this, then. Iran, the world's premier state sponsor of terrorism, debuted a five-day exhibit on its "human rights achievements" at the United Nations last fall.

"The promotion of human rights [is] the Islamic Revolution's raison d'être, " declared Iran's foreign ministry in a statement, highlighting a five-day exhibition of slides and posters celebrating its "human rights achievements" at the United Nations (UN) Office in Geneva, Switzerland.

According to Amnesty International, Iran arrested over 7, 000 dissidents in 2018, killing at least 28 of them. Death-row inmates in Iran have their organs harvested "voluntarily" before or after execution. In April, Iran sentenced an award-winning female human rights lawyer to 148 lashes and 38 years of imprisonment for defending Muslim women's prerogative to remove the Islamic Republic's mandatory hijab in public.[153]

I could go on, but I think you get my drift: woke ideology's One World international organizations are not only *not* living up to their professed visions and purposes. They are taking us for a ride we never wanted. And they get away with it because we can't hold them democratically accountable because they are unelected.

As if that isn't bad enough in terms of the psychological frustration of the voters finding no outlet for justified democratic outrage, Russia's attack on Ukraine in the spring of 2022 has been the final nail in the coffin of the post WWII Woke internationalist system: the U.N.'s Security Council, the supreme arbiter of international law and order has been shown to be impotent ,because it is one of its own veto-wielding powers, Russia, which committed the crime.

---

[152] National Review, March21,2020
[153] Breitbart, Nov. 24, 2019

And Russia is blocking any U.N. attempt to intervene in the crisis.

Part III: Woke´s Long March Through the Institutions

Chapter 4: Woke´s One World Internationalism: the UN and Climate Change Panic

xxxxxxxxxxxxxxxxxxxxxxxxxxxxxxxxxxxxxxxxxxxxxx

"Adults keep saying we owe it to the young people, to give them hope, But I don't want your hope. I don't want you to be hopeful. *I want you to panic.* I want you to feel the fear I feel every day. I want you to act. I want you to act as you would in a crisis. I want you to act as if the house is on fire, because it is. "
   Greta Thunberg, 2019.

xxxxxxx

Extinction Rebellion slogan: It´s Not About Climate Change-It´s About Systems Change.
   From a slogan an XR demonstrator was carrying on TV

xxxxxxx

Albert Gore, former US President, Bill Clinton´s vice-president famously said when asked how to teach people the seriousness of climate change: **"We need to create** *fear*".

   From Factualism by Hans Rosling[154]

xxxxxxxx

"The United Nations may resort to *military action* against states that defy its mandates on global climate action"

   Ole Wæver, international relations professor at the University of Copenhagen, ABC Australia News, Breitbart, 3 December, 2019.

xxxxxxxx
- The United Nations has blamed human-induced climate change for mass migration: "Climate change means extreme weather events are happening more often and with greater force. Rising sea levels, drought, floods, wildfires, and other natural hazards are forcing people to flee their homes, "
"Most are displaced inside their own countries, but people may also cross borders to find safety".

---

[154] Hans Rosling, Factualism, p. 229

UNHCR Video: "Climate change and displacement-how are they linked?", COP 15, Madrid, Breitbart, 3 December 2019.

xxxxxxxx

- "For years, several versions of climate change denial were in circulation. Today, luckily only *a handful of fanatics* deny the evidence," ..."No one can escape this challenge by themselves. There is no wall that can protect any country, regardless of how powerful it is. ".

Pedro Sanchez, Spanish socialist interim Prime minister, COP15, Madrid, 2 December 2019.

xxxxxxxxxx

The Swedish author Astrid Lindgren in the 1930s wrote some of the most successful and long-lived children´s stories ever known. Her most endearing character was Pippi Långstrump (Pippi Longstocking) a little befreckled girl with pig tails, supernatural physical powers and a way of setting adults straight if they needed to be taught a lesson or two.

Almost a hundred years later Pippi´s reincarnation this time in the flesh, a little Swedish teen-age girl with pigtails and supernatural powers, Greta Thunberg, is at it again. She has been speaking about climate change in such august and venerated institutions as the French National Assembly and the General Assembly of the United Nations and her message to us is clear: "Shame on you" ;"Do better", " Stop climate change", "Do something" or the name of your generation will live in infamy.

Greta "Pippi" Thunberg was even nominated for the Nobel Peace Prize. And why not? Former US President, Barack Obama, was awarded the Nobel Peace Prize *before* he had hardly set foot in the Oval Office and before having put his signature on any official legislation. Why? In recognition of his being the first *black* man to hold US presidential office, although strictly speaking that was to his parent´s credit and none of his own doing; and, of course, because of his flowery oratory about his *intentions* of bringing about harmony and peace.

Greta is likewise hailed for representing rather than *being* something: a cute teenage girl who courageously sets the adults straight. Like Pippi Langstrump it is, of course, pure fiction. Anyone with a head on their shoulders or with teen-age children ,will know that the child is obviously being used by some activist *adults* in a blatantly political act to scold other adults of a different persuasion. But the media fawn over her and nobody double fact-checked her father, Svante, when he denied scripting his little girl´s statements. We now know the truth: he was lying through his teeth.

A recent bad code update on Facebook allowed anyone to see which accounts posted Facebook Pages, including those of celebrities and politicians. Among the pages exposed by the bug was Greta Thunberg, whose posts are mostly authored by her father Svante Thunberg.[155]

Woke ideology´s strategy is clear from the quotes above: instill fear and claim that the science behind the fear is *undisputed* except by a "handful of fanatics".

---

[155] Breitbart Jan. 14, 2020

Fear has been used since man's first day on earth to gain control of people's minds and…money. Think Catholic Church and the four horsemen of the apocalypse, think Dante's Inferno.

But you have got to hand it to them: Gore and Greta have succeeded beyond anyone's wildest beliefs in making us panic.

The European Parliament on one of its first days in office declared a climate "emergency" and vowed to increase the EU's CO2 emissions reduction target from 40 percent to 50 percent by 2030. That's in 7 years, my friends. At a staggering cost in money and jobs lost.

By way of example, a German Government report estimates that "More than 400, 000 jobs could be lost in Germany over the next decade as its auto industry shifts towards electric vehicles… In a worst-case scenario, Germany's workforce could shrink by almost 1 per cent by 2030 if carmakers such as Volkswagen and Daimler are forced to rely on *imports* to meet targets for electric vehicle sales. The vast majority of vehicle batteries — the most valuable component of electric cars — are manufactured in Asia."[156]

And those *imports* just got more expensive. For the EU Commission, not to be outdone has drawn up a New European Green Deal which includes new carbon *taxes* on *imports* from countries that are deemed to have failed in meeting their international climate commitments. By way of example, Indonesia, a very poor country, is seeing the EU reducing its import of palm oil - its main export- from this country because the palm olive plantations are considered to be emitting too much CO2.

Brazil's former President, Jair Bolsonaro, has called the EU's New Green Deal colonialist and a way for the EU to force its standards on everyone else. Indeed. And Indonesia has lodged an official complaint against the EU with the World Trade Organization, which adjudicates international trade conflicts.

Germany's new budget plans to help the country meet the EU's ambitious new CO2 emission goals and avoid fines from the EU, recently resulted in massive protests by German farmers who with their tractors blocked all access roads to Berlin.

Are voters going to take all this pain lying down, once the real cost of this climate change hysteria settles in?

Common sense would argue no.

Aren't the successes of Donald Trump and Brexit and the "populist movements that have destabilized Europe's ancient regimes "rooted in a perception, more than half-true, that those near the bottom of the pile were burdened with bailing out the elites responsible for the financial crisis. The left-behinds rather than the bankers bore the brunt of austerity" as the Financial Times argues?

Wouldn't the fact that the elites' obsession with cutting carbon emissions will hit normal people the most mean that such radical policies are less likely to be adopted because those who need to drive to work in the ancient, gas-guzzling cars that spew out the most carbon, who live in households least likely to have decent insulation or do not have the cash to replace fossil fuel boilers mean that voters, once they realize the personal cost of climate change, would vote for climate change *critics* in increasing numbers?

---

[156] Financial Times, Jan. 13, 2020

That would seem a reasonable assumption, given that these are the voters to whom Trump is speaking and the same ones who have fueled the rise of populist parties across Europe. Most often they live in small towns and villages beyond the big cities where sustainability has become a fashion statement. If anyone doubts their anger, they need only look at the gilets jaunes in France, whose year of protest against Emmanuel Macron began with an increase in fuel taxes.[157]

But so far, the opposite is the case: Green Parties from Bilboa to Berlin are riding high in the polls, not least virtually sweeping up almost all of the votes of young people between 18-24 years of age. The voters, especially the young ones, it would seem, are in a panic.

The problem is that panic is a neurological brain reaction meant to help humans decide how to escape imminent mortal danger. It offers two escape routes: fight or flight.

In the case of climate change woke ideology has chosen both: fight *and* flight. Flight by leaving science, i. e. common sense behind; and fight by choosing as its solution the solution that is going to be the costliest of all: exclusively targeting *man-made* CO_2 emissions.

I call it the hair-shirt solution. A hair shirt is a shirt made of rough uncomfortable cloth which some religious people used to wear to punish themselves. By saying that someone is wearing a hair shirt, you mean that they are trying to punish themselves to show they are sorry for something they have done. That's the "solution" woke ideology has chosen.

Let's take the *fight* scenario: the UN in 1988 set up an International Panel on Climate Change (IPCC) which since then has been the driver of the goal of reducing man-made CO_2 emissions or getting to net zero as it says.

It's worth taking a closer look at this United Nations body which has acquired tremendous and largely uncontrolled power.

How can groups of scientists collaborating on scientific reports get such power? Well, they are not the *prime c*ulprits, although, as I explain below, some have engaged in dodgy practices. But it's the UN *bureaucracy* behind the climate reports that uses its power of final conclusions and summaries that has grabbed that power. Let me explain.

IPCC since 1990 have published climate forecasts, or projections. Most if not all of them have been proven wrong or exaggerated. Everybody makes mistakes but when it happens with this degree of frequency, a bit of skepticism is in order. Furthermore, we know that the IPCC sometimes does *intentionally* mislead. One example out of many: glaciers. In 2010, one report author admitted that the claim that Himalayan glaciers would be melted by 2035 was included purely "to put political pressure on world leaders, "and was not properly vetted.[158]

The IPCC itself attributes varying degrees of probability to its forecasts often with reference to "the consensus of the scientific community". As we shall see below this "consensus" is somewhat contrived but suffice it to say that "scientific" consensus is not a reliable metric and has often been proved wrong including well after the Catholic Church had the sun circling the Earth rather than the other way around. And threatened anyone, including Galileo, who dared question the "consensus of the scientific community" with extinction. Not to mention the "science" of Covid-19 lockdowns and mask mandates.

---

[157] Financial Times, Climate change How populism will heat up the climate fight, Jan. 23, 2020
[158] Issues and Insights, Nov. 15, 2019

Furthermore, the UN is misdirecting: science is not something you vote on. It is not opinion-based but fact- based.

Worse, the IPCC deliberately has led people to believe that IPCC studies include *all* causes of climate change when in fact, they only seriously look at one: *man-made* CO_2 emission changes. They get away with it because almost no one actually reads the underlying science reports because they are too complicated and scientific.

But they *do* read the Summary for Policymakers (SPM). Only the SPMs are not written by scientists but by UN bureaucrats and government representatives who also have to approve them. The SPM is consequently a highly *political* document. Why? Tim Ball, former climatology professor at the University of Winnipeg, explains:

"What is systematically *omitted* from the Summary for Policymakers are precisely the uncertainties and positive counter evidence that might *negate the human interference theory*. Instead of assessing these objections, the Summary confidently asserts just those findings that support its case. In short, this is *advocacy,* not assessment"[159]

In other words, the government and UN bureaucrats have *already* decided the conclusions of the IPCC reports, now their job is just to find the facts that support their case.

That´s not just unscientific; that´s dishonesty on an industrial scale.

So, what does the IPCC do when the facts and intervening new scientific discoveries negate their forecasts as has happened multiple times since IPCC started publishing its reports in 1990?

It covers up.

The IPCC in its reports stipulates that they are "Subject to correction, copy-editing, layout and trickleback". As the abovementioned Tim Ball points out, trickleback begins with "trick" and the "trick" is to adjust the underlying science report to ensure that it is in conformity with the Summary. Only, no one reads the science reports nor the trickleback reports which often arrive long-time after the IPCC report. And no science journalist who has *already* commented on the main conclusions of the report has the time or inclination to go back and tell his readers that, er…, please, disregard the nonsense I wrote 2 years ago.

But is that a real problem, I hear you say? Do climate scientists get it wrong that often? How would you react if I were to say that not a single one of the 41 climate change predictions going back to the 1970s mentioned below, have come true?

LIST OF DOOMSDAY PREDICTIONS THE CLIMATE ALARMIST GOT WRONG

1. 1967: Dire Famine Forecast By 1975
2. 1969: Everyone Will Disappear In a Cloud Of Blue Steam By 1989 (1969)
3. 1970: Ice Age By 2000
4. 1970: America Subject to Water Rationing By 1974 and Food Rationing By 1980
5. 1971: New Ice Age Coming By 2020 or 2030
6. 1972: New Ice Age By 2070
7. 1974: Space Satellites Show New Ice Age Coming Fast
8. 1974: Another Ice Age?

---

[159] Washington Times, Why UN climate report cannot be trusted, Oct. 15, 2019

9. 1974: Ozone Depletion a 'Great Peril to Life
10. 1976: Scientific Consensus Planet Cooling, Famines imminent
11. 1980: Acid Rain Kills Life In Lakes
12. 1978: No End in Sight to 30-Year Cooling Trend
13. 1988: Regional Droughts (that never happened) in 1990s
14. 1988: Temperatures in DC Will Hit Record Highs
15. 1988: Maldive Islands will Be Underwater by 2018 (they're not)
16. 1989: Rising Sea Levels Will Obliterate Nations if Nothing Done by 2000
17. 1989: New York City's West Side Highway Underwater by 2019 (it's not)
18. 2000: Children Won't Know What Snow Is
19. 2002: Famine In 10 Years If We Don't Give Up Eating Fish, Meat, and Dairy
20. 2004: Britain will Be Siberia by 2024
21. 2008: Arctic will Be Ice Free by 2018
22. 2008: Climate Genius Al Gore Predicts Ice-Free Arctic by 2013
23. 2009: Climate Genius Prince Charles Says we Have 96 Months to Save World
24. 2009: UK Prime Minister Says 50 Days to 'Save The Planet from Catastrophe'
25. 2009: Climate Genius Al Gore Moves 2013 Prediction of Ice-Free Arctic to 2014
26. 2013: Arctic Ice-Free by 2015
27. 2014: Only 500 Days Before 'Climate Chaos'
28. 1968: Overpopulation Will Spread Worldwide
29. 1970: World Will Use Up All its Natural Resources
30. 1966: Oil Gone in Ten Years
31. 1972: Oil Depleted in 20 Years
32. 1977: Department of Energy Says Oil Will Peak in 90s
33. 1980: Peak Oil In 2000
34. 1996: Peak Oil in 2020
35. 2002: Peak Oil in 2010
36. 2006: Super Hurricanes!
37. 2005: Manhattan Underwater by 2015
38. 1970: Urban Citizens Will Require Gas Masks by 1985
39. 1970: Nitrogen buildup Will Make All Land Unusable
40. 1970: Decaying Pollution Will Kill all the Fish
41. 41. 1970s: Killer Bees!

To put it mildly, there is a long history of eco-pessimism, and a nerd on the internet has put together some of the main Media headlines since 1968. It is called: Wrong Again: 50 Years of Failed Eco-apocalyptic predictions. Read them and weep.

Acid Rain Kills Life In Lakes

SPRINGFIELD, Va. (UPI) — Acid rain, which has already wiped out the fish in 107 of New York's Adirondack Mountain lakes, is rapidly killing other lakes in nearby eastern Canada, says a Canadian official.

Raymond Robinson, deputy minister in Canada's environmental agency, told the first interstate summit conference on acid rain Tuesday his country is determined to fight the spreading problem.

"We're simply not prepared to contemplate leaving the generations of the next century with tens of thousands or hundreds of thousands of sterile lakes," he said. "As a practical matter, in Canada, there's no question acid rain is a front page concern."

Robinson was a key speaker at the two-day acid rain meeting, sponsored by the U.S. Environmental Protection Agency. The meeting attracted 200 representatives from a score of Eastern states, government, industry and environmental and civic groups.

Douglas Costle, EPA administrator, said in an opening address the object of the meeting was to reach mutual understanding on the cause and effects of acid rain and to open debate on possible solutions.

"I look at this conference as a first step for building substantial agreement between the states on the seriousness of the problem and the kinds of near-term and long-term remedial actions that are appropriate," said Costle.

Although the acid rain phenomenon respects no political boundaries, Costle believes the main culprits in the United States are old coal-burning electric power plants that lack newly legislated anti-pollution safeguards.

In Canada, where half the acid rain pollution wafts in from the United States, the pollution source seems to be heavy industry and non-feric metal smelters, said Robinson.

The Salt Lake Tribune (Salt Lake City, Utah) · 17 Nov 1967, Fri · Page 9

'Already Too Late'

Dire Famine Forecast by '75

By George Getze
Los Angeles Times Writer

LOS ANGELES — It is already too late for the world to avoid a long period of famine, a Stanford University biologist said Thursday.

Paul Ehrlich said the "time of famines" is upon us and will be at its worst and most disastrous by 1975.

He said the population of the United States is already too big, that birth control may have to be accomplished by making it involuntary and by putting sterilizing agents into staple foods and drinking water, and that the Roman Catholic Church should be pressured into going along with routine measures of population control.

Ehrlich said experts keep saying the world food supply will have to be tripled to feed the six or seven billion people they expect to be living in the year 2000.

"That may be possible theoretically but it is clear that it is totally impossible in practice," he said.

Ehrlich spoke at a science symposium at the University of Texas. The text of his speech was made available here.

Since, in Ehrlich's opinion, it is of no longer any use trying to avoid the coming world famines, the best thing to do now is to look past the "time of famines" and hope to have a second chance to control world population sometime in the future.

"At the moment it is shockingly apparent that the battle to feed humanity will end in a rout," Ehrlich said.

He said we have to hope that the world famines of the next 20 years will not lead to thermonuclear war and the extinction of the human species.

"We must assume man will get another chance, no matter how little he deserves one," he said.

Rising seas could obliterate nations: U.N. officials

UNITED NATIONS (AP) — A senior U.N. environmental official says entire nations could be wiped off the face of the Earth by rising sea levels if the global warming trend is not reversed by the year 2000.

Coastal flooding and crop failures would create an exodus of "eco-refugees," threatening political chaos, said Noel Brown, director of the New York office of the U.N. Environment Program, or UNEP.

He said governments have a 10-year window of opportunity to solve the greenhouse effect before it goes beyond human control.

As the warming melts polar icecaps, ocean levels will rise by up to three feet, enough to cover the Maldives and other flat island nations, Brown told The Associated Press in an interview on Wednesday.

Coastal regions will be inundated; one-sixth of Bangladesh could be flooded, displacing a fourth of its 90 million people. A fifth of Egypt's arable land in the Nile Delta would be flooded, cutting off its food supply, according to a joint UNEP and U.S. Environmental Protection Agency study.

"Ecological refugees will become a major concern, and what's worse is you may find that people can move to drier ground, but the soils and the natural resources may not support life. Africa doesn't have to worry about land, but would you want to live in the Sahara?" he said.

UNEP estimates it would cost the United States at least $100 billion to protect its east coast alone.

Shifting climate patterns would bring back 1930s Dust Bowl conditions to Canadian and U.S. wheatlands, while the Soviet Union could reap bumper crops if it adapts its agriculture in time, according to a study by UNEP and the International Institute for Applied Systems Analysis.

Excess carbon dioxide is pouring into the atmosphere because of humanity's use of fossil fuels and burning of rain forests, the study says. The atmosphere is retaining more heat than it radiates, much like a greenhouse.

The most conservative scientific estimate is that the Earth's temperature will rise 1 to 7 degrees in the next 30 years, said Brown.

The difference may seem slight, he said, but the planet is only 9 degrees warmer now than during the 8,000-year Ice Age that ended 10,000 years ago.

Brown said if the warming trend continues, "the question is will we be able to reverse the process in time? We say that within the next 10 years, given the present loads that the atmosphere has to bear, we have an opportunity to start the stabilizing process."

He said even the most conservative scientists "already tell us there's nothing we can do now to stop a ... change" of about 3 degrees.

"Anything beyond that, and we have to start thinking about the significant rise of the sea levels ... we can expect more ferocious storms, hurricanes, wind shear, dust erosion."

He said there is time to act, but there is no time to waste.

UNEP is working toward forming a scientific plan of action by the end of 1990, and the adoption of a global climate treaty by 1992. In May, delegates from 103 nations met in Nairobi, Kenya — where UNEP is based — and decided to open negotiations on the treaty next year.

Nations will be asked to reduce the use of fossil fuels, cut the emission of carbon dioxide and other greenhouse gases such as methane and fluorocarbons, and preserve the rain forests.

"We have no clear idea about the ecological minimum of green space that the planet needs to function effectively. What we do know is that we are destroying the tropical rain forest at the rate of 50 acres a minute, about one football field per second," said Brown.

Each acre of rain forest can store 100 tons of carbon dioxide and reprocess it into oxygen.

The Guardian

US edition

Sat 21 Feb 2004 20.33 EST

Now the Pentagon tells Bush: climate change will destroy us

- Secret report warns of rioting and nuclear war
- Britain will be 'Siberian' in less than 20 years
- Threat to the world is greater than terrorism

Climate change over the next 20 years could result in a global catastrophe costing millions of lives in wars and natural disasters..

A secret report, suppressed by US defence chiefs and obtained by The Observer, warns that major European cities will be sunk beneath rising seas as Britain is plunged into a 'Siberian' climate by 2020. Nuclear conflict, mega-droughts, famine and widespread rioting will erupt across the world.

But I think you are getting the message: not only have predictions of impending doom proved incorrect at the margins, but they have also been spectacularly wrong.

What that means is that a bit of skepticism is in order, and that the "climate alarmists" calling climate sceptics, of whom you will meet many in the pages below," climate deniers" or "a handful of fanatics" as does Spain's Prime Minister quoted above, is, perhaps, a bit of a stretch.

How do you spot a climate alarmist? Do they wear Extinction Rebellion buttons and Greta Thunberg t-shirts? They might, but some of them might slip through this particular filter.

The simplest test is they conflate weather with climate.

Weather you can observe and feel.

Climate is changes or non-changes over time. You can't observe it but you can falsify it. So, let's falsify.

Hurricanes, floods, and fires have climate alarmists coming out of the woodwork. But only if they are caused by anything that can be related to *warming*. A heavy spell of global freeze causing untold misery to humans, is not newsworthy. That's the first hint, somebody's lying to us.

Secondly, media coverage of 2 recent, devastating fires in 2018-19 in California and Australia, which killed respectively 100 and 26 people, ravaged thousands of homes and killed hundreds of thousands of animals, shows us we are being manipulated.

In both cases the media was right on cue and wanted you to panic: what better proof of the climate change emergency and that the planet was heating beyond our control, than devastating wildfires?

Michael Mann, arguably the world's no. 1 climate alarmist, whom we shall come back to below, writes, while on holiday in Australia, that he is "watching climate change in action". But climate change by definition takes place over long periods of time, so what he is observing is weather.

So, what *did* cause the conflagrations in Australia and California?

The answer: the Australian and Californian wildfires were caused by humans, not climate change. To be more specific: Government authorities decided under pressure from Green environmental groups not to carry out controlled burns to do away with dry shrubs that could leak to bigger trees burning and causing much more havoc.

Er…, I hate to say it but the fires in Australia and California, were caused by the insane policy priorities of the very same woke, green lobbies who are now screaming global emergency climate crisis: the environmentalist lobby. They didn't want controlled shrub burns because it would kill small animals; and ended up with uncontrolled burns that killed humans.

Did global warming, i. e. dramatic changes in rainfall, rise in temperatures, wind patterns, etc. cause the climate catastrophe? The first answer is that there were no dramatic if any changes in the climatic conditions and that Australia had suffered similar wildfires before. In fact, severe wildfires in the 1960s had led to the adoption of those controlled burning techniques that were later dropped due to the lobbying of environmental activists, techniques.

The scientific Mass Weather Blog asked the same question and arrived at the same answer:

"Was Global Warming a Significant Factor in California's Camp Fire? The Answer is Clearly No."

Furthermore, the blog notes," beyond the heart-wrenching losses, it is doubly tragic that this disaster was both foreseeable and avoidable, resulting from a series of errors, poor judgment, lack of use of available technology, and poor urban planning. It is more than unfortunate that some politicians, environmental advocacy groups, and activist scientists are attempting to use this tragedy as a tool for their own agenda and make the claim that the Camp Fire was result of global warming.[160]

Patrick Michaels & Myron Ebell, of the Competitive Enterprise Institute make the same point about the Australian and Californian wildfires : "Bottom of Form Alarmists have been quick to blame climate change for the recent, horrific fires in Australia and California. Although human actions do bear a large share of the blame for the scale of this ongoing tragedy, the cause is primarily bad management policies, not dreaded climate change. Governmental decisions, made under pressure from environmental groups, have made what would normally be big fires into hellish conflagrations. "[161]

That is a pretty damning indictment of the climate alarmist lobby. And its UN co-conspirator, the IPCC.

Especially if you consider all the other arguments against the coming climate "emergency".

The first and rather obvious one, is that the IPCC, as a UN body, is institutionally incapable of pursuing scientific truth, because the truth would undermine the reasons for U.N. dealing with the subject in the first place: namely that climate change respects no borders and therefore there can only be an *international* solution to the problem. Of course, to be carried out by…. the UN. In short, the UN has a very obvious conflict of interest.

Another problem is that IPCC and climate change has become a giant money-making machine for thousands of climate researchers all over the world. Research has to be funded and to a high degree funding comes from governments. But governments are increasingly the ones wedded to the human interference model and research that goes against" consensus" IPCC opinion is unlikely to get government funds.

But don´t take my word for it.

Greenpeace co-founder, and scientist, Patrick Moore, says: "scientists are co-opted and corrupted by politicians and bureaucracies invested in advancing the narrative of "climate change" in order to further centralize political power and control {and} you´ve got the green politicians who are buying scientists with government money to produce fear for them in the form of scientific-looking materials {but} There is no truth to this. It is a complete hoax and a scam"[162]

This has unsurprisingly led to corruption, one example of which is documented by Judith Curry, former Head of the Department of Earth and Atmospheric Sciences at the Georgia Institute of

---

[160] Mass weather blog, Nov. 20, 2018
[161] Competitive Enterprise Institute, Jan. 8, 2020
[162] Breitbart, Greenpeace Founder: Global Warming Hoax Pushed By Corrupt Scientists Hooked On Government Grants, March 15, 2019

Technology, who in an interview with City Journal says that in 2005, she had a conversation with Rajendra Pachauri, an Indian railway engineer, who remade himself into a climatologist and became director of the IPCC, which received the 2007 Nobel Peace Prize under his tenure.

"Pachauri told me" she says, "without embarrassment", that, at the UN, he "recruited only climatologists convinced of the carbon-dioxide warming explanation, excluding all others. "[163]

Another example of this collusion between researchers and governments is "Climategate" which came to light because someone, we still do not know who, leaked a series of emails which showed that top climatologists in England and the US with climatologist Michael Mann, professor at Pennsylvania State University, at the center, were conspiring to coordinate their efforts to prove that climate change was man-made by leaving out evidence to the contrary. Mann went as far as to manipulate facts to completely exclude a global warming medieval period with CO2 levels and temperatures as high or higher than today's from his new "scientific" method which was duly used by a later IPCC report to confirm the threat of man-made global warming.

When confronted by independent climatologists, notably the above-mentioned Tim Ball, who joked that Mann should be in the "State Pen, not Penn State", Mann failed to see the joke, sued in court and lost.

The *reason* he lost is interesting. In a defamation case, the judge will want to know if Tim Ball's comments were true and in order to assess that he asked Mann to produce the data underlying his scientific results. Mann refused. As he has refused to allow other fellow climatologists access. In science no theory can be taken as proven unless other scientists independently can reach the same conclusion. It is the flipside of Karl Popper's falsification theory and what Popper says is simply that any theory that cannot conceivably be refuted is not science.

Verdict? Mann withheld his evidence because he knew it -literally-wouldn't stand up in court.

Woke's tendency towards totalitarianism is no place more evident than in the climate change debate and in its intolerance of dissenters. As Curry says, "a person must not like capitalism or industrial development too much and should favor world government, rather than nations"; think differently, and you'll find yourself ostracized. "Climatology is becoming an increasingly dubious science, serving a political project".[164]

Indeed. Beware of ideologues and politicians who think they have all the answers. Curry, in the same piece, warns us not to think our computer models can tell us everything. By way of an example: "between 1910 and 1940, the planet warmed during a climatic episode that resembles our own, down to the degree. This warming couldn't be blamed on industry, because back then, most of the carbon-dioxide emissions from burning fossil fuels were small. Natural factors thus had to be the cause. None of the climate models used by scientists now working for the United Nations could explain this older trend. Nor can these models explain why the climate suddenly cooled between 1950 and 1970, giving rise to widespread warnings about the onset of a new ice age".[165]

---

[163] City Journal, From Climate Change to Myth Buster, Judith Curry interview by Guy Sorman, Winter 2019
[164] City Journal, From Climate Change to Myth Buster, Judith Curry interview by Guy Sorman, Winter 2019
[165] All Judith Curry quotes from the abovementioned interview in City Journal

In the late 1960s and early 1970s the world was in a similar panic as today, this time about the planet being in the grip of an annihilating *deep freeze*. According to a group of scientists, we faced an apocalyptic environmental scenario—but the opposite of the current one.

But aren't major storms, floods, increasing hurricanes signs of impending doom? Aren't the images of polar bears drifting on ice floes warnings of the global warming that's melting the polar ice caps, aren't they symbols of the threat to the earth posed by our ceaseless energy production—above all, the carbon dioxide that factories and automobiles emit?

Actually, no. Hurricanes aren't increasing, sea levels aren't rising any more than normal in a period of warming which is what we are in. You don't believe me, do you? Look it up. These are facts not opinions.

In its latest assessment, even the IPCC notes that "no robust trends in annual number of tropical storms, hurricanes and major hurricanes…have been identified over the past 100 years in the North Atlantic Basin"[166]

So, before you put on your hair shirt, here's a few facts you need to wrap your mind around.

The first one is honesty. For example, honesty about going vegan and driving an electric car while banning all other cars from city centers as green activists want you to. Here's the honest truth: it won't make a bit of difference.

Bjørn Lomborg, author of The Skeptical Environmentalist, who is a statistician by profession and one of the world's foremost climate change experts, and critics, and also a vegetarian who doesn't own a car, says that we need to be honest about what such choices can achieve: Going vegetarian actually is quite difficult, he says: "One large US survey indicates that 84% of people fail, most of them in less than a year. But a systematic peer-reviewed study has shown that, even if they succeed, their vegetarian diets reduce individual CO_2 emissions by the equivalent of 540 kilos — or just 4.3% of the emissions of the average inhabitant of a developed country.

Furthermore, there is a "rebound effect" as money saved on cheaper vegetarian food is spent on goods and services that cause additional greenhouse-gas emissions. Once we account for this, going entirely vegetarian reduces a person's total emissions by only 2%.

Likewise, electric cars are branded as environmentally friendly, but generating the electricity they require almost always involves burning fossil fuels. Moreover, producing energy-intensive batteries for these cars invariably generates significant CO_2 emissions. According to the International Energy Agency (IEA), an electric car with a range of 400 kilometers (249 miles) has a huge carbon deficit when it hits the road and will start saving emissions only after being driven 60, 000 kilometers. Yet, almost everywhere, people use an electric car as a second car and drive it shorter distances than equivalent gasoline vehicles."[167]

In his new book, "False Alarm: How Climate Change Panic Costs Us Trillions, Hurts the Poor, and Fails to Fix the Planet", he explicitly warns that *"This alarmism is not only false but morally unjust. It leads us to make poor decisions based on fear, when the world not only has gotten better, but will be even better over the century."*

---

[166] Bjørn Lomborg in an opinion-piece for Project Syndicate, Your electric car and vegetarian diet are pointless virtue signaling in the fight against climate change. What's really needed is more green-energy R&D, Dec. 28, 2019

[167] IPCC report, Sept. 8, 2019

He explicitly criticizes Greta Thunberg for her scaremongering which he claims keeps 6 out of 10 American teenagers awake at night.

Remember, says Lomborg, that the world today is much better in almost every measurable way. In 1900, the average life expectancy was 32. Today, it has more than doubled to 72. The disparity in health between the rich and poor has reduced, the world is much more literate, child labor has been dropping and we are living in one of the most peaceful times in history. Indoor air pollution, previously the biggest environmental killer, has halved since 1990. Four out of five people were extremely poor in 1900 and today — despite the intense impact of the coronavirus — less than one in five is. He shares this book's concern with alarmist modelling citing a paper from last year, which claimed that future sea-level rise would flood 187 million people — without assuming that we would adapt over the next 80 years. This scary predictive number was 600 times too large.

Even the much criticized UN Climate Panel's middle-of-the-road estimate for the end of the century is that we will be even better off, says Lomborg. There will be virtually no one left in extreme poverty, everyone will be much better educated, and the average income per person in the world will be 450 percent of what it is today. Yet, because climate is a real challenge, it will leave us less well off. Based on three decades of studies, the UN estimates that global warming will reduce the 21st century welfare increase from 450 percent to "only" 434 percent of today's income.

Clearly, says Lomborg, this is a problem. But a 3.6 percent reduction by the end of the century is not an existential threat. Resorting to panic and hysteria is unlikely to help, indeed, one of the UN Climate Panel authors warned against this: "We risk turning off the public with extremist talk that is not carefully supported by the science."[168]

Indeed. This trumped-up rhetoric leads woke ideology to make unrealistic promises. We have mostly failed our climate promises for the last thirty years, says Lomborg, and we are poised to fail our Paris climate promises by 2030 as well. "It also leads nations to make exorbitantly expensive promises of carbon neutrality by 2050, something that will be more costly than permanent coronavirus shutdowns. By way of example, New Zealand has asked for an independent assessment of the cost of its climate policy. It will cost 16 percent of its GDP *each and every year* by 2050, making it more costly than the entire New Zealand public expenditures for education, health, environment, police, defense, social protection, etc."[169]

If cutting CO2 emissions is not the answer, what is then, I hear you ask?

Smart R&D says Lomborg." Climate economic studies convincingly show that one of the best investments to fix climate in the medium run is to invest heavily in green R&D. Because research is cheap, we can explore many avenues, from better renewables and battery storage to carbon capture and fusion, fission, carbon-neutral oil-producing algae, and more. If we can innovate on the price of green energy down below that of fossil fuels, everyone will switch — not just well-meaning rich people, but also most Chinese, Indians and Africans. The models

---

[168] Excerpts from Lomborg's book adapted by New York Post as ", How climate change alarmists are actually endangering the planet, July 11,2020.
[169] Idem.

show that each dollar invested in green energy R&D will avoid eleven dollars of climate damage."[170]

As if on cue Associated press on Feb. 9,2022,reported that European scientists have taken a significant step closer to mastering a technology that could allow them in 10 to 20 years 'to harness nuclear fusion, providing a clean and almost limitless source of energy.[171]

The technology used to achieve the result, using magnets to control ultra-hot plasma, show that harnessing fusion — a process that occurs naturally in the stars — is physically feasible.

Scientists think that fusion reactors might one day provide a source of emissions-free energy without any of the risks of conventional nuclear power.

Woke when it comes to the "climate emergency" operates on two premises: firstly,that the climate is stable and that any and all deviation, whether too cold as we saw in the scaremongering 50 years ago or too hot as we see today,constitutes an emergency..This is false: the climate is not stable. It never has been, and it never will be.

Secondly, the Thunberg and Extinction Rebellion quotes above let the cat out of the bag. For Woke it isn't really about climate change, it's about *system* change. It is about the same power grab by Woke that we have seen in other chapters.

Hurricanes aren't increasing, polar bears are more numerous than ever, ice caps may be melting but they have melted before, remember? When they were growing wine on Greenland in the Middle Ages.

Does that mean that global warming isn't real? Judith Curry gives the answer: "There is warming, but we don't really understand its causes. The human factor and carbon dioxide, in particular, contribute to warming, but how much is the subject of intense scientific debate."

So, what about arctic ice melting and sea levels rising to disastrous levels. Steady now, Curry says: "Sea levels are rising, but this has been gradually happening since the 1860s; we don't yet observe any significant acceleration of this process in our time." Here again, one must consider the possibility that the causes for rising sea levels are partly or mostly natural, which isn't surprising for "climate change is a complex and poorly understood phenomenon, with so many processes involved."

So much for "the facts are not in dispute" argument. They *are i*n dispute when it comes to how big a role, if any, man-made warming plays. And that's the crux, isn't it? Man-made warming, we can do something about although at astronomical cost. Solar shifts and the earth's

---

[170] Idem.

[171] Scientists Hail 'Big Moment' for the Future of Nuclear Fusion as a Clean Energy Source, AP, Feb.9.2022

oscillations, not so much. Therefore, Woke, cue Frankfurt School of Critical Theory and Herbert Marcuse, wants it to be all about humans and senseless capitalism.

The Thunberg and Extinction Rebellion quotes above let the cat out of the bag. It isn't really about climate change, it's about *system* change. It is about the same power grab by Woke that we have seen in other chapters.

But the problem is, the IPCC tries *too* hard, and people like me start suspecting that we are being manipulated. Exhibit no. 1 in terms of climate alarmism is the 1, 5 Celsius degree deadline beyond which humanity will pass the point of no return. Where did that figure come from and what does it mean?

Let's take a look at the IPCC report itself on the 1,5 Celsius warming threshold, entitled, <u>Global Warming of 1.5 °C. An IPCC special report on the impacts of global warming of 1.5 °C above pre-industrial levels and related global greenhouse gas emission pathways, in the context of strengthening the global response to the threat of climate change, sustainable development, and efforts to eradicate poverty.</u>

First the background because it explains a lot of what is really going on in climate change politics. The reason the IPCC had to write this "special report" is-according to another report called "What does 1.5C mean in a warming world? - "that over the three years from 2015-18, climate scientists have changed the definition of what they believe is the "safe" limit of climate change.

For decades, researchers argued that the global temperature rise must be kept below 2C by the end of this century to avoid the worst impacts. In fact, the Paris Agreement speaks only of "pursuing efforts" to limit the rise in average global temperature to 1.5°C above pre-industrial levels and achieving net-zero emissions sometime "in the second half of this century." The more aggressive timetable came three years later, when the Intergovernmental Panel on Climate Change (IPCC) produced its 1.5°C special report. In that document, the IPCC asserted that emissions must reach net zero by around 2050 and, by 2030, emissions should be cut by about 45 percent from 2010 levels.

So, scientists now argue that keeping below 1.5C is a far safer limit for the world. Why has the goal changed?

In a word - politics.

The idea of two degrees as the safe threshold for warming evolved over a number of years from the first recorded mention by economist William Nordhaus in 1975.

By the mid-1990s, European ministers were signing up to the two-degree limit, and by 2010 it was official UN policy.

However, small island states and low-lying countries were very unhappy with this perspective, because they believed it meant their territories would be inundated with sea water as higher temperatures caused more ice to melt and the seas to expand.

They commissioned "research" which showed that preventing temperatures from rising beyond 1.5C would give them a fighting chance.

And by the time of the Paris negotiations in 2015, 1.5 C won the day as French diplomats sought to build a broad coalition of rich and poor nations who would support a deal in Paris.

It worked. But remember, even the Paris Agreement only spoke about "pursuing efforts" to limit the rise in average global temperature to 1.5°C.

So, the reason the IPCC had to release this special report directly relates to the dilemma of the IPCC: how does it, the IPCC, explain to a wondering world that the idea of a safe threshold of 2.0 C. for warming, evolved by scientist over 40 years suddenly is no longer valid? How does it explain that the deadlines of the "end of the century" and "by the second half of this century" suddenly become 2030-52? Without admitting that the whole thing is political.

By massive manipulation of data that's how.

Let me back that up with some facts and you decide whether you agree with me:

The first thing that strikes the reader is the *baseline which* the IPCC chooses for reaching the conclusion that by 2030-52, global warming of the world will have reached the unsustainable threshold of 2.0 C., sorry, the unsustainable threshold of 1,5 C.

To reach the conclusion that present-day temperatures are *too* high, IPCC, obviously has to ask compared to what? It's called a baseline and IPCC picks that of *pre-industrial* temperature levels.

But why pick the years 1850-1900 as *pre*-industrial? The standard historical definition of the beginning of the Industrial Period, which is the transition from hand made to machine made production, is around 1750.

So why pick a baseline that is 100 years *later* when the industrial revolution was already well under way? I smell a rat:

We know from the IPCC discussions that scientists were not involved in choosing this baseline. In fact, scientists, financially independent of the IPCC are still discussing the validity of picking this particular baseline. So, it is fair to say that this decision was political not scientific.

We know that 1850 marks the end of the little ice age and was preceded by the Medieval Warm Period (also known as the Medieval Climate Anomaly). Why pick a baseline from the little ice age?

Could the answer be that this is the most favorable baseline for backing up the climate alarmist conclusion of the IPCC-report?

I think so but even more to the point is that it ties right in with the IPCC's political agenda which is that climate change is anthropogenic, man-made. It cannot pick a period like the Medieval Warm Age where temperatures were like to-day's because it would seriously undermine the man-alone-is-guilty-of-global warming theory behind the IPCC's global warming alarmism.

Call me a cynic, but given the politicized background of the report, it can't be excluded.

OK, I hear you say, but these are details. The bigger concern is that the World is coming to an *end*.

Let us use our falsification tools on this prediction and scrutinize what according to the IPCC will be the effects of this climate emergency:

- Sea levels are *expected* to rise between 10 and 32 inches (26 and 82 centimeters) or higher by the end of the *century*.
- Hurricanes and other storms are *likely* to become stronger. Floods and droughts will become more common. Large parts of the U.S., for example, face a higher risk of decades-long "megadroughts" by *2100*.
- *Less freshwater* will be available since glaciers store about three-quarters of the world's freshwater.
- *Some* diseases will spread, such as mosquito-borne malaria (and the 2016 resurgence of the Zika virus).
- Ecosystems will continue to change: Some species will move farther north or become more successful; others, such as polar bears, won't be able to adapt and *could become extinct.*[172]

Notice the language? Sea levels *expected* to rise by *the end of the century*, hurricanes *likely* to get more common, *by 2100?* Where have we seen this before? In the long list of failed predictions, I entertained you with at the beginning of this chapter. Why should we believe it this time? No reason at all.

But I think you get the picture: The UN through the IPCC picks an arbitrary baseline date at the closing of the last ice-age, and calls it the pre-industrial age, although historically it is about 100 years off. It makes no attempt at comparing this baseline with earlier baseline data, say from the Medieval Warm Age.

We are then invited to believe that *only* anthropogenic, i.e. human emissions about which we *can* do something, matter; to the detriment of other plausible causes such as sun oscillations, which we *can't* do anything about.

And by the end of the exercise, since global warming *may* lead to rising sea-levels and *could* lead to fewer polar bears(which we now *know* is not true) we are invited to be panicked into undertaking enormous changes to our existing political and economic system, the most successful in the history of mankind, by drastically limiting our CO2 emissions, which not only will hit the poorest part of our populations the hardest but will mean a massive transfer of wealth from the developed world to the developing world.

With a strong likelihood that this transformation of the West, will have absolutely no significant effect on the climate, not least because 85% of the World´s anthropogenic emissions come from Non-Western countries.

Which by any clearheaded observation have no intention of impoverishing their own populations, by introducing climate change measures that are likely to lead to massive political

---

[172] National Geographic on internet search: What are the consequences of global warming according to IPCC?

unrest; and threaten the powers of the local political elites, as we saw most recently in the popular riots in Chile and Sri Lanka, set off by massive crop failures and increases in fuel prices caused by climate change measures from a government trying to implement the Paris Climate Agreement.

All this in a context where the IPCC has a massive conflict of interest. And has been proven to have a political agenda ranking from downright lies about glaciers over manipulation of scientific data to hiring as "experts" only those scientists who already are believers in *anthropogenic* climate change to the exclusion of all other evidence.

Call me cynical, but it's a scam and a hoax as Patrick Moore and Judith Curry, and lately President Trumps science advisor, Will Happer, have pointed out. Happer is Cyrus Fogg Brackett Professor of Physics, Emeritus, at Princeton University and — till September this year — senior director at the National Security Council's Office for Emerging Technology, but more importantly, a spectroscopist. Spectroscopy is the study of the composition, physical structure and electronic structure of matter to be investigated at atomic scale, molecular scale, macro scale, and over astronomical distances; but other than that, best known for inventing the sodium guide star which is used to correct for atmospheric turbulence (which in his opinion is the main cause of global warming).

This is what Dr. Happer, said when asked if it would help if California went 100 per cent "zero carbon", as green activists are demanding:

"I think it would be very helpful. It would be bad for the poor citizens of [California] but it would be good for the rest of the world. One of the advantages we have in the United States over other countries is that we have states, and so a state can try out something which might be a good idea, or which might be a terrible idea without affecting the entire country. So, we should take advantage of this. Let California do everything that the Greens demand them to do. Let's see what will happen. I know what will happen…

It will be a disaster. Jobs will be lost, there will be blackouts, it will be the ultimate morality play. We'll see how some of the movie stars like what they've created.[173]

Another environmental policy expert, Rupert Darwell, author of "Green Tyranny: Exposing the Totalitarian Roots of the Climate Industrial Complex" (2017) and former adviser to the Government of John Major, calls the IPCC report " a blueprint for the extinction of capitalism as we know it." Indeed, he says, "the 1.5°C report is the most ideological of any IPCC report so far."

Why? Because the 1.5°C target "creates the opportunity for "intentional societal transformation." In language closer to Sanders's than any believer in capitalism, the IPCC says hitting 1.5°C implies "very ambitious, internationally cooperative policy environments that transform both supply and demand."

Under this vision, the energy, industrial, construction, transportation and agricultural sectors are all slated for policy-induced restructuring. A dietary shift from meat and dairy is envisaged to reduce pastureland by up to 11 million square kilometers, or 4.2 million square miles, an area

---

[173] Breitbart, Dec. 8, 2019

greater than the U.S. (which is roughly 3.8 million square miles). The industrial sector is to cut its emissions by between 67 percent and 91 percent. [174]

How can this happen, without inducing a contraction that makes the Great Depression of the 1930s look like a mild recession?

It can't of course. And ordinary people are going to be the big losers. Money- wise and politically.

The IPCC held its 1919 climate meeting in Madrid, Spain. It was meant to be held in Chile. But riots in Chile meant it had to be moved. What were the riots about? People were taking to the streets because of rising gas prices and ensuing increases in transportation costs. Why were prices increasing? Because the left-wing government of Chile was trying to implement the targets of the Paris Agreement by introducing more solar and wind projects, which are expensive, and cutting down on fossil fuels energy, which is cheap.

Who got hurt the most? Normal people and especially low-income people. But Woke does not take that into its social justice equation when it wants us to vote green. The loss of wealth in the West is going to be astronomical, if Woke has its way: keep voting for them and you will see your income drastically reduced to the tune of 70 trillion dollars a year, more than 3 times the annual GDP of the US

With low-income groups who depend on fossil-fueled transportation and the use of cheap plastic getting hit especially hard. Remember the riots in Chile and multiply by several orders of magnitude.

But wait. It's already happening. In another of the world's poorest countries: Sri Lanka. Sri Lanka's Socialist government in April 2021 in an effort to go green and meet the goals of the Paris 2015 Climate Agreement banned imports of chemical fertilizer and told its farmers to use locally sourced *organic* fertilizers instead. Unsurprisingly, this led to widespread crop failure, which in turn led to such widespread riots that the President not only resigned but tried to flee the county.

Will the growing perception among voters that the cost of climate change far outweigh any potential risk far down the road at the end of this century, change anything? Maybe. Because politicians, contrary to what you think, are not the ideologues driving the climate change bandwagon. Woke ideology is. Politicians have two strong desires: to get re-elected and get to power. To realize those ambitions, they have developed an uncanny smell for the way political winds are blowing. And right now, they're blowing Green.

So, politicians are caught between their sense of realism and the electorate's radicalism. Woke ideology has voted into the European Parliament, the European Commission, and all sorts of national governments in countries ranging from Germany to Greece, so-called watermelon

---

[174] Growth will be a thing of the past if businesses choose 'net zero', by Rupert Darwall, March 7, The Hill.

parties, green on the outside, socialist red on the inside, that will take us for a ride we never wanted.

We therefore face three political problems we: firstly, Woke is in the process of seriously reordering our lives and neither they nor their hand-picked experts are totally honest about the facts driving that decision. The proof that Woke manifestly has an agenda is that it wants to focus on man-made climate change to the exclusion of other explanations including solar changes and the natural oscillations of the Earth. And that it only hires so-called experts who share its opinion to do its work for them.

Secondly, Woke has deliberately created a climate of hysteria and fear that disadvantages, demonizes, and sometimes threatens dissenters´ careers and precludes rational discussion of other possible explanations such as the above-mentioned solar shifts and the oscillations of the earth.

Five years ago at the time of writing (June 2023) Greta Thunberg predicted in a since deleted tweet, that if we did not get rid of fossil fuels the world would come to an end in …. five years.

The UN´s woke organization for climate change, the IPCC, also in June 2023 published a report warning that temperatures had risen 2.3 C since 1850.

1850 was the culmination of a climate period with much colder temperatures than today called The Little Ice Age. That temperatures have gone up since then is not surprising since the baseline chosen by the IPCC was so low.

Why not choose a baseline from a period when the Earth was going through a warming period, say around the year 1000 when they were growing wine in Greenland?

The answer is, of course, that such a baseline would show that temperatures haven´t risen since then, and then there wouldn´t be a climate *emergency,* would there? Nor an IPCC.

The real question, the IPCC doesn´t ask is: have temperatures risen enough lately, say in the last 30 years, for me to worry?

And the answer is: very little. A recent report from the Big Barrier Reef in Australia showed that temperatures on the reef had risen by 0.8 degrees since 1908.That´s 0.006 per year.

Third, Woke is lying through its teeth to us about the real cost of the hair-shirt option. Not just in terms of money but in civil and social unrests. Just in the last couple of years , farmers from Berlin to Amsterdam have been blocking access roads with their tractors in protests against ever increasing climate change-based taxes. There is a good chance that politicians in the West will soon have to face the reality of the consequences of Woke´s reckless pandering to the Climate Change Crowd.

But they won´t pay the price. Ordinary people will.

It won´t be pretty, because the unelected, faceless, international elites from Woke´s failed One World institutions won´t give up their power without a fight.

The summer of 2023 was unusually hot due to the El Nino phenomenon (a natural, not climate change-related phenomenon in the Pacific, which tends to boost global temperature in years when an event occurs whereas its cooler counterpart, La Niña, drags temperatures down)and consequently the media was fuller than usual of.... hot air, warning us that this year's hot temperatures show that fossil fuels are already making Earth unlivably hot.

The truth is that this year's hot temperatures are part of a slow warming trend on a planet where far more people die from cold than from heat, and where we need fossil fuels to protect us from both; but the problem is that each turn of the panic-wheel intensifies the call for the Woke's preferred solution: anti-fossil-fuel policies, with former presidential candidate going as far as blaming MAGA Republicans on the hot summer temperatures.

Climate change alarmism is not only fashionable and popular, but is *unopposed* by the young; not only because it seems so obviously right and furthermore a cause without serious cost but because it seems so mindless:as Greta Thunberg says:"What in the world are the adults thinking?"

Nothing could be further from the truth.

For controlling the debate on climate change is Woke's trojan horse in transforming the consciousness of society and undermine capitalism.

Its main tool is ESG, Environmental, Social, and Governance (ESG) investing.

Environmental criteria consider how a company **safeguards the environment,** including corporate policies addressing climate change, for example. Social criteria examine how it **manages relationships with employees, suppliers, customers, a**nd the communities where it operates. Governance deals with a **company's leadership, executive pay, *audits*, *internal controls*, and shareholder rights.**

According to Investopedia, an internet website for investors, ESG is a powerful tool, to direct energy investments away from fossil fuels in directions favored by Woke through the following actions:

- Environmental, social, and governance (ESG) investing is used to *screen* investments based on corporate policies and to encourage companies to act *responsibly.*
- Many mutual funds, brokerage firms, and robo-advisors now offer investment products that employ ESG *principles.*
- ESG investing can also help portfolios avoid holding companies engaged in *risky or unethical practices.*
- The rapid growth of ESG investment funds in recent years has led to claims that companies have been *insincere or misleading* in touting their ESG accomplishments.

Notice the language, *screen* for investments, *encourage* companies to act responsibly, *risky* or unethical practices, flagging companies that have been *insincere or misleading* in touting their ESG accomplishments.

This is positively Orwellian and a blueprint for Government takeover of the economy:*who* does the s*creening,*who *encourages* r*esponsible investments,*who decides what is a *risky investment,* who decides whether a company has been *insincere*?

Why Woke Government, of course.

Surely, I am exaggerating?

Judge for yourself-

What is the consequence of Governments pursuing non-fossil policies,like Germany phasing out the combustion engine and the diesel car and the EUs favoring so-called Net Zero policies by 2050? What are the consequences of Government encouraging companies to address climate change *responsibly*, which is short-hand for not investing in fossil fuels?

That those companies that don't and still favor fossil fuels will be put on a blacklist.

So, controlling the debate on climate change is Woke's attempt to transform the consciousness of society and undermine capitalism with huge consequences for all of us, including the most ardent activists of Stop the Oil and Extinction Rebellion the young and restless.

That is the reason why debunking the myth of the "boiling" planet as the nominal head of the IPCC, the Portuguese woke socialist, Antonio Gueterres, calls it, is so important.

I offer 4 answers[175] to the deceptive myths offered up to us by the Woke and any young activist blocking main highways, spraying paint on Picassos and Wimbledon's green green, grass, to make the rest of us finally realize that "the end is nigh":

Deception nr.1: Cold-related deaths > heat-related deaths.
When Woke discusses the warming of the planet, it treats warming as obviously bad. But while they portray the planet as already "too hot," the fact is that far more human beings die of cold than of heat.

Study after study has found that deaths from cold outnumber deaths from heat by 5–15 times. On every continent, cold is more dangerous than heat. Even in many countries we think of as especially hot, such as India, cold-related deaths significantly exceed heat-related deaths:

---

[175] These answers are based on a paraphrasing of Alex Epstein's piece in National review, The Myth of an Overheated Planet, which in turn leans heavily on Bjørn Lomborg.

Lancet: More Cold Death Than Heat Death Everywhere

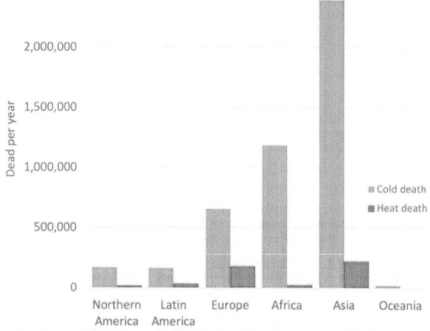

Annual dead from heat and cold across world 2000-19. Latin America includes the Carribean. Sources: "Global, regional, and national burden of mortality associated with non-optimal ambient temperatures from 2000 to 2019", Lancet July 2021, https://www.thelancet.com/journals/lanplh/article/PIIS2542-5196(21)00081-4/fulltext, table 1, twitter.com/bjornlomborg

(Bjørn Lomborg)
    The fact that far more human beings die of cold than of heat means that, for the foreseeable future, even without accounting for the heating and cooling benefits of fossil fuels, fossil-fueled global warming will <u>save</u> more lives from cold than it will take from heat:

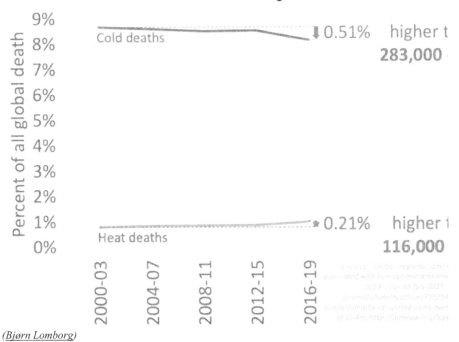

(Bjørn Lomborg)

Deception nr.2: . Earth is warming slowly — and less in warm places.
So far, we've had ~1°C of warming from a cold starting point in Earth's history 150 years ago. And future warming will be limited by the diminishing nature of "the greenhouse effect" — as well as being concentrated in colder places.
If we remember that cold kills more than heat, and we compare the ~1° C (~2° F) average warming that has occurred over the last 150 years with the wide range of temps we deal with every day/month/year, we will not be scared at all. So climate catastrophists use deceptions to scare us.

2a)**The "compressing the Y-axis" deception**:

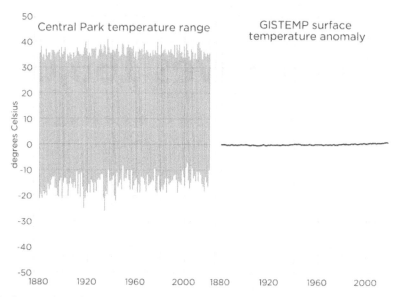

To make the slow warming we have experienced look scary, climate catastrophists like to show warming, not on a human-temperature scale but on a compressed Y-axis where 1°C is huge. This is like measuring weight gain on a scale where one pound is huge:

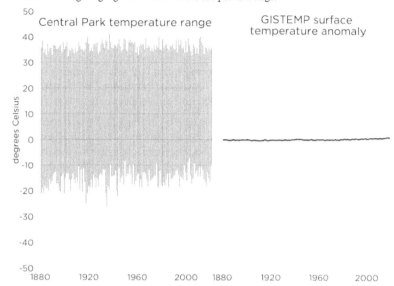

2b)The "hottest on record" deception: We hear constant alarming-sounding claims that we are in or near "the hottest year on record." But given that records began at a cold time, and we're experiencing slow warming, of course any given year we can expect a new record. So what?*NASA)*

Given our limited temperature records, alarming us about a "hottest year on record" during a slow warming period is like a doctor alarming a patient who gains 1/10th of a pound of muscle by saying that it's his "heaviest year on record."

2c)The "hottest ever" deception: Climate catastrophists often absurdly equate a month or year being "the hottest on record" — which refers to the fewer than 200 years we have detailed temperature records — with being "the hottest ever." Even though Earth was 25°F warmer for millions of years!

2d)The "treating local extremes as global" deception: Given the slow pace of global warming, local temp changes tend to be much larger than global ones. To scare us, catastrophists take the hottest local temps and portray them as global so we think everywhere is very hot.

An example of treating local extremes as global has been the national media's focus on Texas when Texas has been "abnormally" hot while ignoring the many places that have been "abnormally" cool.

For some true perspective on heat waves, look at the U.S. Annual Heat Wave Index from the EPA, which says "longer-term records show that heat waves in the 1930s remain the most severe in recorded U.S. history." *(EPA)*

2e)The "treating El Niño warming as global warming" deception: On top of slow global warming, we experience additional warming due to the change from La Niña to El Niño. This is a temporary phenomenon, not a climate trend, but catastrophists exploit it to exaggerate global warming:*(CarbonBrief.org)*

Warming so far has been slow and benign. But will future warming make the world unlivably hot? No, given two facts almost universally acknowledged by climate scientists: 1) the diminishing warming impact of CO2 and 2) the concentration of warming in colder places.

The warming impact of CO2 diminishes ("logarithmically") as it increases in concentration. Every new molecule of CO2 we add to the atmosphere has less of a warming effect than the previous one. Warming will diminish as emissions increase — the only question is at what rate. (Equilibrium climate sensitivity is defined as a warming in °C per doubling of greenhouse-gas concentrations in the atmosphere. The IPCC – the Intergovernmental Panel on Climate Change — estimates it to be between 2.5°C and 4°C. Other analysis suggests it to be below 2°C.)*(Alex Epstein)*

Even the most wildly implausible "scenarios" from the anti-fossil-fuel IPCC include diminishing warming and a highly livable world with an increasing population:

Deception nr.3: **Fossil fuels make us safer from dangerous temperatures**.

Not only is the warming from fossil fuels' CO2 emissions slow and in many ways beneficial, but the uniquely cost-effective energy also we get from fossil fuels makes us safer from both cold and heat.

The portrayal of warming temperatures as a huge danger is based on the fallacy of only looking at the negative effects of something (in this case, warming), not the benefits. Opponents of fossil fuels also commit this fallacy by ignoring the temperature-mastery benefits of fossil fuels.

The key to being protected from dangerous temperatures is to master them by producing different forms of temperature protection, such as: insulated buildings, heating, and air-conditioning. All of these things require energy — which means for most people they require fossil fuels.

Fossil fuels are the only source of low-cost, reliable energy that, for the foreseeable future, can provide energy to billions — in a world where 3 billion people still use less electricity than a typical American refrigerator.

"Studies" that claim future warming will make the world unlivably hot are denying temperature mastery. E.g., one assessment used by the EPA absurdly assumes that if a city like Chicago got as warm as some of today's Southern cities, it won't adapt and just suffer mass heat death!

It should be common sense for reporters and leaders that if we're going to be looking at the temperature side-effects of fossil-fuel use, we also need to consider the enormous temperature-mastery benefits that come with them. But this common sense is almost never practiced.

Deception nr. 4: Anti-fossil-fuel policies increase danger from cold and heat.

The number one thing that will determine people's safety from cold and heat for decades to come is the availability of cost-effective energy. Anti-fossil-fuel policies will increase both cold deaths and heat deaths.

On a planet where people die much more from cold than from heat, but both are major threats, the key to safety is to have energy be as affordable and plentiful as possible so as many as possible can afford heating and air conditioning. For the foreseeable future, this means more fossil fuels.

Even though billions need fossil fuels to protect themselves from cold (above all) and heat, today's media and leaders pretend that heat is the only problem and the solution is to follow anti-fossil-fuel policies that will supposedly cool the Earth. This is breathtakingly dishonest.

Not only do anti-fossil-fuel policies deprive people of the energy they need to protect themselves from both cold and heat, but these policies also cannot cool the Earth for at least several decades, and only then if the whole world, including China, follows them absolutely.

Even if 100 percent net-zero energy is just decades away (absurd) that won't even have a tiny cooling impact until emissions are zero (or negative) and today's warming energy dissipates.

To portray anti-fossil-fuel policies as cooling in any way anytime soon is dishonest:

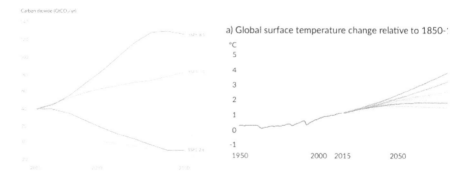

Dangerously cold and hot temperatures are by far the most problematic for *poor* people. What they need is more fossil-fuel energy for air conditioning and heating now, not a climate and energy policy that prevents real future low-emission solutions and makes energy expensive now.

Anyone offering advice on how to deal with hot temperatures, including young eco-activists is obligated to give advice that will actually help human beings for the foreseeable future. Pretending that supporting anti-fossil-fuel policies will help people anytime soon by cooling the Earth is a lie.

Not only is it a lie that anti-fossil-fuel policies will protect people anytime soon by cooling the Earth, it is a deadly lie — because in practice it means preventing people from acquiring the air conditioning they need to deal with warm temperatures today and in the future.

The only moral and practical way to reduce CO_2 emissions — a global phenomenon — is innovation that makes low-carbon energy globally cost-competitive. So long as fossil fuels are the most cost-competitive option, especially in developing nations, they will (rightly) choose to emit CO_2.

Reducing CO_2 emissions in a humane and practical way means focusing on liberating alternatives — especially the most potent, nuclear — to try to truly outcompete fossil fuels in the future. Depriving us off fossil fuels now and pretending China will follow suit is immoral and impractical.

Part III: Summary

The West´s turn to Woke internationalism started when Woke EU leaders in the 1990s and onwards ignored the results of referenda in Denmark, Ireland, Holland and France which clearly showed that voters were not ready for any more integration efforts.

Western leaders regardless continued their path towards a world without borders with internationalist institutions at the helm.

But it wasn´t until the fateful years of 2015, 2016 and 2020 when 4 events rocked the ordinary man in the street that the masks came off our political class:

The first one was when former German Chancellor, Angela Merkel´s Open Door immigration policy let 1 million *economic* refugees jump the external borders of the EU in Greece and Italy; and block the motorways and train station and border crossings all over the EU heading for the nirvana of northern EU-countries with their open doors and welfare handouts.

It was chaos and a huge set-back for everything the EU thought it stood for: multi-culturalism, diversity, open borders and tolerance. And it split the EU down the middle.

But Merkel drunk with hubris after the successes of the Single Market, the introduction of the Euro as the EU´s single currency and Eastern Enlargement, in a phrase whose arrogance more than anything symbolized the leader of a political class that had lost its head, said:" Wir schaffen das"(We can do it).

Only she couldn´t and her fellow Europeans wouldn´t. As they said, mockingly:" Wir schaffen das… nicht".

After that came Brexit in June 2016, another big shock to the EU Establishment who were so full of themselves that they had confidently predicted that no one in their right mind would voluntarily leave their paradise on earth.

And after that the third whammy: the election of a nationalist, Make America Great Again, Donald Trump as U. S. President. And after *that* the Covid19-crisis with its subsequent loss of trust in the system Woke had set up. And their self-serving narrative about it.

And that´s the reason the EU is in the crisis that it is now.

Only, the truth is: the EU elite *created* the crisis by closing their eyes and ears to reality and refusing to recognize, let alone acknowledge, what was happening: that by not listening they had lost the trust of ordinary voters. To this day the EU political class *still* don´t acknowledge that they have failed their own people.

Around the same time, the UN became the world´s number one promoter of Open Borders, touting the benefits of immigration-legal and illegal. Through its Global Compact on Immigration, adopted over the protests of the U.S. and many EU-countries in December 2018, but promoted relentlessly by its originator, Germany led by its Woke chancellor, Angela Merkel, it has effectively erased the distinction between refugees, whom countries under international rules must accept, and economic migrants-whom they must not.

On climate change, the big Woke turn -around was 2015 and the Paris Climate Change Agreement.

Up until then, European ministers were signing up to a two-degree limit, and by 2010 it was official UN policy.

However, small island states and low-lying countries were very unhappy with this perspective, because they believed it meant their territories would be inundated with sea water as higher temperatures caused more ice to melt and the seas to expand.

They commissioned "research" which showed that preventing temperatures from rising beyond 1.5C would give them a fighting chance.

And by the time of the Paris negotiations in 2015, 1.5 C won the day as French diplomats sought to build a broad coalition of rich and poor nations who would support a deal in Paris.

Since then, Woke has voted into the European Parliament, the European Commission, and all sorts of national governments in countries ranging from Germany to Greece, so-called watermelon parties, green on the outside, socialist red on the inside, that will take us for a ride we never wanted.

We therefore face three political problems: firstly, Woke is in the process of seriously reordering our lives and neither it nor its hand-picked experts are totally honest about the facts driving that decision. The proof that woke manifestly has an agenda is that it wants to focus on man-made climate change to the exclusion of other explanations including solar changes and the natural oscillations of the Earth. And that it only hires so-called experts who share its opinion to do its work for them.

Secondly, Woke has deliberately created a climate of hysteria and fear that disadvantages, demonizes, and sometimes threatens dissenters' careers and precludes rational discussion of other possible explanations such as solar shifts and the oscillations of the earth.

Third, Woke is lying through its teeth to us about the real cost of climate change for ordinary people. Not just in terms of money but in civil and social unrests. Just in the last couple of years, farmers from Berlin to Amsterdam have been blocking access roads with their tractors in protests against ever increasing climate change-based taxes. There is a good chance that politicians in the West will soon have to face the reality of the consequences of Woke's reckless pandering to the Climate Change Crowd.

Radical reengineering of internationalism is the hallmark of Woke.

But it isn't working. Voters say so and have been telling Woke for years.

Yet, our Woke internationalist elites persist.

Why?

The answer is that open doors immigration and climate change are only tools used by Woke for a higher purpose: undermining capitalism by and transforming the consciousness of society.

Mass immigration is already transforming the West, by allowing in millions of new citizens with no connection and no loyalty to the system that feeds them.

As they organize politically, their power will grow incrementally and Woke is counting on their votes going its way.

Some federal states in the U.S. notably very liberal ones like California and Illinois, and some EU countries are already offering *illegal* immigrants social services, the right to vote, drivers' licenses and yes ,the opportunity to serve as policemen, official upholders of the....*law*.

The purpose, though hidden behind flowery phrases of international citizenship and one world solidarity is to undermine the very concept of the nation state and its demands of government of, by and for its people.

Controlling the debate on climate change similarly translates into Woke's attempt to transform the consciousness of society and undermine capitalism.

Controlling the debate on climate change is Woke's trojan horse aiding and abetting this process.

Its main tool is ESG, Environmental, Social, and Governance (ESG) investing.

Environmental criteria consider how a company **safeguards the environment,** including corporate policies addressing climate change, for example. Social criteria examine how it **manages relationships with employees, suppliers, customers, a**nd the communities where it operates. Governance deals with a **company's leadership, executive pay, audits, internal controls, and shareholder rights.**

According to Investopedia, an internet website for investors, ESG is a powerful tool, to direct energy investments away from fossil fuels in directions favored by Woke through the following actions:

- Environmental, social, and governance (ESG) investing is used to *screen* investments based on corporate policies and to encourage companies to act *responsibly.*
- Many mutual funds, brokerage firms, and robo-advisors now offer investment products that employ ESG *principles.*
- ESG investing can also help portfolios avoid holding companies engaged in *risky or unethical practices.*
- The rapid growth of ESG investment funds in recent years has led to claims that companies have been *insincere or misleading* in touting their ESG accomplishments.

Notice the language, *screen* for investments, *encourage* companies to act responsibly, *risky* or unethical practices, flagging companies that have been *insincere or misleading* in touting their ESG accomplishments.

This is positively Orwellian and a blueprint for Government takeover of the economy:*who* does the *screening,*who *encourages* r*esponsible investments,*who decides what is a *risky investment,* who decides whether a company has been *insincere?*

Why Woke Government, of course.

Surely, I am exaggerating?

Judge for yourself-

What is the *rationale* behind Governments pursuing non-fossil policies, like Germany phasing out non-electric cars and the EUs favoring so-called Net Zero policies by 2050?

> "Climate change is already affecting the entire world, with extreme *weather* conditions such as drought, heat waves, heavy rain, floods and landslides becoming more frequent, including in Europe. Other consequences of the rapidly changing climate include rising sea levels, ocean acidification and loss of biodiversity.
>
> In order to limit global warming to 1.5 degrees Celsius – a threshold the Intergovernmental Panel for Climate Change (IPCC) suggests is *safe* – carbon neutrality by mid-21st century is essential. This target is also laid down in the Paris agreement signed by 195 countries, including the EU.
>
> In December 2019, the European Commission presented the European Green Deal, its flagship plan that aims to make Europe climate neutral by 2050. This target will be reached through the European Climate Law that sets climate neutrality ***into binding EU legislation***."(my underline)[176]

There you have it: conflating weather with climate change, postulating that 1.5 degrees Celsius is somehow safe, without offering the slightest reason why and threatening that the target of 1.5 will be implemented through binding EU legislation.

Orwell weeps.

What are the consequences of Government encouraging companies to address climate change *responsibly,* which is short-hand for not investing in fossil fuels?

That those companies that don't "address climate change" and still favor fossil fuels will be *breaking the law.*

Until that happy day, Woke will do everything in its power and use all the social and political control it can muster to further ESG investment.

That means encouraging institutional investor, including big state investment funds, pension funds which are subject to government regulations like those of woke teachers' unions and other investors subject to governmental stakeholder intervention, to investment in ESG-approved companies.

Think I am exaggerating?

ATP, Arbejdernes Tillægspension, is a state mandated pension fund to which all Danish workers are legally obliged to contribute throughout their working lives. It invests 1500 billion kroner a year(roughly 200 billion Euros).

---

[176] EP News, 12.04.2023- What is carbon neutrality and how can it be achieved by 2050?

Its website brags that its ambition is to be Denmark´s biggest green investor, adding:" Vi inddrager hensynet til klima, miljø, sociale og ledelsesmæssige forhold (ESG) og investerer dér, hvor vi kan skabe et godt afkast."(We include considerations regarding the climate,the environment,social and company governance(ESG) and invest where we can make a good return).[177]

Like it?

Sounds a bit like state directed investment …ahem…socialism, to me.

But this is not the way capitalism, the most successful economic system in world history, is supposed to work, indeed *can* work: for in a capitalist economy *risk*-taking is decided by private actors who screen their investments according to their business profile and the prospect of profit.

And whether a business partner is *insincere* is judged by the marketplace or if disputes arise adjudged by the courts.

Not by Government whose sole and only task in a capitalist economy is to set up a legal system that allows the free exchange of goods and services and the protection of property rights.

Not if Woke has anything to say about it.

.

---

[177] ATP Website.

Part IV: From Free Speech to Hate Speech-How Woke Crushes Dissent.

xxxxxxxxxxxxxxxxx
"You can´t say anything about anything important ever without offending!"

> Jordan Peterson, Canadian psychologist in a podcast entitled "Free speech and the right to offend". [178]

xxxxxxxxxxxxxxxxxxxxxxxx

"We have freedom of expression,"… "But freedom of expression has its limits. Those limits begin where hatred is spread. They begin where the dignity of other people is violated!" …" This house will and must oppose extreme speech. Otherwise, our society will no longer be the free society that it was,"

> Former German Chancellor Angela Merkel in a speech to the German Parliament in November 2019.

xxxxxxx

"I will take a series of actions as president to further address the spread of disinformation: Push to create civil and *criminal* penalties for *knowingly disseminating false information about when and how to vote in US elections.*"

> Liz Warren´s official campaign website. Warren obtained tenure at Harvard by lying about her Native American ancestry.

xxxxxxx

"Oppressed language does more than represent violence; it is violence."

> Toni Morrison, Nobel Lecture in Literature, 1993. (Tony is a black woman).

xxxxxxx

The one who utters hate speech is responsible for the manner in which such speech is repeated, for reinvigorating such speech, for reestablishing contexts of hate and injury.

> Judith Butler, Excitable Speech: A Politics of the Performative

J

Xxxxxxx

"We are living in an age where honesty is seen as aggression, and truth must be sugared over or else be rejected as hate speech."

> Mike Klepper, American writer, author of **Gone the Sun.**

xxxxxxxxxxx

---

[178] YouTube podcast entitled "Free speech and the right to offend", March 15,2018.

"The term "cancel culture" is a right-wing American term. It's a term crafted to gaslight and vilify changing progressive voice.
There's no such thing as "cancel culture". It's "consequence culture"; and demands more than an apology for transgressions of harm.
"Consequence culture" aims to deplatform a person's social capital until they make meaningful change."

<u>Annastacia Dickerson, Canadian writer and editor.</u>

Xxxxxxxxxxxxxxxxxxxxxxxxx

"First Amendment freedoms are most in danger when the government seeks to control thought or to justify its laws for that impermissible end. The right to think is the beginning of freedom, and speech must be protected from the government because speech is the beginning of thought."

<u>Supreme Court Justice Anthony M. Kennedy,</u> Ashcroft V. Free Speech Coalition

xxxxxxxxxxxxxxxxxxxxxxxxxxx

Nobody likes to be called on their lies and Woke is no exception. The negative counter-reaction of Woke to criticism of its narrative has been threefold: political, legal, and social.

It was woke students who in 1964 orchestrated a free speech movement at Berkeley University, California, that through civil disobedience tactics such as sit-ins forced authorities to abandon their restrictions on political activities on campus, an achievement that ranks as high in the Woke trophy cabinet as the Freedom Riders and Anti-Vietnam War protests.

Yet, on Feb.7,2022, the U.S. Department of Homeland Security released a National Terrorism Advisory Bulletin that states, "The United States remain in a heightened threat environment fueled by several factors, including an online environment filled with false or misleading narratives and conspiracy theories and other forms of mis-dis-and mal-information (MDM)".

Free speech even if false or misleading is now terrorism? A threat to homeland security? Has Woke gone off the deep end?

Our governments will have us believe that it is us, their voters, who either through misinformation or ignorance are spreading misinformation, and that we are a threat to national security.

The truth is that it is Woke *governments*, both nationally and internationally. that have filled *us* with "false or misleading narratives" and accused *us* of "conspiracy theories" when we question their science.

As Supreme Court Justice, Anthony Kennedy, says, it is *government* seeking to curtail our free speech we should be afraid of.

It was our *government* who told us to lock down our businesses and schools and restaurants. But today we know that lockdowns had minimal to no effect on saving lives but caused massive losses both economically and in terms of mental health for us and for our children.

It was the democratically elected *government* in one of the most democratic countries in the world, Denmark, which unconstitutionally and without any basis in virology, with a stroke of the pen eliminated a whole sector of its economy, mink-farming, siccing police on recalcitrant farmers, lying about it and then when caught red-handed, had its parliament adopt a law after the fact-a big no-no in any democracy- justifying and legitimizing the whole sorry affair.

It was *government* that mandated vaccines for truckers in Canada in January 2022, even as the pandemic was largely gone and certain countries like Denmark had already done away with all pandemic-related restrictions.

And it was *government,* like that of Canadian Prime Minister, Justin Trudeau, who called the truckers' protests and exercise of free speech "unacceptable", forced banks to close accounts worth 10 million dollars donated to truckers via GoFundMe and who, when that did not work, invoked the Canadian Emergencies Act, an act meant to be used in times of war, allowing him to dispense with constitutionally guaranteed rights such as freedom of assembly and free speech.

It was our *government* that chased people off beaches and other outdoor spaces from Florida to Portugal even as they knew that outdoor transmissions of Covid-19 were about as common as unicorns.

It was out international bodies like the World Health Organization that withheld and denied vital information about the transmissibility of Covid-19 and protected China's role in causing the pandemic by allowing the virus to escape from a Virology Institute in Wuhan.

It was the former White House chief medical advisor, Anthony Fauci, who previously claimed that attacks on him "are attacks on science." And who said,

> " "I worry about the country a lot because what we're seeing — and I think anybody who just takes a deep breath and looks at what's going on — that we are in an arena, an era, of what I call the normalization of untruths,"
>
> "There are so many misrepresentations and distortions of reality and conspiracy theory, that it almost becomes normalized," he added. "We should not accept that as the new normal because when facts are no longer accepted as facts, when distortions occur and when reality is distorted, that will undermine the foundations of the social order and of our democracy. And history has shown us that."

But Fauci, who left government work at the end of last year, who was a noted distributor of untruths throughout the pandemic.

Former CDC director Robert Redfield testified in March that Fauci's suppression of the Covid-19 lab-leak theory was "antithetical to science."

And it was Fauci, who actively worked to debunk the lab theory in favor of the Government's failed narrative of transmission from animals to humans as the House Select Subcommittee on the Coronavirus Pandemic has revealed:

> "On February 1, [2020] Fauci held a call with several scientists to discuss the origins of the virus. During the call, a group of evolutionary virologists suggested that Covid may have stemmed from *a lab accident* and may have been genetically engineered, according to the memo.

Just three days later, four of the experts who attended that meeting wrote a paper, later published in *Nature Medicine*, that argued Covid had "mutations" that supported the explanation that it had been transmitted to humans from *animals*."[179]

Correspondence between Fauci and the experts show that Fauci, who was in charge of government contracts for the study of Covid 19, exerted "inappropriate" pressure on the experts.

As we have seen in the climate change debate, toeing the government line, because government has the power of the purse, comes with a psychological price-tag: dishonesty.

And it was *government* like Spanish Premier, Sanchez, that willfully and with intent stoked the climate change "crisis" by deliberately promoting "false and misleading narratives" and called sceptics "climate change deniers".

And it was *government*, like U.S President Joe Biden´s spokesperson, Jen Psaki, that called upon social media to censor websites and people who questioned the Administrations pandemic policies.

So, Woke asks us to believe that *private citizens* are now the main purveyors of "an online environment filled with false or misleading narratives and conspiracy theories and other forms of mis-dis-and mal-information (MDM)"?

Politically, Woke´s increasing intolerance of dissent, is demonstrated by President Joe Biden´s Democratic Party, who frustrated by the U.S.Federal system which does not allow him to turn winning the popular vote.into political majorities in the houses of Congress, is threatening to abolish several of the most important constitutional institutions of the U.S. such as the Electoral College, the backbone of American Federalism; do away with an important Senate rule, the filibuster, which for almost 200 years has acted as a democratic brake on the excesses of the majority party in power; or change the number of Supreme Court justices to partisan advantage- the so-called court-packing-which last was tried 85 years ago by Democratic President, Franklin Roosevelt, in 1937 and soundly defeated then by enraged voters.

Historically, the indictment of former president, Donald J. Trump on charges of mishandling government documents which is normally treated as a misdemeanor but was jacked up to charges of espionage, is unique, as was the nightly raid on the residence of the 45th President of the U.S, Mar-a-Lago, by the sitting President's, Democrat Joe Biden´s FBI, on August 8,2022.

In fact, it was the first time in U.S. history that a former President had his residence and de facto Republican HQ raided by the politicized Department of Justice of the sitting President, his former and perhaps future political rival.

It was a politicized move which the Department of Justice under Donald Trump refused to make even when there was credible evidence of Obama being informed of and perhaps even being behind the FBI´s decision to spy on Trump´s campaign, or when Hillary Clinton used a private server to deal with highly classified secret government documents.

We know it was not only unprecedented but also *political* because Steven D'Antuono, then in charge of the FBI's Washington field office, told House investigators in June 2023 that he questioned why headquarters assigned the raid to Washington—not Miami.

According to the Wall Street Journal:

---

[179] National Review,June 23,2023

"He also voiced his concerns that no U.S. attorney was assigned to oversee the case—the usual step. Instead it was left in the hands of the Justice Department's chief of counterintelligence, pit bull Jay Bratt. Mr. D'Antuono said he pushed back against the department's demand for an immediate raid, arguing the FBI should first attempt to get consent for a search—which would have been "the best thing for all parties"—"for the FBI, for former President Trump and for the country."[180]

When special counsel, Jack Smith, charged Trump with yet *another* federal crime for inciting the Jan.6,2021 Capitol riots and *defraud the public*, Woke crossed the Rubicon into revolutionary territory: never before in American history had a former President and leading candidate to replace the sitting President, been so obviously targeted for removal for political reasons by the ruling elite.

"Obviously targeted?

Here's what The Wall Street Journal's Kimberley Strassel had to say:

> In 2014 the {Supreme Court} justices held unanimously that President Barack Obama had violated the Constitution by decreeing that the Senate was in recess so that he could install several appointees without confirmation. It was an outrageous move, one that Mr. Obama's legal counselors certainly warned was a loser, yet the White House vocally insisted the president had total "constitutional authority" to do it. Under Mr. Smith's standard, that was a *lie* that Mr. Obama used to *defraud* the public by jerry-rigging the function of a labor board with illegal appointments.
>
> What's the betting someone told President Biden he didn't have the power to erase $430 billion in student loan debt. Oh, wait! That's right. He told himself. "I don't think I have the authority to do it by signing with a pen," he said in 2021. The House speaker advised him it was illegal: "People think that the president of the United States has the power for debt forgiveness. He does not," Nancy Pelosi said. Yet Mr. Biden later adopted the *lie* that he did and took action to *defraud* taxpayers by obstructing the federal *function* of loan processing—until the Supreme Court made him stop.[181]

The good news is that Courts are calling out Woke's abuses.[182] This July Fourth (2023). Judge Terry Doughty issued a preliminary injunction in *Missouri v. Biden.*

Judge Doughty issued the injunction (which is an order to *desist* and stop doing what you are doing) against **eight** federal agencies—including the Justice Department, the Federal

---

[180] WSJ, July 13,2023, It's a Shame About Christopher Wray.

[181] The Unprecedented Jack Smith,If lying politicians can be prosecuted for 'fraud,' as he proposes in the Trump indictment, we'll need a lot of new prisons.WSJ,Aug.3,2023

[182] "A Key Ruling Against Social-Media Censorship,"The judge in Missouri v. Biden likens the federal government's suppression of dissent to the 'Ministry of Truth' in '1984.'July 4,2023,Wall Street Journal.

Bureau of Investigation, the Department of Health and Human Services and the Centers for Disease Control and Prevention whom he accused of a massive assault on *free speech*.

Judge Doughty <u>observed</u> in the injunction that "The United States Government seems to have assumed a role similar to an Orwellian 'Ministry of Truth,' "..."threatening, pressuring, or coercing social-media companies in any manner to remove, delete, suppress, or reduce posted content of postings containing protected free speech."; and furthermore kept the federal government's use of social-media platforms to censor Americans *secret* through two election cycles".Not to mince word he called the actions of the Biden Administration, "the most massive attack against free speech in United States' history."

The second weapon being used by Woke to stop criticism is legislation. Hate speech in the United States is not regulated, in contrast to that of most other Western democracies. The US Supreme Court has repeatedly ruled that hate speech is legally protected free speech under the First Amendment. The most recent Supreme Court case on the issue was in 2017, Matal v. Tam, when the justices unanimously reaffirmed that there is effectively no "hate speech" exception to the free speech rights protected by the First Amendment.

In the EU, we are not so lucky, and hate speech legislation is common.

Several prominent European politicians have been convicted of hate speech which generally in the EU is defined as speech that attacks a person or a group on the basis of protected attributes such as race, religion, ethnic origin, national origin, sex, disability, sexual orientation, or gender identity.

As we saw in the LGTBQ chapter, where an employment judge found in favor of a company which had fired an employee who had said that transgender males are not women, courts can go very far in interpreting such legislation.

But remember that politics are downstream from culture, and it is the culture of free speech that is being targeted by woke ideology.

The Merkel and Liz Warren quotes above are just a symptom of this broader war on free speech.

When former German Chancellor, Angela Merkel, says free speech has its limits and those limits begin where *hatred* is spread and that they begin where the *dignity* of other people is violated, she is coming down in favor of the Woke world view of oppressor and oppressed.

The EU's definition does the same: Illegal hate speech is defined in EU law (Framework Decision on combating certain forms and expressions of racism and xenophobia by means of criminal law) as " the public incitement to violence or hatred directed *to groups* or *individuals* on the basis of certain characteristics, including race, color, religion, descent and national or ethnic origin".

This is a very different animal from the classic Enlightenment definition of free speech, still followed in American jurisprudence but long ago abandoned in the EU, of there being no limits to hate speech including that of expressing disparagement of certain groups on the basis of race, religion or sexual orientation.

Hate speech legislation in the EU, in short, is devised not just for the protection of individuals but certain *groups* of individuals. That's where the confusion begins: a person can either have individual human rights based on his membership of the human race or rights according to his membership of a certain religion, a certain race or gender but under Enlightenment logic not both.

Although it is pretty ironic to be lectured about political "lies" on Facebook, by a woke politician, Elizabeth Warren, who made her career by not only lying about her Native American background to get tenure at Harvard, but also about her kids not going to private schools (they did) and being fired from her job because she got pregnant (she wasn't).

Liz is deadly serious. A dangerous ideologue. But don't take my word for it.

According to her campaign website she wants CEOs and other company leaders to be held accountable for failures to protect user privacy. She has introduced legislation in Congress proposing jail time for corporate executives found liable for data breaches or other privacy violations that affect a certain amount of users, a bold measure that could implicate high-profile CEOs like Facebook's Mark Zuckerberg or Google's Sundar Pichai.

Warren has cast the measure as part of a crackdown she envisions on executive wrongdoing. The bill would empower state and federal regulators to punish executives found liable for privacy violations with up to a year in jail for first-time offenders and up to three years for repeat offenders.[183]

You will argue that political speech always is and always has been characterized by attempts to make your political opponents seem extreme or outside the mainstream, as we saw in the climate change chapter, where Spanish Prime Minister, Pedro Sanchez, at the COP 15 said," For years, several versions of climate change denial were in circulation. Today, luckily only a handful of fanatics deny the evidence,"

Maybe. But, politically, the Biden Administration, Jen Psaki's and Pedro Sanchez 'naked authoritarianism, show that Woke is ready to go much further in using the weapon of controlling and reducing free speech than before. Forcing internet companies to censor and remove "hateful" content on the internet is *new*. Threatening to criminalize social media platforms for the dissemination by their users of false information, is *new*.

And they are not alone. In Canada, legislation (Bill C-36) supported by PM Justin Trudeau's administration is making its way through the Canadian Parliament which would allow citizens to be taken to court and penalized if they are suspected of simply *intending* to post "hate speech" online.[184]

The proposed law encourages Canadians to report other Canadians to the authorities for *intent* to post hate speech online and allows courts to punish Canadian citizens for things they haven't done yet. You couldn't make this up. Woke is going full Orwellian.

Both France and Germany go further than threats and have passed legislation under which internet companies like Google, Twitter and Facebook must remove hateful contents from their website within 24 hours on penalty of heavy fines.

Countries all over the West have in effect outsourced speech control to new censors: social media. But who are the new corporate censors?

Studies show that politically employees at Google, Twitter and Facebook are overwhelmingly left of center. Twitter before it was taken over by Elon Musk went as far as deleting a sitting President's ,Donald Trump's,account.

---

[183] Warren 's campaign website.
[184] "Breitbart, Allum Bokhari, Feb.24, 2022

Woke´s Brave New World is taking shape. Woke argues that the internet has changed the rules of free speech, and that we, meaning herself and other Woke leaders, cannot "allow", meaning will prohibit, "hate speech" (Merkel).

In other words: political censorship, which otherwise had been abolished in the West by the French and American constitutions, more than 200 years ago.

What is fact and what is fiction in this argument?

Woke argues that freedom of speech is dangerous because only the wealthy and corporations can afford to buy the electorate.

This argument refers to studies which show that there is a correlation between getting elected to political office and the size of your campaign chest. But correlation is not causation. At the 2016 US election, Hilary Clinton largely outspent her opponent, Donald Trump. And lost.

The US and the EU, furthermore, already have campaign laws limiting the size of corporations´ and individuals´ contribution to political candidates.

Corporate financing constituted less than 1% of all spending in the last US election. The rest came from individual small donations that are capped by law, from voters who exercised their free speech.

So that dog won´t bark.

Joseph Stiglitz makes a more sophisticated argument in favor of political censorship in an op-ed piece in Financial Times. [185]

But he sets up a "straw man" argument: all economic studies, he says, show that unregulated markets for *goods* don´t work, therefore unregulated markets for *ideas*, i.e., free speech *won´t* work either.

Why won´t they work? Because experience shows that markets without regulations do not work: "Much of the thrust of economics over the past half century has been to understand what regulations are needed to ensure that markets work. We have tort laws that ensure accountability if someone is injured, and we don't allow companies to pollute willy-nilly. We have fraud and advertising laws to protect consumers against *deceptions* — recognizing that such laws circumscribe what individuals may say and publish."

The problem is these examples of tort and fraud, and advertising laws are about regulation of goods and services not political advertisements. Yes, consumer protection laws circumscribe what individuals may say and publish.... about their *products*. Not about their political opinions.

The answer to Stiglitz and the woke is therefore, that the marketplaces of ideas and goods differ in one crucial aspect: control.

If we as consumers, want to avoid unscrupulous producers of goods and services causing us bodily harm we must be given enough information to make our consumer choice. By Government.

Furthermore, Government has a duty to not even allow products that are noxious to our health in the marketplace. That and giving us enough and correct information about the goods and services we are about to choose is one of Government´s most important jobs. Because we don´t have sufficient information, we can´t control those who seek to misinform us.

---

[185] All quotes from Stiglitz´ op-ed in Financial Times, Jan. 20, 2020

Ideas, political advertising, propaganda we can *control*. By not listening, reading, watching, or by turning it off. We don´t need health advertisements.

I don´t have any control over someone wanting to sell me contaminated food but I *can* choose to ignore someone calling me an idiot for voting for Joe Biden.[186]

But more importantly, consumer protection and protection of free speech have two completely different *rationales*.

The *purpose*, of consumer protection is to protect us against deception from *unscrupulous producers* of goods and services.

The purpose of protecting free speech is to protect us against deception and censorship from an *unscrupulous Government*.

Stiglitz mixes two vocabularies, the economic one, i. e. the marketplace, and the political/ legal one, to confuse us in order to better advance his real agenda: limiting free speech for those who disagree with him.

So why is Woke both in the US and the EU, playing Russian roulette with one of the most important foundations of the success of the West?

Because it is under pressure. Its transformation of the consciousness of society, its gender politics and its anti-populist and internationalist pro-immigration narrative is failing.

However, if political pressure and legislation fail, Woke has another serious arrow in their quiver: social control a.k.a. cancel culture.

Social control is what our friends, our families, our neighbors and yes, our employers do to us if we cross the line.

Social control is what some Muslim families do when they threaten their daughters and sisters who won´t wear the hijab or date non-Muslim boys with exclusion from the family and, in some cases, death in the mislabeled form of "honor killings".

It´s what Soviet Union plenary sessions looked like when delegates did not dare be the first one to stop clapping, for fear of being the next one on Stalin´s death list.

And it is alive and well and well and with us today. It is there when a Cambridge don, Noah Carl, is fired because his fellow scientists claim his research on race and I. Q. is "racist".

It is there when former member of the Executive Board of the Deutsche Bundesbank, Thilo Sarrazin, writes a book critical of Muslims´ well documented inability to integrate into Western society, <u>Deutschland Schafft sich Ab</u>, (Germany commits suicide); and is promptly fired for his heresies.

And the reasons given are always the same. As Merkel says in the quote above: yes, you have free speech in principle, but there are limits and "Those limits begin where *hatred* is spread. They begin where the *dignity* of other people is violated".

I think it is fair to say her message to us is you are not allowed racist, xenophobic, or sexist remarks, as defined by ME. And if you do make them, somebody out there with an agenda who is just dying to be offended will claim to be hurt or offended by your book or your speech, and ultimately your career will be *cancelled*. With my approval.

---

[186] Hicks, Explaining Postmodernism, p. 242

Offended by sexism? Daniel Korski, former advisor to former U.K Prime Minister David Cameron and official candidate for the office of Mayor of London, in June 2023, stepped down. Why? Because a woman accused him of groping 10 years ago. Without proof or any kind of corroborating evidence.

That may look like justice to Woke feminists, but an undermining of basis human rights to others: what happened to "innocent until proven guilty in a court of law"?

Social control always starts with the same thing: cancelling out your speech.

The last time it happened in US history was during the 1950s´ McCarthyism. The time when researchers and professors at public universities, such as f. ex. the University of California Los Angeles, better known as UCLA, had to take oaths of loyalty to the US as a precondition to being hired. Now we are at it again.

Today, guess what, some teachers in California, before being hired have to sign a loyalty oath, this time to diversity. Don´t believe me? Check out this little story from University of California professor, Abigail Thompson:

"In 1950 the Regents of the University of California required all UC faculty to sign a statement asserting that 'I am not a member of, nor do I support any party or organization that believes in, advocates, or teaches the overthrow of the United States Government, by force or by any illegal or unconstitutional means, that I am not a member of the Communist Party,'" Thompson says. Those who refused to sign were fired.

Now, "Faculty at universities across the country are facing an echo of the loyalty oath, a mandatory 'Diversity Statement' for job applicants."

The "professed purpose" of these statements is to identify candidates "who have the skills and experience to advance institutional diversity and equity goals," Thompson writes. But "in reality it's a political test, and it's a political test with teeth. "[187] It´s another code word for the same thing. If you´re not with us, you´re against us. And we will fire you.

Behind this attempt at social control is an idea popular among the woke, namely that language, i. e. ideas, can be as violent as actions. It is called the "language is violence" meme and woke ideology has had great success in making even fairly level-headed people believe it.

As witnessed by the initial quote from Toni Morrison, "Oppressed language does more than represent violence; it *is* violence".

Noam A. Chomsky, the famous radical left linguist, is highly dubious of this theory of language as power and therefore its ability to physically hurt as claimed by the woke.

Chomsky is, if you swallow the woke line, *controversial,* because doesn´t agree with its theory of gender, race and social class being socially constructed.

He thinks that humans are born with certain *innate* linguistic and grammatical instincts which make us understand language as a function of *context*; and that by understanding context we humans avoid misunderstandings and misinterpretations of what our fellow humans want to communicate.

His famous example is the sentence:" He likes her cooking" which depending on *context* can mean anything from *he* likes it as opposed to *others*, he likes *her* cooking rather than *him* having

---

[187] Inside Higher Education, Nov. 19, 2019

to do it, to his actually liking it when she is stewing in the pot. It follows that language is *not*, as the Postmodernists claim, a vehicle for the oppressor to oppress.

Furthermore, as George Orwell, whose dystopian, futuristic masterpiece, *1984,* takes place in a land, Oceania, where totalitarianism, *the Party*, has taken over control of its citizens' lives and thoughts, where they have lost all freedoms, says: *language* is the key to power. Or as he puts it: If liberty means anything at all, it means the right to tell people what they do *not* want to hear.

Unfortunately, not everybody got the memo as the following little story written by Heather MacDonald, a noted conservative author, shows: At West Madison High, Wisconsin, a black student stole an I-phone from another student and was caught by an assistant female principal, whom he proceeded to physically abuse. She called in a guard who happened to be black who tried to control the student which led the thief to call the guard a nigger.

When the guard told the thief not to call him a nigger, the assistant principal used her phone to record the episode whereupon the *guard* was fired- for using the "N-word".

It turned out; the guard had violated the Madison Metropolitan School District's (MMSD) zero-tolerance policy toward the N-word. Any iteration of the word, with whatever intent, by school staff would result in the user's firing. According to Interim School Superintendent Jane Belmore, the district adopted the policy in order to "unequivocally protect" black students.

A Madison district spokeswoman told the Wisconsin State Journal in reference to the incident: "It has simply never been OK for an educator to use a racial slur with children. " The N-word "is based in extreme hatred and violence and causes deep harm", the spokeswoman said. "It is essential to our core values and beliefs that we do not tolerate that kind of harm to our children, our families and our *staff*." (My underline).

Apart from the rather obvious fact that the only one to suffer harm *was a member of the staff*, i. e. the black guard, her statement, though heavy on political correctness, suffers from a glaring defect: it ignores the *context* completely; or as Heather MacDonald says," it misunderstands the distinction between *using* and *mentioning* a word". The black student cum thief used the N-Word as a slur, the black guard mentioned the N-Word in defense against the slur.[188]

But the obvious absurdity of a student who was caught stealing and abusing staff only to get off scot-free while the person upholding the rules was fired, led to such a storm of protests that the guard was reinstated.

A North Texas University, law professor, Caitlin Sewell, wasn't so lucky. In a seminar on free speech, she used a racial slur to illustrate the point that the First Amendment protects offensive speech. "Gonna say a lot of offensive things in here, because it's impossible to talk about the First Amendment without saying horrible things," Sewell said during the speech. "Um, you know, you're just a dumb n**** and I hate you. That alone, that's protected speech."

Several students got so enraged they jumped up on the stage and took over her microphone. She was fired. Woke's cancel culture at work for all to see. Why?

---

[188] The Hill, 29 Oct. 2019

In a statement, University of North Texas President, Neal Smatresk, acknowledged that Sewell was trying to make a point about the broad protections of the First Amendment. However, he went on to suggest that the use of the slur is contradictory to the campus' values.

"We strongly believe in a culture that embraces, and vehemently defends inclusion. While Ms. Sewell was trying to make a point about First Amendment speech, the references used are never condoned in our community, which prides itself in our diversity and caring nature,"[189]

Defending inclusion? Diversity and caring community, huh? Tell that to Sewell. It´s pretty obvious that nobody wanted her opinion *included* nor did the university *care* to protect her *diverse* opinion.

This is doublespeak and it is at the core of the Woke project. It serves to hide the real purpose, namely changing the old order for a new woke one and shutting down the speech of everyone who doesn´t agree.

---

[189] Breitbart, 10 Nov. 2019

Part V: Epilogue.

When I was a child, I spoke as a child, I understood as a child, I thought as a child; but when I became a man, I put away childish things.

1 Corinthians 13:11

xxxxxxxxxxxxxxxxx

The rainbow is a perfect metaphor for Woke: it is an optical illusion that only children believe is real.

xxxxxxxxxxxxxxxxxxxx

It´s Never Too Late to Blame Your Parents.

Old Danish Saying.

xxxxxxxxxxxxxxxxxxxxxx

Psychoanalysis operates on a principle different from medicine: It is not prescriptive. Psychologists after each therapy session don´t hand out a prescription for a medicine meant to cure whatever ailment has been diagnosed.

The therapy session *is* the cure.

Psychoanalysis is like peeling the layers off an onion until only the core is left.

What are the results of this book´s historical psychoanalysis of the Woke mind-set? What kind of Woke core does it leave us?

This book´s historical psychoanalysis has uncovered 4 separate characteristics of Woke core: idealism, rebelliousness, intransigence and intolerance.

Idealism:

Woke, firstly, is aspirational, even idealistic. It wants to save the world from real or imagined dangers, like Holden Caulfield in the Catcher in the Rye. It sees the world binarily, through the prism of oppressed and oppressor and sides unequivocally with the weak, the poor, the downtrodden.

Psychologically, this translates into identity politics, feminism, anti-racism and transgender activism, and concretely into nationalized health services, a strong Welfare state, affirmative action for blacks and women and transgenders, and an overall quest for equality of outcomes, in Woke terminology called DEI, Diversity, Equity, Inclusion.

Politically, Core Woke translates into internationalism, globalism, open borders, anti-nationalism and anti-populism, Woke politicians in the West are overwhelmingly in favor of military support to Ukraine, open borders to help immigrants, international solidarity in the EU and the U.N. and ever more resources to the Welfare State allegedly to help the poor.

Woke claims it always comes down on the side of the weak. But it adds a tweak, namely that it comes down on the side of the "oppressed". Which is a different kettle of fish, because to be oppressed means that there must be an "oppressor". Which in Woke metaphysics are those who hold power in society, which according to Woke are overwhelmingly…. themselves.

To solve that fairly obvious conundrum, Woke must find the oppressor somewhere else, hence the vague use of "society"," systemic" racism, deplorables, populists and clingers.

Psychologically, Woke, at its core is Utopian, which literally means the place that is not there. In the words of Robert F. Kennedy of the famous Kennedy clan and attorney general in his brother's Administration, who was assassinated in 1968 while running for President:

> Some men see things as they are and ask, ""Why?"" I *dream* of things that never were and ask, "Why not?"

Psychologically, dreams are products of the subconscious.

Woke's dreams as we have seen, are heavily influenced by Nietzsche's ideas of the authentic, autonomous individual, ideas which in turn influenced the Neo-Marxist philosophers of the Frankfurt School of Critical Theory, including Herbert Marcuse and his call for sexual freedom and a fight against capitalism; they are influenced by Existentialism and its angst and depression, and last but not least, Postmodernism, and its emphasis on humans as being nothing but a product of collective social structures.

The end-product of Socialism in the view of these philosophers is Communism as envisioned by Karl Marx, who rewrote a passage from the Gospel of Matthew:" From each according to his ability, to each according to his needs".

This brings us into religious territory, although Woke, heavily inspired by Nietzsche, rejects Christianity.

John McWhorter, who is black, in his book <u>Woke Racism</u>, argues that Woke historically is like a religion complete with the "original sin" of White Privilege, the weaponization of "cancel culture" against non-believers, which is akin to The Inquisition, and the fury of "the woke mob" and its parallel in the Crusades.

Our deconstruction reaches the same conclusion.

For Woke is clearly more than a political programme.it has a coherent *meta*-physical narrative the essence of, which is that the arc of *moral* history may be long but it bends towards social justice.

Those words were spoken by Dr. Martin Luther King, Jr. Baptist minister, a man not much appreciated by Woke today, but the <u>social justice</u> part has remained part and parcel of Woke metaphysics, its narrative and its language.

Cynics may argue that the arc of history like the rainbow ends nowhere, but Woke, as we have seen, believes in historical determinism or to quote a phrase it often uses: "to be on the right side of history". Woke not only believes itself to be right, but it is also convinced that it is on the right side of *history*, and that history moves along a predetermined trajectory towards what is just.

Two World Wars, 100 million people killed by Communism, and Russia´s aggression in Ukraine have not disabused Woke of this notion.

The chief reason for this development is that the Woke mind-set has wholly absorbed the Nietzschean idea that man must throw away Christian values and create his own, i.e., the idea that his mind is a blank slate upon which man can imprint his own values and character. The idea that there is no such thing as an a priori human nature, biologically or otherwise, only socially constructed identities.

Hand in hand with that goes a childlike tendency to downplay or ignore *reality*, a direct consequence of Heidegger and the Frankfurt School of Critical Theory. When Ted Dalrymple, the U.K. psychiatrist working with battered women discussed earlier, points out to a young girl that, being weaker than them, she can always be physically battered by her boyfriends, and she should avoid situations that lead to her being beaten, she denies that she is physically weaker, chanting "That's sexist!", and goes back to get beaten some more. Reality-based views of masculinity and femininity have as a consequence disappeared entirely from polite discourse.

Furthermore, the Woke mind-set, to its detriment, has adopted the philosophy of nonjudgmentalism: the idea of that one thing or action is or can be better, more worthwhile, or more moral than another.

A concomitant part of the Woke mind-set is that it has wholly absorbed the religion of emancipation, a life without personal limits, of unfettered freedom to do exactly as it pleases. This idea played out strongly in the first stage of the evolution of the Woke mind-set, again inspired by the Frankfurt School of critical Theory, mainly Herbert Marcuse, and his insistence on throwing out traditional repressive bourgeois morality and replacing it with a morality of unrestrained erotic, sexual and social freedom.

As a consequence, the Woke mind-set downplays or denies aspects of personal responsibility. Dalrymple, notices the frequency of the passive voice describing the actions of hardened criminals, such as when a man stabs someone, he says "The knife went in."

A culture idealizing a mind-set depriving man of agency, of responsibility and accountability, psychologically will promote child-like behavior which in turn may have devastating effects in terms of loss of identity.

Albert Camus wrote of a man who wanted to be guilty in The Stranger and so did the Danish writer, Henrik Stangerup in the novel, The Man Who Wanted to be Guilty (Manden der ville være skyldig)(1973).

And Kevin Williamson in his Big White Ghetto, J.D.Vance in Hillbilly Elegy and Jon McWhorter in Woke Racism,offered the same criticism of the woke mind-set: depriving us of agency and pride in the name of social justice will erase our identity.

Rebelliousness:

 Core Woke, psychologically in its permanent rebelliousness, exhibits traits of immaturity and adolescence. Telling truth to power may work as a slogan when you´re a child but not when you´re a parent and *in* power." Defund the police" works on the sophomore level when you´re living with your parents but not when you are alone, and the bad guy is knocking on your door at 2: a.m.

As Rusty Cohle in True Detective says when asked whether cops are bad guys: "The world needs bad guys, to keep the other bad guys from the door".

Adolescent immaturity allows Woke to hold deeply contradictory *simultaneously*. Psychologically this irrational duality is at the core of Woke.

Thus, Woke can rightly be accused of incoherence or worse schizophrenia, when it on the one hand tells us that all truth is relative but on the other hand insist that *its* narrative tells it like it really is.

Or when its narrative on one hand tells us that all cultures are equally deserving of respect, but that Western culture is uniquely destructive and bad.

Woke is hypocritical when it posits that tolerance is good and intolerance bad but plays down the fact that as it has come to power it has wasted no time in turning back the clock on free speech and instituting a system of government induced political correctness and repression of free speech not seen in the West since the McCarthyism of the 1950s.[190]

It is preposterous when woke ideology claims that the West is deeply sexist while ignoring the fact that Western women were the first to get the vote, contractual rights, and career opportunities that most women in the world are still without.

The woke narrative is historically anti-capitalist but it defies logic on the one hand to hold that Western capitalist countries get rich off the backs of their poor while ignoring the fact that the very poor in the West are far richer than the poor anywhere else in the world both in terms of material assets and opportunities to improve their condition.

Finally, Woke is duplicitous when it promotes a narrative that says that the West is deeply racist, and that America was founded not as an outpost of personal and religious freedom but to preserve slavery, while Woke knows very well that slavery was a World-wide phenomenon, where white men enslaved other white men in greater numbers than those of black enslavement and where blacks enslaved blacks; in short that it was ubiquitous and not racist but economic in nature and that the West, including America, ended slavery first and long before any other cultures.

Intransigence.

Woke, not only is *not* working, but has proven hugely divisive socially, politically, and morally. Only Woke has failed to admit it.

Why has Woke proved so divisive?

Firstly, because we live in a world of scarcity. This means we live in a world of trade-offs.

Woke politicians may decide that black Americans have a *right* to go to Harvard, but seats at the Harvard table are limited, so any Harvard seat going to a black but less qualified candidate, which is brought about by lowering admission criteria for blacks, will meet hostility from those other candidates who were left out.

They resent it and sue Harvard for discrimination as happened recently in the case brought against Harvard by Asian-Americans.

In June, 2023, an official report in the U.K. concluded that the RAF, the U.K.'s Royal Air Force had *discriminated* during its recruitment process against men, in favor of …women.

There are only a limited number of spots open for new RAF recruits. Those who are well-qualified will resent that lesser qualified candidates are recruited ahead of them.

---

[190] The preceding paragraphs are a paraphrasing of Hicks, Postmodernism Explained, pp.184-85.

Affirmative action, which is nothing, but discrimination, is Woke's favorite tool, to solve the problem of scarcity of resources because it favors its ideology of Oppressor v. Oppressed.

That's divisive

Woke may decide that climate change is the existential challenge of our times and impose stifling taxes on fertilizers to limit global warming without thought to the economic consequences, but farmers resent this because it drives them out of business and they decide to lock down the whole country in protest as happened recently in Holland and Sri Lanka.

That's divisive.

The Woke may decide that critical theory about systemic racism and queer theory should be taught to kindergarten children, but non-Woke and Christian parents will disagree with transgender activists and verbally and sometimes physically clash with each other at school board meetings as is happening almost every day in the West.

Now that's divisive.

Woke has proven divisive because its deep anti-enlightenment, neo-Marxist, skepticist, relativist and collectivist philosophical roots clash directly with the traditional Enlightenment values which saw the West bypass all other countries in the world in terms of democracy, individual freedom and wealth: values such as a belief in the individual's ability to make informed rational choices, values such as truth, objectivism, empiricism, and science.

Woke, philosophically, is a paradigm shift too far.

Woke has split the West down the middle because it refuses to recognize that its Core ideology pits groups of different ethnic, racial, and social cultures against each other in a merciless struggle for power that is not *working*.

Put differently, Woke has not fared well when implemented in *real life*.

The #MeToo-movement, a particular manifestation of identity politics in Western culture, , which insists that women always and everywhere must be believed, has taken several hits in the 21st century inter alia when it came out that New York's governor, Andrew Cuomo, who was forced to step down after accusations of sexual harassment, based his defense on a dossier compiled by the local N.Y. chapter of …# Me-Too.

Transgenderism, another form of identity politics, treated as a "civil right" by woke ideology, has also suffered some setbacks when implemented in the real world. What with the transgender woman, who when he was still "identifying" as a man, killed two women, and who after serving his sentence re-identified as a woman and promptly killed a third, or the transgender "woman" who impregnated two women in a women's jail, the movement is losing credibility; and the political support of even the our most fanatical woke ideologues, as evidenced by legislatures all over the West increasingly barring transgender women from women's sports.

Radical feminism, another sub-group of identity politics, suffered a hit when the U.S. Supreme Court in the summer of 2022,[191] reversed one of U.S feminism's most prized legal victories, namely the constitutional right to abortion up until and sometimes after childbirth, and sent the matter to the federal states.

Another sub-category of identity politics, Woke's radical anti-racism stand which saw many violent protests in both the EU and the U.S. in the summer of 2020, took a blow when the main

---

[191] Dobbs v.Jackson Health Organization.

instigator of the riots, Black Lives Matter, not only was revealed to be a Marxist organization with terrorist connections, but was accused of using its donations for self-enrichment and even worse, financial fraud.

That put a bit of a damper on the self-serving demonstrations of political piety by footballers and other athletes in the West who for a year had been taking a knee in support of anti-racism, indeed to such a degree that sports organization like the FA, the English football association organizing the English Premier League, in view of this turn of events but also persuaded by the ever increasing boos of the fans decided to wind it down.

Historically, reality caught up with Woke´s credo of unlimited internationalism and anti-populism with Brexit and the victory of a new nationalism in the US as represented by Donald Trump´s victory and his policy of Making America Great Again.

It came further apart when two members of the United Nations´ Security Council flaunted the U.N.´s own charter: China, by respectively crushing democracy in Hong Kong, putting restive dissidents, the Uighurs in prison camps and threatening an independent neighboring country, Taiwan with invasion and war; and Russia by invading Ukraine in 2022. While the U.N., whose very existence is predicated on its ability to prevent war, stood helplessly by.

It took a heavy blow when China kept the transmission of the artificially lab-strengthened coronavirus from humans to humans from the world and from the WHO, the international body whose very job is to prevent pandemics like the Covid-19. And got worse when WHO covered up China´s lies.

Woke´s Open Doors policies on immigration, with Germany in the lead, have led to a groundswell of popular opposition, not just in Eastern Europe, where anti-immigrants political parties have risen to power in Poland, Hungary, Czech Republic and Slovakia, but in the Mediterranean states bearing the brunt of African and Middle East immigration of Greece (Golden Dawn), Italy (Fratelli d´Italia) Spain (Vox) and Portugal(Chega).

The Climate Change movement has been Woke´s biggest casualty. Not only has the war in Ukraine and the subsequent sanctions on Russia which led to massive gas and oil shortages in the EU, exposed the hypocrisy of Woke as climate warriors, such as the coalition government in Germany of which the Green Party is a prominent member, which under pressure to meet its energy needs switched to, wait for it, not nuclear energy which has no CO_2 emissions but…fossil fuels.

But climate change policies have also led to political rebellion from countries like France where the Yellow Vests protests over increasing gas prices had to be violently put down, to Holland where farmers at the time of writing are still blocking main roads in protest against its government´s green policies which threaten their livelihoods.

<u>Intolerance.</u>

Fourthly, Woke, because it is convinced that it is right, indeed because psychologically like a child it cannot countenance the consequences of not being right, abhors compromises.

Consequently, Woke is always only one step away from repression. As David Horowitz, Director of the Freedom, Center quoted above, says:" Inside every progressive is a totalitarian screaming to get out".

When Woke German Chancellor, Angela Merkel, in 2015 against the wishes of her voters and, indeed, her EU fellow member states opened Germany's borders to uncontrolled immigration, and declares "Wir schaffen das" she let her inner totalitarian out of the bag.

When Woke French President, Macron, in 2023, against the will of the voters whose protests in the streets he crushed violently and against the democratically expressed wishes of the French *Parliament*, implemented his own preferred pension reform by presidential decree *anyway*, he was letting his woke totalitarian out of the bag.

When Obama and Hillary Clinton vent their contempt for "clingers" and "deplorables" they are letting their Woke totalitarian cat, American style, out of the bag.

When a Danish Prime Minister, with a stroke of a pen with no legal jurisdiction abolishes a whole industry, mink farming, lies about it and retroactively uses her slender parliamentary majority to adopt a law allowing the illegal measure *after the fact*, it's a Danish totalitarian cat that's leaving the bag.

Woke intolerance, predictably, has had another casualty in the West: free speech.

The Canadian truckers against whom Canadian Prime Minister, Justin Trudeau, that Boomer of all Boomers, in early 2022 invoked a law meant for war emergencies, the Emergency Act, after they blocked roads and government buildings in protest against mandatory Covid 19 vaccinations, called their protest movement the *Freedom* Convoy.

90% of the truckers were vaccinated and their protest was not really about vaccine mandates. It was about freedom.

Freedom Convoy was a pretty obvious reference to woke ideology's saintly and mythical Freedom Riders.

But Justin Trudeau didn't see it that way. When asked why he was ready to sit down and talk to the BLM protesters in 2021 but would not meet with the Freedom Convoy leaders in 2022, he said that it was because he agreed with the BLM leaders but not with the truckers. That's about as authoritarian a definition as it comes of what has become of constitutional civil rights to freedom of speech and assembly in the West.

At about the same time Trudeau was taking the Canadian truckers' civil rights away from them, an aging 1960s American rock icon, Neil Young, was giving a music and podcast streaming platform, Spotify, an ultimatum: either remove your high-earner podcaster Joe Rogan, from your platform or I'll pull my music. Rogan had upset Young by interviewing some Covid 19 experts who were skeptical about the vaccines and the mandates.

So here we have a 1960s activist, who calls his concerts *freedom* tours and routinely rail against the capitalist system, using a capitalist corporation, Spotify, to cancel a fellow artist who believes in free speech the way that Neil *used* to do, namely that free speech is only free if it gives you the right to say things people do *not* want to hear.

When it comes to freedom woke ideologues have come full circle: from demanding freedom of speech from *their* parents in the 1960s to suppressing *their own* children's right to freedom of assembly and free speech in 2022.

Only as the following little anecdote illustrates, Woke doesn't see it that way.

Northampton University in the U.K.in January 2022 issued a trigger warning to its students about George Orwell's dystopian novel <u>1984</u>, a novel which warns about the very dangers of *progressive* totalitarianism which Woke has come to represent.

Orwell, a self-confessed socialist, who fought on the Communist side in the Spanish Civil War from 1936-39, was warning left wingers about the dangers of letting their political leaders manipulate language to distort the reality of their oppressive system. Orwell's imagery such as the concepts of Big Brother, Thought Police, double-speak, double-think, War is Peace, Freedom is Slavery, Ignorance is Strength, etc. serve to illustrate his point: when we give up our freedom of speech and let our leaders distort reality, we lose our identity and, in the end, our minds.

Trigger warnings, as Orwell would have been the first one to recognize, are the quintessence of Big Brother, Thought Police and Double Think.

When irony- free woke administrators issue a trigger warning about Orwell to us, their own children, they are unself-consciously demonstrating the Orwellian nature of their own narrative.

Our Woke leaders tell us that all will be well if only we stop listening to "populist," and "nationalist" voices. But we know that culture drives politics, so blaming our deeply divided politics on Trump in the U.S. or a slew of alleged nationalists and populists like Boris Johnson or Viktor Orban in the EU, is only killing the *messenger*.

June 28/29,2023, saw an unprecedented legal reversal of Woke´s main theory of rights, including gender diversity, affirmative action, feminism and anti-free speech.

The U.S. Supreme Court in the court case mentioned above filed by a group of Asian students against Harvard, declared race-based criteria used in the admission processes at practically all American universities for unconstitutional. This was a heavy blow to the Civil Rights Act of 1964, which introduced the principle of protected classes of people into American jurisprudence in direct opposition to the equal protection clause of the 14th Amendment of the U.S. Constitution.

A similar blow was dealt by the Supreme Court to the LGTBQ, a class of people also protected under the Civil Rights Act: the Court held that this protection didn´t amount to limiting other people´s rights to exercise their 1st Amendment guaranteed rights of free speech in refusing to create same -marriage websites or bake cakes celebrating same sex-marriage.

Jordan B.Peterson,who, as we have seen earlier, was heavily fined for refusing to call transgender people by their own selected gender pronouns because it infringed on his right of *free speech*, would have felt vindicated, despite the fact that he is Canadian.

Speaking of free speech, psychologically, the worst part of Woke is that it encourages, indeed, demands self-censorship.62% of Americans admit to self-censorship according to a YouGov survey[192] and not saying what you mean and not meaning what you say, as any psychologist will tell us, is not good for our mental health.

Woke diversity took another heavy hit at that very same time(end June,2023), when, as mentioned earlier, an official report in the U.K. concluded that the RAF, the U.K.´s Royal Air Force had *discriminated* during its recruitment process against men, in favor of …women.

In other words, by prioritizing diversity, it had violated another supreme Western value: equality. That all human beings are created equal.

Mainstream media in the U.S went bonkers at the Supreme Court with outrageous claims of a return to separate diner counters, blacks in the back of the bus and transgenders as 2nd class citizens.

---

[192] "Poll: 62% of Americans Say They Have Political Views They're Afraid to Share", YouGov, July 22,2020.

But perhaps most telling was the reaction of one of the wokest of the Supreme Court judges, Sonia Sotomayor, who not only strongly dissented, but implied her fellow judges were…racist:

> "Despite the Court's unjustified exercise of power, the opinion today will serve only to highlight the Court's own impotence in the face of an America whose cries for equality resound. As has been the case before in the history of American democracy, "the arc of the moral universe" will bend toward racial justice despite the Court's efforts today to impede its progress."[193]

The Supreme Court may just have denied Woke the use of affirmative action in college admissions, but the reaction of Woke´s defenders from President Joe Biden, over Judge Sotomayor on down to mainstream media, shows that Woke has every intention of not obeying this decision and to fight against it. Including by stacking the Supreme Court with pro-diversity judges.

And in Europe, French President, Macron, is busy putting into practice a pension reform his voters did not want, Denmark recently officially exonerated all government officials and elected political leaders responsible for the mink-scandal, while the European Parliament has just (July,2023)adopted a program for meeting the "Emergency Climate Change Challenge" so ambitious and expensive that the EU, if it is implemented is looking at almost certain political gridlock, division and bankruptcy.

Our historical psychoanalysis leads to the conclusion that Woke at its core suffers from arrested development, a psycho-social ailment first diagnosed by a Swedish psychologist called Erik Erikson.

In the late 1960s, Erikson proposed a framework to map and understand human psychosocial development that segmented general *age ranges* that corresponded to lessons to be learned along the way.[194]

> "An example of this paring is how individuals from the ages of birth to around 2 years old learn about trusting the world. At this time, babies learn about their relationship with caregivers and whether the world itself is safe enough to be trusted. If they learn that their caregivers and the world are generally dependable, then they can progress onto the next stage. If not, their emotional state will stall at that point."

This does not mean that adults that have suffered trauma and lack of trust in their caregivers when they were young speak gibberish and want to wear diapers when they are 45-year olds, but it does mean that adults who are *stuck* may end up functioning like emotional teenagers.

Being "stuck" means having and internalizing a narrative that is not working.

Which, as argued in this book, is Woke in a nutshell.

---

[193] STUDENTS FOR FAIR ADMISSIONS, INC. v. PRESIDENT AND FELLOWS OF HARVARD COLLEGE SOTOMAYOR, J., dissenting, p.69.

[194] Quoted from Eric Erikson, Internet, "Arrested Psychological Development: You maybe younger than you look…psychologically speaking…".

How do individuals get to a place where they are stuck emotionally? What does it take to keep someone from progressing normally? In general, says Erik Erikson, there are only a few different ways that keep people from progressing in emotional maturity. The first is *trauma* as result of an event or experience and the second is the *inability to express* feelings due to ignorance or insolence.

Both apply to Woke. The 60s psychologically were an event where youth lost trust in their elders. "Don´t trust anyone over 30" may sound like just a slogan but hides a deep sense of distrust and trauma and a concomitant search for other authorities and other belief-systems so characteristic of Woke.

Woke´s inability to express its emotions about its own narrative honestly is substantively documented in this book; and its attempt to crush dissent and inability to engage in adult dialogue about it is, indeed, per Erikson, reminiscent of the behavior of an emotional teenager.

What´s the therapeutical prognosis? Not good.

Dealing with arrested development is notoriously difficult. At the very minimum it requires patience and time.

The problem is that psychoanalysis, apart from dialogue and therapy, also operates on another principle, namely that it can only work if the patient is cooperating with the counsellor; or at least is able to take responsibility for whatever conclusions are reached during therapy. In other words, psychoanalysis only works if the patient is willing to adopt or change a narrative that is manifestly not working for him or her.

Clearly, Woke is not cooperating. In fact, the patient shows all the classic clinical signs of being in denial, which according to my Handbook of Psychology are types of "defense mechanisms that involve ignoring the reality of a situation to avoid anxiety" and "strategies that people use to cope with distressing feelings" which "can involve not acknowledging reality or denying the consequences of that reality."

I started out this book by referring to Hamas´ barbarous attack on Israeli civilians on Oct. 7,2023, as being the day, the masks fell, the day the true nature of the Woke project became clear for all to see.

My ambition all along has been to make clear that Woke´s mission from day one always was to transform the consciousness of the West in order to bring about radical social change. October 7,2023,and the mass demonstrations in favor of the atrocities perpetrated on innocent civilians by Hamas simply showed that it has succeeded beyond its wildest dreams in having the establishment elites in our international institutions, the EU and the U.N, in our government, our universities, the media and whatever passes for our cultural institutions like Hollywood, swallow hook line and sinker that old Neo-Marxist binary canard that the world is made up of oppressed and oppressors.

The problem is that to the other half, October 7,2023 showed the true nature of the Woke project and that ordinary voters, as demonstrated by the surging popularity of nationalist parties all over the West, from Geert Wilders in Holland to Marine le Pen in France, from Giorgia Meloni in Italy to Alice Weidl of the AfD in Germany, from Viktor Orbán in Hungary to Donald Trump in the U.S. are not onboard that particular Ship of Fools..

The West is obviously heading for troubled waters. Woke politics with its mixture of righteousness and zealotry have proven extremely divisive leading to continual culture wars in the West, yet Woke is likely to double down on its rhetoric of fighting a quasi-holy war against fascists and enemies of democracy as long as it thinks it is a battle it will win.

But civil wars rarely produce outright winners. On the contrary they often as in the case of the Spanish Civil War (1936-39) or the American Civil War (1861-64) leave problems like the race question in the U.S. and the independence of Catalonia in Spain unsolved like a festering wound.

Therefore, from a historical psychoanalytical perspective, I wish to give Woke one piece of unsolicited advice: beware of what you wish for.

And on that unhappy note I rest the therapy.

Made in the USA
Middletown, DE
31 May 2024